ON THE BRINKS

A MEMOIR

ON THE BRINKS

Sam Millar

Wynkin deWorde

2003

Published in 2003
by

**Wynkin
deWorde**

Wynkin deWorde Ltd.,
PO Box 257, Tuam Road, Galway, Ireland.
e-mail: info@deworde.com

A CIP catalogue record for this book is available from the British Library

ISBN: 0-9542607-7-5

Typeset by Patricia Hope, Skerries, Co. Dublin, Ireland
Cover Illustration: Roger Derham.
Jacket Design by Design Direct, Galway, Ireland
Printed by Betaprint, Dublin, Ireland

I dedicate
On The Brinks,
to the memory of my father,
Big Sam,
a rebel and nonconformist
in the true sense of the word.

Acknowledgements

I would like to express my sincere appreciation to the many people who have helped me on the road to completing *On the Brinks*, be it by their encouragement or sheer single-mindedness. Once again I find myself facing the prospect of leaving so many people out, and once again I can only say a big thank you to each of you for your help and consideration. I would however like to thank two writers in particular for their encouragement over the last two years.

Liz Curtis, author of *The Propaganda War* and other works was the first person to see the manuscript and despite her own exhaustive schedule, she took the time to not only read but edged me in the direction of positive criticism, for which I will be forever grateful.

Gaye Shortland, author of *Rough Rides in Dry Places*, and other works simply never surrendered her belief in the manuscript. If ever a writer should be fortunate enough to have someone fighting in their corner when things appear to be at rock bottom, then that person is Gaye. A simple thank you seems rather redundant, but she will know it means a lot more than that.

I would like to thank all at Wynkin de Worde; Roger and Brenda Derham for the commitment shown and to Valerie Shortland, whose editorial professionalism never waned despite my attempts to sabotage it.

Also to my family circle here in Ireland as well as Europe, Argentina, Canada and USA and all my relations and friends for their support of my previous book, *Dark Souls*. To all the clans: Millars, O'Neills, Morgans, Clarkes and McKees, a big thank you. It was heart lifting. A special thank you goes to my brothers and sisters, Mary, Danny, Joe and Phyllis.

Finally, and most importantly, a big kiss and thank you to my wife Bernadette, and children, Kelly-Saoirse, Ashley-Patricia, Corey and Roxanne. Now that *On The Brinks* is ready for the printers, I no longer have an excuse not to cut the grass, make the tea, see the latest movie, go for a walk, stop drinking so much coffee . . .

Prologue

"Hollywood couldn't have done it better."

New York's IRISH VOICE

When I met him later that night, he was smiling, his hand outstretched, as if greeting me for the first time in years.

'Don't say a word in the car,' I whispered, a plastic grin on my face. 'It's bugged.'

We drove down Lake Avenue, towards the beach, in silence. Upon reaching the beach, I parked the car and removed a few *Buds* from the back seat. When we were far enough away, I came to the point. 'How'd you like to make some serious money?'

A young couple sat on a grassy hill eating greasy sandwiches, watching people on the beach pack and leave. It was late evening but the heat was still horrendous. Crickets made smalltalk and mosquitoes bit on my ears as I watched calmness come to splintered waves. A seagull hovered effortlessly, killing itself laughing. Later, I would remember the albatross in the "Ancient Mariner". Much later, I would remember a seagull in Long Kesh . . .

'How serious?' he asked, taking a slug of *Bud*, balancing his words, remaining noncommittal.

1

'Maybe a million,' I answered nonchalant, placing the beer to my lips.

The *Bud* hit the back of his throat, making him cough. 'Are you shittin' me?' he asked, wiping the spillage from his chin.

"Security guards told the police that they were surprised by assailants who had somehow evaded the sophisticated security system. They could not say how many robbers there were . . . it appears to be one of the biggest robberies in U.S. history."

NEW YORK TIMES, FRONT PAGE

I knelt on the sand and, with my finger, started to draw. Before long, I had sketched the rough layout of a bird's-eye view of a building, a collage of rectangles and squares. I didn't speak. Even when the waves slowly crept in, erasing my work, I said nothing, waiting for it to disappear.

'Let's go,' I said, eventually, brushing the sand from my jeans while rays of rolling water embraced the sand, kissing it before retreating like a chased child. Slowly, we walked along the beach, whispering like lovers on a first date, as an old lady walked by, exercising her dog. Shaking her head with disgust, she watched us disappear behind sand dunes.

When the time came, and I looked back on that eventful day, I realised I had been shittin' him. It was more than a million. A lot more. History was about to be made . . .

"Federal agents have suddenly netted a veritable Sean O'Casey farce of circumstance and suspects. Bags of money scattered in a dim tenement apartment; Millar, an Irish revolutionary hiding out in America as a comic book dealer in Queens, New York; O'Connor, an Irish American cop and 'Father Pat', a classically ascetic Irish priest."

FRANCIS X CLINES, columnist for the *New York Times*.

PART ONE
Belfast

1

The House

April 1965

"As each of us look back into his past, a door opens upon darkness."

EM FORSTER

I was born in Belfast and lived in Lancaster Street, a street whose most famous son was the Irish artist, John Lavery. Among his many paintings was that of Kathleen Ni Houlihan on the first Irish Free State banknotes; his wife, Hazel, was used as the model. We never spoke much of the man for the simple reason that he committed one of the most unpardonable sins: accepting a "knighthood" from the British Empire. From a street that would see three-quarters of its male population interned without trial, or sent to Long Kesh by the infamous non-jury "trials" of Diplock, it was easy to understand why.

My mother was a workaholic, scrubbing and cleaning and always smelling of *Daz*, bleach and carbolic soap that stained her hands the colour of raw wounds. While my father worked as a merchant seaman, she ran a semi-boarding house that contained the grand total of one lodger. She never made a penny from the house and was perpetually in debt because of it. Her purse was testimony to that. It was a fat, working-class purse: Fat. Fat with the pain of pawn tickets and IOU's. Fat, like the false swelling bellies of starving children in far away Africa.

Each night before my father's departure, they would argue over her loneliness and his need to be free.

Silently, I would creep to the door, tapping meekly on it, hoping neither would hear, clearing my conscience with the provoked rational of a coward trapped in his own paralysis, before quickly slithering back to bed, relieved the door had remained shut, dreading the distorted looks on their faces, knowing they would hate me for what I knew.

One time when I returned from school, the next day, she was sitting on the sofa, smiling strangely to herself. She leaned to kiss me, but I could only push her away, as if betrayed. 'You've been drinkin',' I accused. 'And after all you said.'

She smelt strongly of mints, a smell I dreaded and one which she used in a vain effort to camouflage the horrible stench of dead leaves that settled heavily on her breath; of brandy in all its degrading cheapness transforming her into a mumbling, sobbing wreck. She wiped her flour-covered hands nervously on an apron which was covered with windmills and trumpet-headed daffodils swaying in the breeze. 'Your father'll be home next month. He doesn't need to know, does he?'

Already her words were coming out slurred. Soon she would start her crying, telling me how lonely she was, how my father was to blame, being away for so long. I hated her like this. Did she not know how humiliating it was to sneak into the off-licence, hoping no one would spot me, while the man behind the counter gave me that knowing, sneaky wink that said: *Your ma's wee secret is safe with me. Don't you worry.* His words were slippery, like a snail captured by the sun. I would remember him, years later, when he no longer existed.

She attempted another kiss, burning my mouth with the brandy wetness on her lips.

'Keep away from me! I hate you when you're like this,' I shouted, pushing her back onto the sofa. 'This time I'm tellin' my Da!'

But when she sobbed those terrible sounds, her hands covering her face with shame, I knew I would never tell. I placed my hands on her head, soothing her. 'Don't cry. Everything will work itself out.'

But she couldn't look at me, simply wanted me to leave the room. When I did, she continued her mumbling, whispering, 'Your father need never know, need he?'

As time progressed, she began to pick at the wallpaper with her fingernails, leaving them a bloody mess and the walls devastated like leprosy. Neighbours began to talk about her, the state of the house.

It was shortly after that she solved it all, choosing to live alone in the shadow of the dead in exchange for the debt of the living. And while we all slept, in some far-off place, the rain against the window filled her head with a reservoir of eerie dreams, easing the pain that had crushed her for years.

2

Leaving

May 1965

"The thought of suicide is a great consolation: by means of it one gets successfully through many a bad night."

NIETZSCHE

As a child, Saturday mornings always attracted me to the local pub. Outside, crates of empty *Guinness* bottles were pyramided, their smell fermenting in the early sun, their contents gone with last night's dreams. Flies, vile and lazy, nestled drunkenly on bottlenecks buzzing angrily at their hangovers.

'Whaddye want?' asked the barman, scrubbing brush in hand.

'Nothin',' I replied. 'Just lookin'.'

'Then go look elsewhere.' He hated anyone watching him struggle with the vomit that permeated the ground, staining it like great maps of the world.

'Not want me to kill the flies for ye?' I asked, showing him my *Irish News* rolled into a peeler's baton.

He stared at me for a few seconds, then skyward for Divine guidance. 'Okay . . . but don't eat 'em.'

He grinned, but I only nodded solemnly and turned to the task of transforming fat-bellied flies into perfect dead inkblots. A dog came to watch then, bored, chased itself in an odyssey of arse-sniffing circles, as if fascinated by its own hairy hole. A minute later it was gone, leaving me behind with the flies. Sometimes, if the barman remembered, he brought me a *Coke*, making me swear to Our Lady that I'd return the empty bottle. I always did, no matter how much I wanted to keep it for target practice. The dog returned and sniffed suspiciously at a dead sparrow, its anorexic legs protruding like miniature branding irons towards the sky.

'Can ye hear 'em?' asked the barman as he swept dirt from the pub's door.

Of course I could hear them. The lexicon of Clockwork Orangemen floated acoustically from Clifton Street where they had gathered en masse below the pigeon-stained statue of King Billy. From there they would march to the Field, unfurling their banners of intolerance and hatred, flanked by benign old ladies resplendent in their Union Jack dresses and *"Fuck The Pope"* hats.

As the Orangemen approached the shadow of Saint Patrick's, it was as if they had suddenly become possessed: leaven faces swelled with anticipation; eyes bulging like ping-pong balls, and thick, ruddy necks trafficked with corduroy veins the size of football laces exposing their congenital abhorrence of all things Catholic.

My father always said that Orangemen were full of sour grapes and whine. He should know. His father was one. My grandfather came from a strong Protestant family whose loyalty to God and Ulster was never questioned. He marched to the Field every Twelfth, and no doubt had his eye on becoming Grand Master, with great visions of riding down Clifton Street atop a white horse like his hero, King Billy.

Catholics meant little to him because their strange beliefs and customs were difficult to comprehend. They were an invisible people. There, but not really there; moving, but going nowhere. He believed the dogma that Catholics in the North had only themselves to blame. They bred too quickly and didn't believe in controlling their sexual urges, or at least using methods to curtail them. He built his images of Catholics as composites of pure imagination – his imagination. He told himself he didn't hate Catholics. As long as they "knew their place" and didn't bother him, things would be fine. He was very tolerant, my grandfather. He didn't hate them, but he certainly had no love for them. That was until he actually met one and committed the ultimate crime of falling in love with one.

My grandmother was a staunch Catholic, from the South of Ireland, a fiery woman who took nonsense from no one – including her soon-to-be husband. She laid down the law the first time he proposed to her: 'Any children that God may bless us with, will all be brought up Catholics.' No ifs, ands or buts; 'If you don't like it, end this right now.'

Had he, of course, my life would no doubt have taken a different course.

'Bastards,' said the barman to himself. 'Hope to fuck that a few of 'em die of a heart attack in this heat. That'll take the marching out of 'em.'

Just then the dog bowed its spine, preparing to leave its shitty mark, and there was the sickening sound of wood on bone as the barman cracked the dog over the head with his brush.

'Get, ya dirty bastard!' he screamed, sending the poor creature running for its life. He spat, just where he had spent all morning scrubbing, then walked back to serve a customer who kept tapping an empty glass, annoyingly, against the counter.

The bar counter was lined with pints of perfect *Guinness*. Rivulets of condensation formed on the fat bodies of the pints, which sat sweating tantalizingly close, like a synod of clergy in idle discussion. From the pub's reflective window, I could see a shape jumping up and down.

'Yer da's lukin' fer ye, Sammy!' screamed Gerry Green, waving his hands frantically, from across the street.

Gerry loved bringing bad news. The more distressing, the happier he became. He was the local bully, but an unusual one because he had a conscience and only hit you when you deserved it – which was usually twice a day, except on Fridays when he got his pocket money. He never touched you on Friday. A decent bully, really. He was about my age, I guess, with glass-cutting blue eyes. A family of pimples inhabited his entire face. He'd be a horror to look at in later years.

'He's shoutin' all over the place like a mad man fer ye. Luks like yer in fer it!' he claimed, as I crossed over to the other side of the street.

To see someone "in fer it" could bring tears of joy to Gerry's eyes. He was practically wetting himself with glee as he escorted me back down Lancaster Street, fearful I would escape justice. As I approached the towering figure of my father, a rosary of knots formed in my stomach, warning me.

'Where've you been? Didn't I tell you not to be going away from the door?' My father was putting on his coat as he handed me a bag of fruit. His shoes were gleaming, as usual, because he was a great believer in the *Cherry Blossom* legend: *a shine on your shoe says a lot about you.* 'Get your coat and let's get going. We're late.'

Gerry was devastated. Not a boot up the arse. Not even a slap on the head. For a moment, I thought he would complain to my father about his misguided leniency. Instead, he simply walked away, head down.

'For heaven's sake, will ye cheer up a bit? It's the hospital; not O'Kane's . . . not this time, anyway.'
O'Kane's was the local undertakers, but as far as I was concerned there was little difference between them and the dreary wards of the Mater Hospital that we now entered.

'How is she today, doctor?'
'A slight improvement from yesterday, Mr Millar. We hope to give her some soup, later. She had some tea last night, but couldn't hold it down for long. It's a slow process.'
A soft breeze rallied the combined stenches of piss, vomit,

disinfectant and the dry-talc smell of death, filling the corridors with the universal dread of all hospitals. My mother lay motionless in the bed, her pallid complexion as one with the linen sheets, almost invisible.

It wasn't her first attempt at suicide, but it was her most imaginative as well as elaborate. Instead of simply opting for an overdose, she had decided to slash both her wrists, also. This time she almost made it, having been pronounced DOA by the doctor on duty. Her effort was frustrated only by the attentive eyes of my older brother, Danny, who, upon hearing the doctor's verdict, became maniacal and demanded a medical miracle. It worked. She lived to die another day.

I knew she could hear me whisper in her ear as my father sat silently, chained to the guilt of wasted memories that were cemented in the heat of anger and fury. 'You could've waited,' I accused. 'I told you my exam results were due and that I would do well. But you don't care, do you? Too selfish. I hope you die, next time.'

But she ignored me, feigning the death she had yet to perfect. A log, stiff with shame and loneliness. Suddenly, her exhausted eyes turned dark. The way a beetle's eyes appear against a raindrop.

It was the last time that I would ever see her again as she fled into shadows a few nights later. And when neighbours insinuated she wouldn't be back, I knew they were mistaken. They didn't know what I knew: she had only smoked two of her *Park Drive*. She'd be back for the other eight.

But even the pictures on the wall knew better. The Sacred Heart became more melancholy, while the vulpine grins of the "princes" of Rome and Camelot mocked my naiveté. They knew.

3

A Very Hot Summer

August 1965

"Everything that deceives also enchants."

PLATO

A madness of sorts possessed my father now that he was "on his own". For a while, things were great, as he pitied me more than himself. But as the cold reality began to bite at him, he slowly reversed his feelings in favour of himself, finding fault with every thing I did. I had to run like hell when he sent me on an errand, timing me, always criticising with a "what the hell kept you?". It would have made no difference had I broken the world record, it would still be "what the hell kept you?".

Friday mornings, before school, were bad, having to deal with George Flanders, the greengrocer from hell.

'How many, young Millar?' asked Flanders, a giant with tight clothes, lamb-chop side-burns, a ruddy complexion and an enormous nose that defied gravity. The kids called him Banana Nose. His eyes had the tight look of someone who scrutinized beaten dockets, hoping beyond hope. But when it suited him,

15

the same eyes could remove skin, burn you with their intensity.

'50, Mister Flanders,' I squeaked, hating this part: the barter of apples from my father's tree.

Flanders handled one of the apples, rubbing his thumb against the texture, smelling it with his giant nostrils. 'Four cabbages. Howsabouthathen?' He said this as one word.

'My da said *five* cabbages, four carrots and a quarter stone of blue spuds.' I always wished Flanders would speed it up, in case one of my mates came in for an apple, to witness my humiliation.

'Ha! Yer da's arse is out the window! I'm a greengrocer. Not green,' laughed Flanders who was now juggling some of the apples, like a clown, into the air, winking as he pretended to allow them to fall.

Dead, supine flies lined the window of the fruit shop like a contiguous military convey debilitated by superior forces, while their air-borne comrades struggled menacingly above, attached to flypaper, tearing off their own limbs. I would always stare at the adhesive, fascinated by its struggling victims trying, in vain, to detach themselves from the sticky graveyard. It always reminded me of the currant buns sold next door in Mullan's bakery. I had never tasted one in my life. Never would. *That's life*, I thought, *one big sticky ending that comes to us all.*

'You've caught me in a generous mood, young Millar,' claimed Flanders, his face a politician on polling day. 'Four cabbages. And here's some carrots as well.'

It was over. He had won. As usual.

As I left his shop, Flanders handed me a pear. It was badly bruised and had his teeth marks in it. 'Here, that's for you. And tell yer da he's gotta git up early ta catch me!'

I could still hear the laughter halfway down the lane. My father would look on the exchange with disdain.

'That's all?' he asked, his voice snide.

Why didn't you go yourself? I would ask, in my dreams. *Afraid of the humiliation?*

But if Friday mornings were bad, Friday nights were always a

16

nightmare, as I had to run to Peter Kelly's for fish and chips. And even though I would run like a madman and the fish and chips would've burnt the mouth off him, he would still greet me with "These are freezing. What the hell kept you?". People were staring at me as if I was completely mad, but I still couldn't find the courage to refuse to run.

But that all changed one Friday night when someone else's madness intervened.

The line at the chippy had snaked the corner, stretching all the way to McCleery Street. Everyone loved Peter's fish and chips so there always seemed to be a queue there, especially Fridays and Saturdays, when working-class people had some money in their pockets. *My da'll kill me*, was all I could think of as I ran even faster to get my place in the queue.

'I watch you every Friday night. Ye think ye are somebody, don't ya?'

He was a bit younger than me. His face was filthy, as if a dirty rag had attached itself to his skin, sucking the life out of him. I was so exhausted I could hardly breathe, let alone answer him.

'What's its name?' he asked, running in perfect unison.

'What? Get away from me, will ye?' Everyone was watching.

'Yer horse, stupid! What's yer horse's name?'

I tried to ignore the head-case.

'They call my horse Silver. Just like the Lone Ranger's,' he replied, as proud as a peacock up at Bellevue Zoo.

My chest was burning. I needed to stop.

'The great thing about Silver is that he's invisible. I'm the only one who can see him.' He then patted the neck of the invisible horse. 'Easy, boy. Easy.' Ignoring the threat on my face, he continued to talk. 'The great thing about Silver being invisible is when he shites all over the street. No one can see it, so they all walk on it! I laugh when I see them walking into their houses, trailing Silver's invisible shite along with them! And the smell! Worse than visible shite, I can tell ye! They all laugh at me, but I always get the last laugh. Don't I, Silver?' Suddenly, without warning, he leapt two feet into the air. 'Easy! Easy, Silver. Good boy.' He began to pat the ghost-rider, reassuring it. Everyone was grinning at us but before I could grab him he shouted: 'See ye! Hi ho Silver, away!'

And away he went, slapping the arse off himself, jumping over bin lids and empty cardboard boxes. That was it, I decided. No more running. My father could do what he liked to me, but I'd been humiliated enough. I was more than surprised when he didn't force the issue and was quite proud of my stand. But pride always comes before a fall and a week later, to my horror, he enrolled me in the local boxing club where I won many friends as a walking punch-bag.

It was many months later that I met the Lone Ranger again. His face was a mask of sweat as he cleared three bins with ease. 'What happened to your horse? And where did ye get the black eyes?' he asked.

He seemed genuinely concerned, so I humoured him. 'He went limp, so I shot 'im. Got the black eyes when I fell from 'im and hit my head on a rock.'

He shook his head. 'That's sad. He was a good horse. Maybe you'll find another one, some day.' He studied the ground for a few moments, then said: 'Well, got to go now. See ye about.'

I hoped not. Then he began to laugh that weird laugh of his. 'What's wrong? Who're ye laughin' at?' I asked.

'You just walked on Silver's invisible shite! Shouldn't have shot your horse!' And with that, he was gone, jumping over boxes, screaming, 'Hi ho Silver, away!'

To escape my father's mood swings in the aftermath of his wife deserting him, I would climb to the top of Saint Patrick's school, impervious to the caretaker's threats to get the "peelers" for me. How could heavy cops master the fragile drainpipe that sighed wearily under my youthful weight? I reasoned.

As I lay there, invisible to all except those empowered with flight, my mind would fill with the imagery of velvet butterflies and cooing pigeons. In the distance, the imposing derrick known as "Goliath", stood guard, a futuristic Orwellian sentinel watching the modicum of Catholics labour below it like inimical bugs. An anathema to Catholics, it was a salient reminder – as if we needed one – of our second-class citizenship, and British and Unionist ascendancy.

But at that time, I knew nothing of such things: of the gerrymandering, discrimination and squalid housing conditions. I was only eleven and didn't care about any of it. That would come later. Right now I was king of the castle, looking down on all my subjects in Lancaster Street. From the roof, I could hear stones breathing; the soft whisper of distant traffic. A handball game was in progress and the ball made hypnotic, heartbeat staccato thumps. I could discern bare hands slapping, slicing, and aiming for points. Despondency and triumph manifested themselves in the voices of the untiring warriors.

Gazing towards the yards, I could see the washing lines full of fluttering clothes resembling gulls scampering for food, and dirty water snaking through the striation of arteries in the pavement, suffusing discarded oil from an abandoned car that lay like a great wounded beast against the scrap-yard wall.

At the end of the street, the horses utilised by the local glazier, now stood in unison, eating, pissing and shitting. They never stopped. Their arses perpetually pushing out fist-size boulders with slivers of undigested straw protruding from it like burnt cacti. Kamikaze sparrows darted in and out between the horses' legs, capturing the spillage.

There was one other place I – along with a few mates – sought shelter, and God help us if ever we were caught in it: the rag store . . .

Sadie reigned as the *de facto* boss of the rag store, irrespective of the grumbling from proprietor, Mister Jacob, to the contrary. She negotiated the prices, hired and fired, and took care of the cats that helped decimate the rat population. She was a pleasant-faced woman with hips as wide as fresh-baked bread. An enormous moneybag rested on those hips with a cosy familiarity, its leather lips worn and scuffed from the constant transactions performed in the store. And, oblivious to the danger of flammable rags, a *Park Drive* dangled perpetually from a gap where a tooth had once been. She often "joked" of having accumulated enough tar in her lungs to cover York Street, all the while releasing menacing plumes of fog from her nostrils like an exhausted dragon. When she spoke – which was rarely in conversation – her voice was a raspy, sandpapery growl.

Sadie's smoking wasn't the only health hazard in the store. The rats topped the list. Sly and bold, they harassed then banished most of the mangy, bounty-hunter cats that turned out to be quite cowardly. Sadie herself had been bitten so many times she seemed immune. Her legs were a constellation of horseshoe-shaped bites, and sometimes on Fridays with too much *Mundies* she'd hoist her flowery gypsy dress, pull down her knickers and slap her arse, saying: 'Whaddya think of 'em, eh? Bit me arse, dirty buggers!'

Had the place been on fire, we couldn't have cleared out faster after being exposed to her sagging buttocks, scarred black-and-blue.

We had been warned, of course, by our parents to steer clear of the store with its fleas, stench and disease. And even though Sadie's name was never mentioned, it was implied with subtle innuendo that she had a history as a loose woman. We were naive to the meaning, but the dark whispers with their torn curtains of resentment were enough to convert us to her side. So most Friday evenings, like moths to a flame, we gathered with jumping fleas and cowardly cats to watch Sadie's bloody ritual of cutting throats and gutting.

'Rabbits!' we exclaimed in unison when first seeing the caged creatures.

'Hares,' she said with the voice of a gangster's moll, cigarette jerking in her mouth.

'No, rabbits,' we insisted.

'Hares,' she reiterated, pulling a squealing creature unceremoniously by the ears, from the cage. It made the sound a hungry baby makes searching for a nipple: a haunting sound so pitiful it reached to the ghetto of my soul, tattooing it forever.

She held the struggling creature inches from our mesmerised faces, its whiskers nervously capturing dust motes, making them dancing rhinestones. Then, with sleight-of-hand, she produced an evil-looking cut-throat razor and, to our shock – but childish delight – she slit the animal's throat, releasing a leaf of blood that covered her fingernails like crimson varnish. Our hands moved instinctively to our throats, as if feeling the pain.

As the day progressed, twenty hares met a similar fate. Sadie's skinning, gutting and curing the hares followed this, though to be honest, we were totally baffled how something dead could be cured. The mercuric entrails, which slipped through her fingers like crimson sand, were deposited into a tin bucket to be sold to the butcher for sausages. The skins, festooned upon the walls and resembling leaves of tobacco, retained their tiny faces, each adorned with grotesque, posthumous grins. Pity and wonder emoted from the scene.

And there, among the rags and pungent attar of cat-piss, we came of age with the knowledge that life is arbitrary to a fickle god who alone understands the strangeness of life and death with their seamless, paradoxical partnership.

Don't pay 'em no heed,' advised Sadie, watching my eyes skim over the dead. 'They're only animals. Nothin' more.' She took a sip of *Mundies* from a chipped cup with "*Made in Hong Kong*" stencilled in bold blue letters on the bottom. The wine glazed her lips, making them fat and obscene. 'You'll be able to do this one day,' she said, nodding her head sagely.

Ice formed in my stomach at her words knowing I could never carry out such a bloody deed.

'Yes you will. Yes you will,' said her slurred voice, a needle stuck in a groove. 'Everyone knows it was you who forced your dear mother to run away.'

I ran home, never stopping, my heart banging in my chest, her words ringing in my ears. I didn't sleep that night. Or the next. I vowed never to return to the store. But I'd forgotten: I was a moth, Sadie the flame.

Eventually it was time to come down from the roof as a coolness brought the pervasive shadow of autumn bleeding into summer. But a wave of dread swept over me at the thought of going home.

Somewhere below, a radio captured Marvin Gaye singing "What's Going On" and I closed my eyes, squeezing in the night, feeling my lids flicker as if housing angry ants. *I don't want to go home*, I whispered to myself. *Not now, not ever . . .*

4

Bloody Naivety

30 January 1972

"What you need is a civil war."
JULIUS CAESAR

"A land . . . where light is as darkness."
JOB, CH.12-V.2

It was about this time that Neal Armstrong made one giant step for mankind, while here in the North, the Unionists were taking their usual two steps back for the Empire. Neal claimed there were no moon men up there, and he was right, of course. They were all down here, in the biggest spaceship mankind would ever witness, in a place called Stormont.

Black people were marching for civil rights in America, and Catholics in the North had the audacity to try and sample some of that pie, also. It was shortly after that my oldest brother, Danny, purchased a car. Not too many Catholics had cars in those days, so it was the talk of the street. It was a sky-blue Mini and it was his pride and joy.

One Sunday, before sunrise, he shook me from a deep sleep. 'C'mon, kid. Hurry and get dressed. We're goin'.'

For two weeks he had been promising me a drive in the car, some place special. But I didn't believe him. I thought he was full of shit. But here I was, squeezing into his tiny car, filled to capacity with three of his mates. It was brilliant. I didn't care where he was going, or that I could hardly breathe through lack of room; just being in the car was heaven.

When we finally reached our destination, he said, 'Out, kid. We're here.'

'What do you call this place,' I asked, my legs buckling with pins and needles.

He laughed. 'Derry.'

I hadn't a clue where Derry was but it sounded magical. I could smell fish and chips in the air and it made me think of Bangor on a Sunday afternoon. It was 30 January 1972 and little did I or anyone else know what a terrible nightmare awaited us. It became the seminal moment in my life, a baptism of fire into the real world of being a nationalist in the North of Ireland.

The smell of fish and chips was quickly swept away by the stench of gas and gunpowder. It followed us all the way home. On the journey to Derry we couldn't stop talking, filled with the delight of navigation on wheels, laughing. But the entire journey home was in stone silence, as if not talking meant it hadn't happened.

My father almost cried as we entered the house, telling us the terrible news. 'They've killed thirteen people. I thought youse were among them,' he repeated, over and over again.

My brother said nothing. His silence said it all: there was no way they would get away with it. The world would make justice prevail.

It was laughable how naïve we all were in those days.

Whenever I would visit my cousins in the staunchly loyalist Tiger Bay, tessellated pavements of red, white and blue surrounded their homes, like talismans, chasing away the Fenian, evil spirits.

The young girl who lived next door to my uncle, was a couple of years older than me. She was beautiful and each time I saw her I could never take my eyes off her.

'See enough?' she asked, catching me watching her, one day.

'I . . . well . . . oh . . .' My face was burning.

'Why're ye takin' a reddener?' she smiled, walking towards me in the street, her gorgeous eyes trapping me.

A couple of days later I saw her again.

'What's yer name?' she asked.

'Sammy. What's yours?'

Little evolved as the months passed. Then came a summer that changed my life forever, a summer filled with rushing daylights that banished the misery of a squeaky voice and spotted skin.

'What kept ye?' she asked. 'I thought ye'd chickened out.' She sat on a dilapidated swing, sucking on a blood-red lolly.

I shouldn't have been there. It was too far from home and my father had always warned me, for some arcane reason, to avoid the park. But Judy had gone on and on, calling me a chicken, a mommy's boy. I had to prove her wrong. 'That lolly makes you look like you're wearing lipstick.'

'So? I do wear lipstick – so there!' She squeezed her lips, and to prove her point produced a tube of lipstick from beat-up jeans and applied it. 'See?'

I was shocked as I took the adjacent swing, the rusted chains staining my hands.

Suddenly she leapt from her swing, stood facing me, then placed the lolly an inch from my face. 'Suck,' she demanded.

It was mushy with her slobbers and dripped on her fingers like melted candle grease. I found it repulsive and jerked my head away. 'No.'

'Snob!' There was anger in her eyes. Dark, challenging anger.

'Am not!'

'Suck if ye're not a snob.'

I wondered if anyone was watching. 'Okay! Okay! Don't stick

it in my gob!' I sucked, disgusted with myself, amazed at what I was doing.

'Ha! Sammy's wearing lipstick! Sammy's wearing lipstick!' She circled my swing, singing.

'You're crazy, wee girl. Know that?'

'Judy. My name's Judy. Say it.'

'I know your effin' name!'

'Say it. Whisper it. Here. In my ear.'

She leaned to me and I could smell *Lifebouy* soap and *Sunsilk* shampoo oozing from her. 'Judy,' I whispered, but not before checking her ear for wax. She slowly turned her face and kissed me hard, causing our teeth to clink like early-morning milk bottles. I could taste the ice on her breath.

'C'mon. Over here.' She pushed me towards the old green hut that functioned as toilet, shelter and storage. Its hoary paint was peeling, revealing initials of lovers long gone. A few yards away, discarded condoms lay guiltily in the grass, pregnant with their owners' imagination. Without warning, she opened her shirt and placed my hand on her breast. It was warm and small, like an egg after a hen goes to feed. 'I love ye. I'll always love ye,' she whispered.

My head was spinning. I never knew things like this existed.

'Say I love ye,' she asked, suddenly coy.

'I love you,' I managed to say, my throat dry with anticipation. At that moment, I would have said anything. I would have said, "Fuck the Pope" and "God save the Queen". I would have become a traitor for this strange magic that was being weaved on me. Suddenly, the sound of released water filled the air and we held our breaths as the "parky" made some tea. A colony of tealeaves danced in the drain's vortex of dirty rainwater. If he spotted us, we'd be dead.

'My da'd kill me if he caught me with ye,' whispered Judy, once the silence returned.

'I know. My da'd kill me if he caught me doin' this,' I agreed.

She laughed. 'No. Not for that. Because you're a Taig.'

'A what?' I was baffled.

26

'A Taig. A Catholic.'

'Why? What's wrong with that?'

She just shook her head. 'Nothin'. Just be careful when ye come to our street.'

Even though I hadn't a clue what "Taig" meant, it made me feel dirty, uncomfortable. It was my first taste into the real world of Catholics and Protestants, into the real world of "Northern Ireland".

After that, my father forbid me to visit my cousins, referring to them as the dung beetle of the insect world: hating the rose but wallowing in its manure. 'Catholics are the saucers in the North of Ireland: close to the cup but never being allowed to savour its contents,' he said, angrily.

It was an anger I hoped never to see again.

I started work in a timber yard near the docks as one of about twelve Catholics from a work force of over a hundred. Needless to say, we weren't given warm welcomes – except near the Glorious Twelfth when, consumed with booze and hatred, our fellow Protestant workers would utilise our tiny tea-hut as a bonfire. If any of us were in it then that was a plus. Not a week went by without some sort of threat – physical or verbal – being made against us.

But the Twelfth was always the worst, forcing the tribal animosity of sowing the bones of the dead into a patchwork of bible and absurdity.

After a few months of walking home backwards for my own survival, I decided a carpenter was not my calling and ended up working in the abattoir, a stone's-throw away from the timber yard. A railway track stretched behind the industrial wasteland. During summer days heat rose off the tracks in crimped patterns that made them look soft and familiar in the baking distance. When someone placed an egg – usually a pilfered seagull's egg – upon the track's gnarled metal, the egg would fry perfectly as if on a kitchen cooker.

In summer, the wasteland had a rough beauty about it, of gossiping insects with their orchestral hum of wings surrounded by yellows, juniper and sage and occasional bursts of purple and red wild flowers, whites and violets, mixing triumphantly with rust and rotting carcasses of dead dogs and cats – making it something that could be tolerated, despite its roughness. In fact, these gritty imperfections gave the industrial wasteland character. There was beauty out there in the rapidly diminishing landscape, something true and necessary and soothing in its quiet reassurances of vastness and power. Unlike the abattoir . . .

Dove-grey smoke drifted upward from a massive chimney, like a ghost, formless yet controlled, as if the building was a living being, breathing steam. Dull lights peered dimly from behind frosted glass and the smell of something floated heavily in the air, at once familiar and strange, and for a very brief moment a specific sensation of everything being unreal. It reminded me of the old black-and-white documentaries of concentration camps I had seen on the television.

The abattoir was a gothic conveyer-belt of transmogrification as live, bewildered creatures entered one way, only to emerge naked, humiliated and dismembered from another. Galvanized by the smell of blood, some, in a futile attempt to escape the inevitable, would leap the barrier, only to break their legs, lying in a mangled heap and quickly set upon by angry butchers who would leave a bloody highway of intricate veins and vestigial nerves strewn everywhere, some ticking with shock.

Each alerted animal had the propensity of craning its neck sidewards, watching the bloody hands and lethal steel do terrifying work. The dismembered bodies were quickly captured on unforgiving "S" hooks giving the scene a grotesque, Bosch-like madness of ruddy violins of sheep carcasses and cello-shaped cows. The place was massive and held no boundaries. It was breathtakingly horrible, like the Sistine Chapel blooded by barbarians, seething with rage in a hideous frenzy of activity. Its dank coldness reeked with tension and void of all things human.

The workers were saturated in blood and were as red as the mangled wreckage of meat they hacked at, distinguishable only by the tiny whiteness of their eyes, teeth and fingernails. They continued working their endless preparation of death as if they were immune, moving in perfect harmony, as if part of some farcical play performed for an invisible audience. They all seemed to be talking at once; loud yet ambient.

Suddenly, my nostrils began to flood with a stomach-churning smell. The same stinking stench from outside the building came at me with force, but more powerful in its taste of rotten flesh, and of fear and hate oozing from the ruins of carcasses and their tormentors.

One group of workers were seated comfortably in a tiny corner of the room, seemingly immune to the chaos all about them, talking and reading newspapers. They devoured their meal of fried eggs and freshly slaughtered meat, wiping their stained mouths with bloody, ragged handkerchiefs.

I felt my stomach move at the thought of eating a creature I had seen alive and well only minutes ago. How could their stomachs hold down the food? I felt my head go light and wondering if I was going to vomit, if my resolve would evaporate?

'Are you feeling okay?' asked the foreman, grinning. 'You look pale.'

'No, don't you worry about me. This is nothin',' I lied. 'Get me my knives . . .' It was then that I remembered Sadie's prophetic words: *You'll be able to do this one day.*

On the plus side, I was able to bring home as much meat as I could carry, each Friday. Some of the Catholic workers refused to take any, perceiving it as an insult to the Fishy Friday imposed by Rome. It didn't bother me for a moment. Steak would beat fish any day of the week, said the Protestant blood in me.

5

Return of the Native

September 1976, daytime

"And this also . . . has been one of the dark places of the earth."
CONRAD

"When one man says no . . . Rome trembles."
SPARTACUS

The van's wipers scythed the windscreen, leaving iridescent ellipses in its wake as I peered tentatively from the grilled windows. In the oblique distance, chalky headlights swathed the silhouettes of starving trees and serpentine hedges, transforming them into a Gothic vignette. I could only steal a quick, last glance of freedom as the ponderous gates of Long Kesh slammed thunderously behind us, making the van quiver.

This wasn't my first "visit" to the Kesh. I'd just been released the previous year from a three-year sentence. In 1973 I'd had the dubious distinction of being the first Irish nationalist to appear in front of the infamous non-jury Diplock court. I had been charged with being a member of an "illegal" organization, a republican,

31

someone who questioned, forcefully, Britain's occupation of the North of Ireland.

'Not to worry,' said my lawyer. 'You'll probably only be fined. Probably about £30. That's what they're all being fined. Cheer up.'

30 quid! Where the fuck was I, an unemployed nationalist who had been forced out of every job I ever had, going to get 30 quid? My da would have a buckle in his eye if he ended up having to find the money. I doubted if he had three quid to his name let alone 30! I didn't know if I could face him.

I needn't have worried. The so-called Judge, Robert Lowrey, sorted it all out. 'There is no doubt in my mind that you are a dedicated terrorist . . .' I glanced at my father's stress-burnt face, wondering what his reaction to having to pay all this money was going to be. '. . . I have, within the law, the power to sentence you to eight years. But I must take into consideration your age . . .' I had just recently turned seventeen. '. . . three years in prison . . .' For one terrible minute, I thought Lowrey had sentenced me to three years. My father was taking the fine a lot worse than I thought. He was screaming something while my lawyer kept patting me on the back, telling me not to worry. 'I can't believe he simply didn't fine you . . . so sorry . . .'

That was 15 Oct 1973.

Now I was back at my old alma mater, probably for ten more years. A place where men made rules but seldom obeyed them. A place where, sometimes, men changed the course of history.

The old Nissen huts were now being replaced with what would eventually become notorious around the world for mistreatment of political prisoners: the H Blocks. They were the jewels of the British Government's doomed-to-failure "Normalisation" policy; a policy they hoped would prove to the world that everything was honky dory in this wee piece of earth and that all the terrible things that were happening were just figments of the imagination.

'Out!' shouted a gruff voice, and out we tumbled – myself and two loyalist prisoners – into the incandescent glare of the Reception, where we were quickly herded into tiny, solo cubicles. The doors, which stood in an uneven wave, de-crucified by time and wear, quickly slammed behind us, their bolts shooting into place. The bolts sounded like old .303 rifles being cocked, and I had no doubt in my mind that the screw at the other side of the door would have loved to have had one in his hands at this very moment.

The narrative walls of the cubicles kept reminding me of something I no longer wanted to remember, but like a long-lost diary you simply had to turn the page. After a few minutes the door suddenly opened causing the light to bleach my eyes.

'Here you! Strip! Put this on! We don't have all fuckin' night!' said the voice, slamming the door.

Resting at my feet, like a dirty pool of water, was a brown prison uniform or "gear", as the prisoners called it. On the wall to my left, someone had scrawled: *"You'll have to nail the gear to my back!"* A nice act of defiance, I thought, but in all honesty it did little to steel me. My heart had not stopped banging in my chest, causing white sparks of pain to dance in my head. The door flung open and once again my eyes stung. My stomach lurched like a trap-door.

'What the fuck's wrong with ye?' said the screw. He was the size of nothing and his over-sized hat kept falling over his eyes, which were bloodshot to the colour of a baboon's arse. His breath stank of last night's whiskey. 'Didn't I tell ye to strip and put the uniform on?'

I had perfected my speech in my head, reiterating it each night on my bunk in Crumlin Road jail. Now that it was time for the main event, my throat had turned arid. 'I . . .' My stomach started to churn, causing purgative acid to ferment in my bowels. I needed to take a crap. 'I refuse to . . . wear . . . the . . . gear.'

There! I'd said it! God, I'd said it! Just like magic, a great weight eased from me, even though, in my heart, I knew what was coming next. The screw stared at me as if he had been struck by lightning, blinked a couple of times then slammed the door, leaving the smell of a starched shirt floating in the air. It made me think of my father, dressed for a Saturday night, and it made me feel so terribly alone and, yet, afraid to be afraid. I could hear the muffled best-of-mates laughter from the loyalist prisoners and screws, the sound fading as they boarded a van for one of the Blocks. I could hear the van's fat tires crunch on the expanse of gravel fading to an echo, then silence.

Suddenly, the Reception became as eerie as a tomb and my nerves began to play havoc with my mind, like a fox waiting in the dark. Anticipation. Silence. Of course, I thought, almost smiling. I knew, from experience, that a perfect measure of silence had the potent power to be as ruthless and as terrifying as the actuality. This was all part of the meltdown procedure, dehumanising.

When the door opened this time, the screw was no longer alone. 'This is your last chance, Millar. Put the fuckin' uniform on *now!*'

Defiantly, I crossed my arms, taut as springs, and waited for the inevitable. It wasn't long coming. On the plus side of being attacked in such close confines is that your attackers usually do as much damage to themselves as they do to you.

'All right now, wee hard man? Bet yer ma 'n' da would be proud of ye layin' there, bollock-naked. We should take a photo of ye and send it to 'em!'

It had only taken them a matter of minutes to literally rip the clothes of my back and give me a "jolly good" kicking into the bargain. Two of the screws lay on top of me, sweating and heaving, cursing and threatening. After they got their breath back I was jerked by the hair and pulled to my feet.

'I'm not going anywhere naked. No matter what you or –' I was kicked in the balls, and collapsed to the floor vomiting, before being dragged into the yard, the rough tarmac surface flaying my skin, embedding it with tiny pebbles.

'Take 'im to 1. They'll sort 'is wagon out for 'im,' said a screw with an English accent.

It was Friday night. I should be in the *Star* drinking a pint and listening to a terrible band doing terrible impressions of Fleetwood Mac. Instead, I was naked; my arse covered in tarmac buckshot and my balls a wicked magenta.

And I still hadn't reached the Block.

6

The Journey Begins

September 1976, evening

"The English have a divine right to fight the Irish on their native soil, but every Irish man fighting against the British government is to be treated as an outlaw."

MARX

"Naked . . . for months on end in a freezing cell . . . beatings . . . whatever . . . Millar went through it all."

Pulitzer Prize winning author, WILLIAM SHERMAN, *Esquire Magazine*

The contiguous bone-coloured cells, whose starkness was augmented by a dark-blue sky, came into view as I descended from the van. A salient moon floated merrily above, its incongruous grin belying the madness at its feet. It was a fat moon, and it reminded me of an Auguste Rodin nude, just like myself at this minute.

From the corner of my eye a tiny red nipple faded in and out amongst the shadows like an SOS beacon. A screw, his face sheltered from the chill, had ensconced himself to a wall as he sucked on a cigarette. A village of discarded butts littered his feet like spent ammo shells. He could easily have been Clint Eastwood in *Hang 'em High*. For a second, I thought he shook his head at me, as if questioning my rationale. But it was probably just the moon playing games.

'Go on! Git yer arse in there!' screamed the screw in the van.

'Take it easy, for fuck's sake!' I shouted back.

'Shutdafackup and git in!'

I took a deep breath; entered.

The astringent smell of polish was overpowering as I entered the "Circle". The floor was constantly polished, buffed and shone making it the colour of horse-eye ebony and as smooth as oil on water. The surrealistic feeling of being on a giant, obsidian mirror came to mind. An orderly – a non-political prisoner – who was buffing the floor stared at me for a second before continuing his mindless task, as if naked prisoners were the norm.

Quickly, I was shoved into a room after a voice had said "Enter", in response to the screw's knock. Four screws dripping with cheap after-shave flanked me. At his desk, pretending to write, sat the "PO", strolling his eyes leisurely along a yellow pad, discerning imaginary mistakes with invisible ink. His hair was the colour of damp straw; a sore, ruddy complexion evoked habitual scrubbing, as did his bleached shirt. Tiny bars of brass rested on his solid shoulders, completing the propaganda poster. After what seemed an eternity, he finally placed the pen down and nodded to the screw beside me.

'Number 606, Millar, *Sir!*' barked the screw. 'Refuses to obey a direct order, *Sir!* Refuses to wear his uniform, *Sir!*'

Straw Head placed his fingers under his chin. 'Is that correct?' he finally said.

'More or less,' I answered.

'More or less, *Sir!*' screamed the screw into my ear. 'You'll address the PO and all members of staff as *Sir*, Millar!'

Sir Millar? That had a certain ring to it.

Straw Head tilted forward and removed an orange from his desk. He nipped its skin, tunnelling under it with his finger. Citrus engulfed the room as he tore the orange in two. 'I

38

remember you,' he said, nodding, and for a terrible moment, I thought he was going to start singing the Frank Ifield hit. Instead, he said, 'Crumlin Road. '73. Remember me?' There was hate in his eyes; not original hate but the secretive, retrospective hate anchored in memory.

Yes; now I remember. His name was Docky Fada, and in those days he held no rank. He was as quiet as a mouse, never looking you in the eye, galvanised by his own shadow. Now here he was all brass and toughness.

He picked up his pen and tapped his finger with it. 'Different days now, eh?' he said, his left eyebrow forming a hairy question mark. 'No more special status. No more ridiculous scenarios of inmates having the audacity to tell staff what to do, now that the tables are turned. The shoe is on the other foot, Millar. Better get used to it.'

'Whatever you say,' I answered sardonically.

'*Sir!* You will address the PO as –'

'It's okay, Wilson. Time is on our side. A few weeks of solitary confinement will teach Millar some respect,' replied Docky. 'You realise, of course, that each day that you refuse to wear the uniform and go to work, will result in loss of remission and all privileges? Think about that in your cell, tonight.'

Somewhere outside in the night, sounds gathered force: the drone of a helicopter sliced the air, drowning out the anxious call of a lost bird and the lonely lament of rain beating on the windows.

'I can tell you're no longer listening, Millar,' said Docky. 'Very well. But let me make one thing clear. If you fuck with my staff, you fuck with me. I don't tolerate disrespect. The rules are simple: when a member of staff, the governor or myself come to your cell, you will stand to attention. Our maxim is: key in the door – foot on the floor. Understand?' He made a motion to dismiss me, but stopped. 'Where did you acquire those cuts and bruises?'

I remained silent, but the screw behind me boomed: '*Sir!* 606, Millar, acquired said cuts and bruises when he slipped on the slick step of the van. We advised 606, Millar, to wear his uniform so as to at least shelter himself from the elements. Our advice was ignored, *Sir!*'

Docky nodded, satisfied with said answer, but had some prudent advice before dismissing me. 'See the doctor in the morning. Those balls of yours look like they're ready to explode.'

7

Bare Soles and Bared Souls

September 1976, nightfall

> *"A great part of the information obtained in war is contradictory,*
> *a still greater part is false, and by far the greatest part*
> *is of a doubtful character."*
> CLAUSEWITZ, *On War*

Papillary lights, each the size of a baby's toe, correlated the entire stretch of the wing. A bluish darkness added to the eerie silence that was ruined only by the plop plop plopping of my bare feet. The door of the cell slammed behind, stinging my ears, making me jump but bathing me with relief as the day's events seeped away, melting with the metal echo. I was in the cell no more than a minute when a voice shouted: 'Sam!'

'What?' I replied through the door's edge, a sliver of freedom.

'Get to your door.'

'I'm at the bloody door! Who is it?' It was disorientating, speaking in the darkness, my voice boomeranging back, hollow and strange.

'Finbar,' replied the voice. 'Any *sceal*, mate?'

Finbar was the present OC of the protesting prisoners, and

41

even though I'd virtually arrived at the embryonic stage of the protest he, together with eight others, had been on protest for at least five weeks. I would soon find out that five weeks without visits, reading material, radio or TV felt more like five months. Adding to the monotonous, mundane repetitiveness was the fact that our mail was at the mercy of the screws' impulses, which were guided by their Alzheimer's disease of forgetfulness.

I began with the little bit of *sceal* – news – I could remember from the night before. 'There was a Brit stiffed in . . .' Slowly, I began to relay all the war news from the last few weeks that they hadn't heard, hoping this might be a lift for morale. But the icy, cynical voice of McJoke soon taught me what was meant by "news" on the protest.

'Fuck that crap! Have you any news covering the protest? *That's* what we want to hear.'

I could hear beds creak as bodies lifted, waiting for my response. I'd already been told what to say by the OC in the Crum: *Tell 'em it'll all be over soon. Anything, so long as it keeps them from leaving the protest . . .*

'The word is that it'll all be over soon.'

'How fuckin' soon?'

Anything, so long as it keeps them from leaving . . .

'Christmas.' I felt my face burn at the lie.

'Christmas?' enquired McJoke. I pictured his eyelids tightening with disbelief, smelling something not right. 'Christmas?' he repeated, giving me the chance to get out of the hole I had just dug.

'That's the word. If not Christmas, definitely January at the latest.'

'Did ye bring any snout with ye?' asked the gruff voice of Teapot.

Snout was tobacco in Block jargon 'No, Teapot. The screw took it from me in the reception.'

'Bastard.'

I didn't know if he meant the screw or me. 'It's freezing in this cell, Finbar,' I said, quickly changing the subject. My nerves probably made it colder.

'The screws turn the heat off in the winter,' replied Finbar, 'and put it up full blast in summer. Part of their moronic strategy to make us come off the protest. You'll soon get used to it, mate. Wrap one of those hairy blankets on ye. Toughen ye up.' He was laughing his contagious laugh.

I immediately grabbed a blanket and felt its coarse, *Brillo*-pad hairs bite my skin. It was torturous, but little did I know then how many years it would be my shadow. 'This blanket's rough.'

'Dry yer eyes!' responded a chorus of voices.

'Who was it told you Christmas?' McJoke was at it again. A dog, refusing to let go of a bone.

'Well . . . I don't really want to mention names out the door. The screws could be listening.' My lie got bigger.

'Never mind him, Sam. How'd the Hammers do on Saturday?' asked Finbar, West Ham United's number one fan.

'Fuck the Hammers,' said McJoke, oozing with diplomacy. 'This is more important than all of –'

'What do ye mean fuck the Hammers? Fuck you,' said Finbar. 'What were we saying, Sam, before we were so rudely interrupted?'

'Never mind all that old political nonsense,' complained Teapot. 'Are you certain you didn't even bring a wee bit of snout?' There was panic in his voice.

'Never mind snout,' cut in McJoke. 'Get one answer at a time.'

'What'd ye mean never mind snout?' said Teapot indignantly. 'You don't smoke. So shut yer mouth. And anyway; this protest is never gonna end. So dry *yer* eyes.'

The verbal jousting went unabated, like table tennis, back and forth. I left the door, walked to the bars and gazed at the night's sky. It was peopled with lucid stars so numerous and washed in God's shadow that it was beautiful. Screaming conquistador starlings flew to the safety of the enormous, mushroom-shaped orbs of the security lights that stood, splashing a pyrite-coloured web over the Block, animating it in charcoal and cheese.

Before I fell asleep, wondering if I should admit I had made the date up, Teapot's voice grumbled in the dark: 'Bastard. No snout. Probably made that date up, as well.'

Tonight would be a long day's journey that I couldn't wait to finish and I would remember forever that things we do not know make us speculate. Information, no matter how delightful, is always dangerous in the aftermath . . .

8

Reality Check

September 1976, dawn

*"I am pent up in frowzy lodgings, where there is not room enough
to swing a cat."*

SMOLLETT

Next morning, reveille was introduced with the screws' orchestral
combination of baton and boots against the cell doors. The screws
stood, their grinning eyes peering through the security-flap, bang
bang banging in staccato until each prisoner got out of bed.

'A beautiful morning like that and still in yer bed! Naughty,
naughty. Up! *Keys in the door – feet on the floor!*' He rattled the
keys, hoping to aggravate.

Occasionally, a prisoner would rise to the bait. "*Work the
keys up yer arse, ye wanker!*"

Unperturbed, the screw continued his woodpecker tap tap
tapping. 'How do ye want yer eggs done, lads? Sunny-side up?
Bacon? Well done? What about a sausage?'

'Ask yer wife,' shouted a gruff voice. 'She was gettin' one last
night while you were on the night-shift!'

'*Ooooohhh*, Teapot. I'm shocked at your language. And you a good Catholic boy!'

Outside, the starlings had left to search for food, but a posse of synchronous homing pigeons skimmed the air, riding the surf that oozed from the sun's golden rays, melting the early-morning darkness. Suddenly, without warning, the birds dropped like blue crashing waves, disappearing behind the horizon.

There was no bacon for breakfast, of course. Not a sausage. Just bland porridge and suspicious-looking bread freckled with blue dots of mould.

Shortly after "breakfast", Finbar provided me with a brief run-down from his cell. 'The screw's comin' to slop us out soon. Go. Even if you don't need to. It gets ye out of the cell, if only for a few minutes. Always remember that we go nowhere naked . . . or with the gear on. Stick the towel on ye.'

The screw was getting closer for slop out, so I sat on the bed waiting. Without warning, the flap went up and a pair of eyes glared in at me. They resembled concentric gob-stoppers that had been sucked and dipped in varnish. He said nothing. Simply stared. I stared back regardless of the disconcerting effect of staring at a green door with bulging eyes. I'd be damned if I would give him the satisfaction of looking away, intimidated. The flap slammed down!

Slowly it opened again. Bulging eyes. Lids closing. Opening . . .

An annoying bastard, I thought, as we began the staring contest again.

'You know the rules, Millar. *Keys in the door – feet on the floor!* Don't have me call for reinforcements.'

I didn't budge, but my stomach tightened at the implied threat.

Slam! Went the flap.

I could no longer see him, but he was there.

The flap opened again. 'Peek-a-boo!' said the voice. 'I see you. Do you see me?'

Sick bastard.

'Last chance, Millar. Four officers are on their way. We'll teach ye a thing or two if you don't stand.' He began a countdown.

'Ten. Nine. Eight. *Seveeennnn.* Six . . . Wise up and save us all the bother, will ye?'

I refused to answer, but my stomach was churning.

'Four. *Threeeeeeeee!* Last chance. Here come the officers now. Two-and-a-half . . .'

His voice was torture. I wanted it over with.

'One!' The door gave a terrible rattle and I held tight to the bed, my knuckles popping.

The door remained closed. Nothing but a sly silence. Then a crazy laugh screamed: '*Ha-ha!* Got you there, Sam! Caught ye lovely! Thought I was the screw, didn't ye! *Ha-ha!*'

I bounced off the bed just in time to see a prisoner known as Polar Bear, zigzagging up the wing, going from cell to cell, shouting: 'Got 'im, lads. Should've seen Millar's gob! *Ha-ha!*' Then he stopped outside Finbar's cell. 'Hey, Finbar? Millar put his feet on the floor, thinking I was the screw.'

That's a load of bollocks, I was about to shout when I realised he was trying to wind me up.

'I thought he was gonna shite himself,' continued Polar Bear loudly for all to hear. 'Wee hard man from the New Lodge, my balls. *Ha-ha!*' He was wiping the tears from his bearded face as he walked back to my cell. 'I'm surprised at you, Sam. Fallin' fer that oul one.'

'I'm too wise to your tricks, Polar Bear,' I lied. 'You're played-out.'

He threw his head back laughing, as if caught in an invisible hook.

Polar Bear was infamous for his *mixes*, pranks on unsuspecting prisoners. In Crumlin Road jail he masqueraded as a doctor or social worker, alternating as his moods took him. But his forte was perfected in the parody of a fire-and-brimstone priest by the name of Foxx whose weekend antics brought "converts" from every landing in the jail. Each Saturday night, with a line of new arrivals, he'd transform his cell into a confessional by partitioning it with a bed-sheet replete with a spy-hole to watch the sinner's reaction:

'Come in, my son,' said the sacerdotal voice behind the sheet.

A carrot-top prisoner, his anxious face a map of freckles the size and colour of rusted nail-heads, entered and sat down.

'Yes, my son?'

The young man coughed to clear his throat. 'It's been almost . . .' his voice trailed as he noticed the solo eye on the white sheet beaming at him.

'C'mon! I don't have all day, ye know!'

'It's . . . it's been almost three . . . months since my last –'

'Three months! What kindda Catholic are ye with no sins in three months? Eh?'

'I'm truly sorry, Father, but this is the first chance I've –'

'Cut the bloody martyr crap, for heaven's sake! Get down to the nitty-gritty!'

Carrot-Top's hands were damp and he wiped them on his jeans, leaving dark snail-stains on them. 'I've had . . . impure thoughts . . . actions. Also –'

'*Hold it!*' screamed Polar. 'Who the hell's in charge here? Take it easy. What kindda impure action?'

Carrot-Top licked his lips. 'You know . . . wanked.'

'Wanked? What's that?' Father Polar was biting his lips, suppressing a laugh-bubble in his chest.

'Well, *master . . . bate*, Father.' The young man shifted nervously on the chair. 'You know what I mean . . .'

'Know? *Know?* How the hell would I know a thing like that? Disgustin'! What did your impure thoughts consist of?' You could hear an audible sucking of air as Carrot-Top prepared for the plunge.

'Well . . . I've had these terrible thoughts about my best mate's girlfriend, you know?'

'As God is my witness, if you have the cheek to say "you know" to me again, you'll feel the hand of God across yer head! I'm a priest, ye big eejit! How am I suppose to "know" stuff like that?'

'Sss . . . sorry, Father. It's just –'

48

'Details! Give me some details about yer best friend's girl, ye Judas ye.'

'I . . . Well, she's lovely.'

'Lovely?' mimicked Father Polar, sarcastically. 'Lovely? Never mind that. How's she built?'

'Oh! Great. She's built really great. Built like a tank,' gushed Carrot-Top.

'Good pair of knockers?' asked Polar.

'Unbelievable!' enthused the young man, warming, loving this liberal-minded priest. 'She makes Dolly Parton look flat! Hee-hee!'

Polar couldn't help but smile at that one.

'Really? What about the rest of her? Her face?'

'Ach, she's gorgeous, Father,' boasted Carrot-Top, elevating her from lovely. 'And the arse on her! Powerful! You know?'

In a split second, Polar's hand came from behind the sheet, crushing down on Carrot-Top's head, spiralling him to the ground. 'Didn't I warn ye about that "know" business? Didn't I?'

'Hey!' shouted Carrot-Top indignantly. 'No need to fuckin' hit, Father!'

'What? What the fuck did ye say? What kindda fuckin' language is that to use in front of a priest? Eh, you dirty-mouthed bastard?' *Whack! Whack! Whack!* More slaps registered to Carrot-Top's head.

'Hey! Hey!' he screamed, getting to his feet as Polar administered a swift kick to his arse.

'Now get the fuck out of here before I tell your mate about Dolly-fuckin'-Parton!'

The unfortunate Carrot-Top tumbled out of the cell, passing the line of sinners, giving advice. 'What ever ye do, don't curse in front of that priest. He's a fuckin' maniac!'

Admittedly, Polar Bear's mixes were childish, but without the likes of him time in prison stretched into an infinite duration; a never-ending shadow lost in its own abyss. He leaned against my cell door, and in a conspiratorial voice whispered: 'I heard what ye said 'bout the protest ending in three months. A load of bollocks, wasn't it?' Before I could answer, he walked away, grinning, but not before he got a last dig in. 'Hate to be ye Christmas morning, mate. A selected memory can only marshal you so far down the path. Don't fuck with people's minds.'

9

The Volunteer

November 1976

"How many things I can do without."

SOCRATES

'Hey, Sam? Get to yer door a minute.'

I was standing at the window, daydreaming. It was a pleasant daydream of walking in the Water Works on a summer day, watching girls in jeans the colour of the sky. I was wearing a *Ben Sherman, Levi's* and *DMs*. I was about to touch for a girl I had had my eye on for weeks when Teapot's growl broke the segue.

'What, Teapot? What is it?'

'Can ye see that screw outside Cell 4?'

I looked through the slit in the door and could just about see the screw. He was opening the doors for "slop-out".

'Yes. What about 'im?'

'We call him the Volunteer. Watch and ye'll see why.'

I watched as the screw neared Teapot's cell, then opened it, releasing Teapot who strolled by and winked at me as he passed the slit in my cell, singing, '*Hi ho, hi ho, it's off to work we go . . .*'

51

Usually the screw would have a sour look on his face at that sarcastic song – part of our protest was refusal to work, and they took it personally – but this one had a grin: very unusual for our environment. He was rocking back and forth on the balls of his feet, scanning the wing to his left. I was about to walk away, bored, when he suddenly bent down to tie his lace. The only problem was it didn't need tying. In fact, for some strange reason, he loosened both laces and then began to re-tie them. Had I not been watching, I wouldn't have spotted the sleight-of-hand as his fingers touched the edge of the cell-mat which was flush to the cell door entrance. This was unusual, also, as we normally kept the remnant in the centre of the cell to walk on.

The screw, still trying to "tie" his lace, was now peeping under his armpit as if looking for sweat-stains. What he actually was doing, I found out later, was watching the other screw between the security grill whose "job" it is to monitor the wings on either side of him. Finally, having learned to "tie" his laces, the screw stood up, stretched, yawned and with the tip of his boot edged the mat back into the cell.

On cue, Teapot returned, singing, 'Oh what a beautiful morning . . .'

Before the screw closed the door I could see him winking, no doubt, at Teapot: operation completed. Later that morning, Teapot explained the strange behaviour. The screw had placed ten cigarettes under the mat. 'Does it every Saturday and Sunday morning when he's on the wing.'

The cigarettes were worth their weight in gold to the men who smoked, more so because as part of the punishment for refusing to wear prison uniforms or do prison work, all "privileges" were denied us. Each real cigarette would be crushed, re-rolled into ten needle-thin Blanket cigarettes then evenly distributed – Teapot taking a tiny commission for his work, of course – amongst the smokers.

I was fortunate in that I didn't smoke, but to those who did it was a windfall that was greatly appreciated knowing it might be a long time before the next one. The monotony which seeped longevity into each day was sustained by the sheer weight of the vacuity: no radio; no visits; no reading material – except a bible; no sweets; no clothes; no tobacco . . . *No! No! No!* On the bright side, of course, having nothing meant the screws and Brits could take nothing else from you. In the interest of sanity, it's always good to look on the bright side.

The Volunteer also handed-out football results each Sunday morning and made sure we received an extra few rounds of bread with our "food". All in all, he behaved like a human being. Had he been caught, he would have been ostracised, at best, by his fellow screws, at worst, fired. He was an enigma but as long as he supplied the cigarettes and football results he could remain one.

10

Squeaks and Drums

12 July 1977

"I am escaped with the skin of my teeth."

JOB

Usually about 1.00pm. the Blocks became as quiet as a tomb. Most screws had gone for lunch, or for a beer in their club. We always took advantage of this by either a quick nap, or learning a bit of the Irish language. I was at the window, daydreaming as usual, when Finbar's voice said, 'Sam? Can ye hear that?'

'What?'

'Someone's in Cell 26.'

Cell 26 was where the screws kept prison uniforms, just in case their wildest dreams came true: that we would all get up one morning and plead with them to allow us to go to work; give their shoes a quick shine, into the bargain. It was unusual that it should be open at that time of day, but he was correct. Someone *was* moving about in there.

The door slammed, and all was quiet except for Cowboy snoring his head off.

'Can ye hear that?' asked Finbar.

'No. What?'

'A little squeak-squeak sound. Such as . . .' Here he paused for effect, '. . . made by a new pair of prison-issued boots.'

I thought he had been reading too much Sherlock Holmes. We had all been on the protest for over a year, now, and perhaps it was just starting to get to him.

'Someone's put the gear on and fucked-off,' he insisted.

I began to laugh. No one had ever left the protest. Yes, men had refused to come *on* the protest, but no one coming on had ever left. It was inconceivable.

'We'll have to find out from Blade, later on. But my money says someone is gone,' insisted Finbar.

Blade was the new OC. Finbar had resigned his position as the stress of the job had become too much. It was a thankless task, and one not for the fainthearted. After siesta, we attempted to wake Blade, but to no avail. He was a notorious heavy sleeper, so we decided to wait until later in the day.

JCB didn't allow us to wait.

'Finbar, Blade isn't in his cell. I saw him leave about an hour ago – oh, by the way, he was wearing the gear.'

JCB said it so matter-of-factly that it took a few moments to sink in. The silence was tangible. Immense. No one spoke, except Finbar.

'I rest my case.' Agatha Christe would've been proud.

The rest of us just couldn't fathom anyone – never mind an OC – leaving the protest. Equally bad was the fact he hadn't had the courage to tell us he was going. It was a blow against our morale and against our ironclad belief that we were infallible.

After this traumatic experience we would look at each other from a different perspective and wonder who – if anyone – would be next. As for Blade, he unknowingly introduced a new phrase into our lexicon: "Squeaky-Booters". But the day hadn't been a complete disaster. Polar Bear was to be released from the madness, and despite the threats from the screws he came to each of our cells wishing us all the best, encouraging us to keep at it and that he would do everything he could to highlight our plight.

The look of powerless hatred on the screws' faces was one we would savour for a long time. Polar Bear had defied them since his first day on the protest. Their 24-hour lock-up, deprivation of all basic human necessities, had all been to no avail, and there wasn't a single thing they could do about it, except stand with their sick smiles and angry eyes.

Of course we were delighted for him – but also a bit envious. In a short while he'd be dressed, eating real food. Tonight he'd be with a woman. God! What we'd give to be in his shoes (when he'd finally get them!). A big hairy grin and a thumbs-up were the last we saw of him as he disappeared, swallowed by the van.

Little did we know that in two months he'd be dead, killed in a car crash on his way home from a meeting to gather support for the protest.

11

Dead Heroes of Our Youth
now breathing

January 1977

"Courage is resistance to fear, mastery of fear – not absence of fear."

TWAIN

A new year. A new beginning.

But as far as we were concerned, it was just another day. We were no longer permitted to wash in the washroom and had to make do with a basin of cold water, once a day. Slopping out had become a game of Russian roulette, never knowing what would happen next as far as the screws' behaviour was concerned. Walking up the wing to slop out was always an occasion for two or three of them to gather round, trying to intimidate. They couldn't resist telling you that it wouldn't be long until you were conforming, cleaning their boots and calling them "Sir". Being called "Sir" by a Blanket-man was a fantasy that lived in the screws' and governors' heads and the foolhardy amongst us would respond to the taunts by issuing a "yellow shower" – pouring the contents of the piss-pot over the screws' heads – despite the inevitable beating that would result.

Outside the window, Stumpy, the paraplegic seagull with one leg and devastated beak, was fighting another bird, healthier, over a scrap of bread. Stumpy was giving as good as he/she got, showing great resilience despite its handicap. Finally, having succeeded in chasing the protagonist, it attempted to shovel the bread into its mouth by scraping its bit of beak along the ground. It took 30 minutes to succeed and was painful to watch. But the lesson was there: Stumpy always endured.

The weather was perfect outside: heartbreaking. You knew God was getting a sly dig at you. A collection of smells suddenly touched me: melted tar cooling in the day's breeze; a soft, faint aroma of washing powder; and eggs frying on a pan. I thought I could hear the clarion tune of a *Mister Softy* ice-cream van and I pictured all the kids lining up for their cones, big solid grins on their tiny faces.

Sometimes you'll hear things that make you remember the days that you thought you've long forgotten, like the childhood days of November with its decaying scent of falling leaves, when time moved so unnoticeably slow. Sometimes you'll hear music that makes you remember memories in some darkened corner of your mind, when everything in the world seemed perfect, less suspect and open to error. I was just about to call Finbar to the window for a conversation when the voice of Hippo, the wing OC quickly spoiled the moment, staining the day.

Hippo was in full flow, lecturing out the window about heroes and martyrs who had died for Ireland. Yet, there was something patronizing about him telling us that what was needed were men of the calibre of Connolly, Pearse or Tone. Perhaps the fact he had only been on the Blanket a couple of months compared to the years the rest of us had done was what really grated.

'Take Tone, for example,' he continued. 'Even when he realised –'

But this was the last place you wanted to hear such talk. 'He's hardly any use to us now, is he?' I interrupted, squeezing my head against the bars. 'He's dead, the last I heard.'

'What? What did ye say?' he asked, incredulously, not believing his ears at such treachery.

'I said they're all bloody dead. What we need is someone like the Incredible Hulk to get us out of this mess.'

A ten-second silence.

'Who? What the fuck are ye rambling 'bout?'

Despite his moaning voice we were, all in all, feeling buoyant that fine day. The screws had even put sugar in the porridge and milk in the tea at supper – though not both in either, of course.

'The Incredible Hulk. That's who. He could knock down these doors with one of his gamma ray farts. Not a load of dust and bones like Tone and the rest. Unless you've got the dragon teeth to bring them to life?'

Laughter from the wing.

'I haven't a clue what yer slobbering about, ye buck fuckin' eejeet. I never heard of the invinsiblewhatever.'

'I'm not slobbering. Simply stating a fact. The Incredible Hulk. Aka Bruce Banner. A scientist hit with gamma rays that turned him green, so obviously he'd be on our side.'

Hippo false laughed, then said. 'Oh, I get it.' Then, returning to his original topic and listener, he said, 'As I was saying, John. The calibre of leadership in those days was nothing less than stellar. Connolly wouldn't even contemplate –'

'I'm serious,' I interjected, squeezing my head tighter against the bars for better acoustics. 'If we had the Hulk, we'd beat the Brits in a week.'

'Lay the fuck down.' he said, anger barely controlled.

'Then there's the Thing from *Fantastic Four*. Not up to par with Hulky in the strength category, but a damn good second.'

There was more laughter from the cells. I was on a roll.

'Listen,' said Hippo. 'I don't tolerate people makin' fun of Ireland's dead. Don't push it.' His voice quivered with emotion.

'*Ooooohhhh*. Better watch yourself, Sam. He'll have ye kneecapped when ye get out!' shouted Cowboy.

'What about Superman? Couldn't he help us?' someone asked, laughing.

'Naw. These doors are really green kryptonite. Deadly to

Superman,' I answered. 'That's why when we summon help we don't lure them inadvertently to their doom.'

'Wise up, the lot of ye!' shouted Hippo. 'The screws are listenin' and laughin' their balls off.'

'What balls? Screws don't have balls!' shouted Joe, bringing more laughter to the windows.

'What about the Lone Ranger?' inquired Cowboy, who then answered his own question: 'Naw. Trigger couldn't get down the wing.'

For the next three days the conversation revolved around the heroes of our childhood, bringing with it the quiet satisfaction of nostalgia. Then, just like us, it burnt itself out.

'Can you imagine what the people out there would think if they heard about all the crap that was talked about in the last few days? They'd think we were nuts. Youse should be ashamed of yerselves, republicans talking 'bout super-heroes on the TV. I only hope this never gets out.' Hippo was talking out the window for all to hear.

Rusted rain began to fall, causing ripples the size and colour of burnt pennies to form in the stagnant piss rings below our windows.

'You just don't get it, do ye, Hippo?' I said, laying on my back, staring at the ceiling.

'Get what? That ye're all a bunch of head-bangers?'

'First: we don't give a crap what anyone *out there* thinks. We're the ones trying to survive; not them. And second: for the last three days we've escaped this place – albeit in our minds, only. But escaped all the same. And it was all thanks to the Incredible Hulk. So stick that up yer arse and sit on it!'

Cowboy chuckled. 'The Lone Ranger, too. He played his part, Sam. Don't forget.'

Forget? How could I ever? That was the day when the new order arrived. The real nightmare had just begun . . .

12

Warts, Water and Joseph Mengele

August 1978

"By the pricking of my thumb, something wicked
this way comes."
SHAKESPEARE

'Was it just me or did I imagine that new order, Sam?'

I couldn't answer Finbar, momentarily, as the contents of my stomach threatened to head south. We were to throw our excrement out the windows, now that the screws and prison governors had refused to give us an assurance that no more beatings would take place. It was degrading, embarrassing and dehumanising, but the alternative was more beatings and more men coming off the protest. Besides, it would probably last only a few days, a week at most. The protest had become sedimentary, finding a comfortable niche of complacency seeping through. This would finish it once and for all.

One month later . . .

'What d'ye reckon, Finbar?' I asked, looking out the window at the rats patrolling the yard, eating the unthinkable.

63

'I thought the screws would've given in by now,' he answered, throwing a piece of rock-hard bread to a rat named Goofy, its buck teeth protruding like tiny planks of wood. 'This place is a disaster. Look at the state of it.'

The cells were now minus all "furniture" as punishment for our "uncivilised behaviour". The sickly white paint had been replaced by even sicklier brown, which, unfortunately, was not paint due to the fact that the screws, with their thick rubber gloves – the same rubber gloves they used to give out our "food" – had thrown our excrement back into the cells, forcing us to spread it upon the cell walls.

Next came the high-powered hoses directed into the cells, turning the grounded mattress into a saturated sponge. If you were unfortunate enough to be at the receiving end of the hose, you would quickly find yourself on the ground, knocked on your arse.

But it was the never-ending stench of shit and piss that made you crave for the friendly smell of *Old Spice, Brut, Lifebuoy* and *Cherry Blossom*. Now I knew how poor Job must have felt, sitting on his dunghill. The only consolation was that this would surely bring the madness to an end. There was no way even the Brits would allow it to continue.

'Two more weeks, Sam. I reckon it'll all be over.'

'Four at the most, Finbar. You know how slow the Brits are to surrender. Stiff upper-lip and all that stuff, old chap.'

'Yea. Yer right, mate. Give them about four. Bastards . . .'

Four months, not weeks, later.

The screws – in another futile move to break us – had now boarded the windows from the outside, cancelling out all light and air. The cell seemed to physically shrink, squeezing every bone tight, cultivating the tiny demons of panic dancing in your head, inducing breathlessness, marrying the insufferable heat and stench.

Worse, the pipes had been turned up full blast to exasperate the stench of piss and shit. It was an overwhelming, claustrophobic torture not for the faint of heart. It made you want to tear skin and hair, rip them clean off, as the cell became an oven and coffin, getting smaller and hotter. The excrement that wallpapered the cells began to flake and detach itself like a shedding reptile, falling on your hair, into your mouth as you slept. Miniature pyramids of decaying food granted life to maggots that found their way into your ears, nose and mouth, as you tried to sleep, forcing you to listen to their never-ending munching.

31 July brought us a visit from Archbishop Tomas O'Fiaich who later was to become Cardinal. Initially, his visit was greeted with a healthy dose of cynicism from most of the prisoners. What had the Church ever done to help our situation? Their usual cowardly response was that they were "working behind the scenes".

While not restoring our confidence in the Church, his visit, overall, did have a lasting effect. What he witnessed he would never forget and he later related his reaction to the world media. It was a testimony to the brutality and horror of the H Blocks:

"Having spent the whole Sunday in the prison, I was shocked at the inhuman conditions prevailing in H Blocks 3, 4 and 5, where over 300 prisoners are incarcerated. One would hardly allow an animal to remain in such conditions, let alone a human being. The nearest approach to it I have seen was the spectacle of hundreds of homeless people living in filth in sewer pipes in the slums of Calcutta. The stench and filth in some cells, with the remains of rotten food and human excreta scattered around the walls, was absolutely unbelievable. In two of them I was unable to speak for fear of vomiting. The prisoner's cells are without beds, chairs or tables. They sleep on mattresses on the floor, and in some cases I have noticed they are quite wet. They have no covering – the men – except a towel or blanket; no books, newspapers or reading material except the bible – even religious magazines have been banned since my last visit –; no pens, or writing materials, or TV, or radio; no hobbies or handicrafts; no exercise or association. They are locked in their cells for the whole of every day and some of them have been in this condition for more than a year and a half."

Then came the wing shifts. Those – including myself – who were naïve enough to believe that O'Fiaich's much publicized criticisms would force the Brits to see sense were in for a nasty surprise when, early one morning we were moved, one at a time, to an empty wing that had just been painted. The move was uneventful as each of us were placed in the shower area, told to remove and shake the tiny cloth that covered us then proceed through the Circle to the newly painted wing. While no force was used, the eerie feeling of a necklace of silent screws watching your every move was unnerving. Despite this, the general consensus was one of "not too bad" and the protest continued, on fresh walls.

Our second move, five days later, while not traumatic, differentiated with the introduction of a seemingly innocuous prop: a mirror; one that would subsequently become a nightmarish phenomenon, and would haunt us to the very end of the protest. And beyond . . .

By the time of our third shift the mood had changed dramatically. Tension lay in the air giving it an almost tangible taste of copper in your mouth. Instead of three screws there were now six. The towel was forcefully pulled from you while they straddled you, naked, over the mirror, forcing you to squat by their sheer force of numbers.

As each new wing-shift came into play, a new brutality would be added: hair-pulling, face slapping, kidney punching, kicks in the genitals, anal probing and spits in the face. Singularly, they were not monumental terror, but collectively they played havoc with your mental and physical stability. The screws had *carte blanche* from the British Government to implement the tortures *du jour*, and they carried them out with relish. We had promotion written all over us: *their promotion*. If they could break us, by hook or by crook, by fist or by boot, then everything was there for the taking. Each prisoner had his own nemesis among the screws and mine was known as the Human Wart.

He was a sadistic pervert whose repertoire of party tricks included urinating in the mouths of sleeping prisoners and watching them through the flap as they went to the toilet. His favourite proclivity was to use a miniature hangman's noose that he carried with him during the wing shift. Once the prisoner had been forcibly squatted naked over the mirror, Human Wart would pull out the noose and swing it like a pendulum, taunting, '*Tock-tick get the dick. Tick-tock get the cock.*'

Then he would place the noose over your penis, laughing at your futile efforts at struggling. 'Hold 'im steady, men. Will ye fer God's sake stop that wrigglin' like a fish! Hold 'im! That's more like it. There, now!'

"There now" meant the noose was tight around the penis. 'Up ye get. Good boy. That's the way.'

He would be pulling hard, forcing you to move like a dummy on a string, his acne-ravaged face grinning from ear to ear. The fear that he would decapitate your penis from the scrotum never left your terrified mind making it easy to hate him. Only two things were certain after that. First, when a naked finger probed your arse, it was the Wart. And second, God ceased to exist from that day on.

The five days it had initially taken the screws to clean a wing were now reduced to three. Bonuses were being used as incentives for them to work continuously, speeding up the wing shifts at a frightening rate. Instead of hearing the dreaded "we're moving!" once a week, we now had to face it twice each week with grinning screws telling us to, 'Keep it up, lads. I'm buyin' the wife a cracker wee car with all this overtime money. Goin' to Spain next week with the kids. We'll buy you a wee poke with a big *Cadbury's* flake stuck right in it.'

Unfortunately, not all the prisoners could "keep it up" as some opted to leave, no longer being able to endure the madness. There was little sympathy for those who left, as each time a prisoner came off it encouraged the screws to step-up the brutality in the false belief that the rest of us could be beaten off the protest also.

A few weeks later.

'What do ye think now, Finbar?' I asked, watching the screws across the yard steam-hosing the wing we had just vacated. We had just been through a rough wing shift and two men had "squeaky booted". Morale was rock bottom.

'Could be worse. Look at H 3. What a nightmare that block is. Everyone seems to have had their nose broke by the screws.'

'That's that animal Paddy Joe, the PO,' said Seamus, a normally quiet prisoner. 'The RA should be goin' out of their way to get that fucker, show the screws that we can get them any time, any place. Stiff a few of 'em, then we'll see how tough they are. Wouldn't be naked prisoners who'll be comin' to their fuckin' house, and it won't be their dicks they'll have in their hands. Fuckers.'

We were all taken aback a bit. Seamus was perhaps the quietist man on the Blanket and he simply never swore, let alone *talk* about killing people.

'You're 100 per cent, Seamus. It's time the RA got the finger out and started putting pressure on these bastards,' I said, though not too loud. You never knew when the screws would be outside the cell, listening.

'Is right, Seamus,' enthused Finbar.

'If only I were out,' said Hippo. 'I'd fix the bastards.'

'We're talkin' 'bout one in the head, Hippo. Not borin' them to death,' laughed Cowboy.

We all joined in the laughing and only stopped when someone shouted there was a civilian coming down the wing surrounded by a bunch of screws.

The civilian turned out to be a "doctor" and one we would never forget. His attire was a tweed jacket with elbow-patches, brown pants, and a green pair of *Dunlop* water-boots that practically reached to his thighs. He wore a bow-tie, which earned him the nickname Doctor Dickey-Bow. He was a mercenary, brought in by the Brits to implement a new policy, one that they hoped would break the protest. Just when we thought we had faced everything they could throw at us, along came the horror of forced washing.

We had all heard rumours that some of the men in one of the other blocks had been made to run the gauntlet of kicks and punches, only to be grabbed by screws and thrown into a bath of freezing water. There they were scrubbed with yard brushes, disinfectant and *Ajax* scouring powder. We all hoped it was only a rumour, but like most rumours in the Block, if they were negative, they were true. Only the good ones were lies, and we soon realised this latest rumour was no exception.

You could hear a pin drop as Dickey-Bow opened each flap on the cell door, stared in for a minute then wrote something in a folder.

'What the fuck do you think he was writin'?' asked JCB, nervously after Dickey-Bow had gone.

We could all hazard a guess, of course, but no one wanted to say it, no one except Hippo. 'Victims. Bet yer balls on it,' he said. 'He's lookin' to see who'll be the one for the Grove Bath. The old rub-a-dub-dub, Blanket-man-in-the-tub routine.'

'Shutta fuck up, will ye, ye morbid bastard,' shouted a voice in the wilderness. 'Hopefully it'll be you.'

'You know somethin', Hippo?' said Cowboy. 'You're the only one who could squeaky-boot and not a word would be said against ye. It would be good for morale if you were to take yourself off.'

Hippo thought he was joking. Little did he know.

'I'll be here when no one else is here, Cowboy. So don't hold yer breath.'

'Water-Melon Head said the exact same words, Hippo, and look where he is now. Up cleaning the screws' boots and makin' their tea. So be careful yer words don't come back to bite you on the arse.'

Water-Melon Head was a reputed "leading" republican and a reputed "hard" man. Unfortunately for him, the Blanket was a lot tougher. He refused, point blank, to attempt the protest citing he had an appeal in against his sentence and that it would look bad if the "judge" were to be told he was on the Blanket protest.

Two days had now elapsed and we could all breathe a bit easier.

'Looks like it was just a rumour, Sam. Old Dickey-Bow

must've taken a powder and blown. Probably couldn't bear the smell,' said JCB.

None of us had dared to mention Dickey-Bow for fear of jinxing ourselves. It was an unwritten rule: don't talk about anything negative that hasn't yet happened.

'Forget about it, JCB,' advised Cowboy.'You know the rule.'

But it was too late and Finbar was the first to hear it. '*Ssshhhh!* Will youse keep quite for one minute? Listen.'

We all strained to hear. It was music. Ghostly. The first music we'd heard in years and it was beautiful. At least until we realised the fiendish significance of the words: *When you're weary, feeling small* . . . A tap was releasing water into a bath. You could almost smell the rust from its years of neglect. *When tears are in your eyes* . . . Laughter was coming from the screws. *I'll comfort you* . . . Footsteps approached, halting. Our stomachs churned, hearts pumped. Thoughts raced in my head: *a perfect measure of silence is as threatening as the actuality when you learn to experience and understand the ruthlessness of silence, how it manipulates*. In the silence of our mind, each of us could hear the flap go up and knew what lurked outside, waiting.

Dickey-Bow, armed with his list of victims, nodded silently to the screw before requesting the door to be opened. It was impossible to hear what was being said but a few seconds later a posse of screws rushed in, trailing a naked prisoner out by the ankles and hair. The man moaned from the pain but Dickey-Bow simply walked behind, nonchalant. It was terrifying to witness and we were powerless to do a thing about it.

Like a bridge over troubled water . . . *water* . . . *water* . . . The screws had deliberately stuck the needle on the last word.

Another door opened and another prisoner was dragged out placing the same thoughts on everyone's mind: *Am I next? What will they do to me? Why doesn't anyone give a fuck about what they're doing to us? If this was happening in Russia there would be a universal outcry* . . . *Fuck you, JCB. You jinxsy bastard!*

There was an absence of movement, a core of quiet, and stillness complete. The blood started throbbing in my head as the screws stopped between my cell and the adjacent one. Dickey-Bow was talking in a whisper. I froze, as if any movement would alert them to my presence. I started to tell God I would believe in Him again if only they would leave me alone – leave us all alone. But when I heard the key turn in the lock, I told God not to worry about the rest, just save me. Take him next door, he's only been here a couple of years. Take Hippo. That bastard deserves it, God. I'll even start going to Mass again if –

But it was all in vain. God was away somewhere. Probably doing a heavenly crossword puzzle, because right in front of my eyes stood the dreaded Dickey-Bow, a phalanx of screws at his side.

'How do you do?' he said as way of introduction. 'I'm a doctor.'

So was Josef Mengele, I wanted to say, but lacked the balls at that specific moment. I refused to acknowledge him, which didn't have the slightest impact.

'You're asked to come for a wash. Will you come, please?'

His voice was void of emotion, the words innocuous yet slippery and evil, like a worm caught by a bird. Trying to prevent your chest heaving at the best of times is an effort, but being naked leaves no room for pretence. My entire body was shaking.

'Answer the doctor!' growled the Human Wart.

'It's all right, gentlemen. Please escort the prisoner to the ablutions where I can make a better observation of his needs.'

My needs? I doubted if they could be facilitated in the wash area.

Refusing to walk voluntary meant being transformed into a Roman chariot and dragged up the wing, your skin on fire as it flayed against the ground.

Water . . . water . . . water . . . water . . .

I remembered sailing through the air, naked, and the truly exhilarating experience of what birds must feel at the start of take-off. A swirl of colours passed over my perspective as I watched my penis wobbling from side to side, making horrible slapping sounds, as it winked at me like a one-eyed pirate. When they dropped me into the bath of freezing water it took my breath, but that was the least of my worries as my mouth and nostrils began to fill and fear of drowning raced in my brain.

Water . . . water . . . water . . . water . . .

'Always the hard way, youse boys,' said the Human Wart as they pulled me up for a few seconds of air. 'I think youse love all this.'

Water . . . water . . . water . . . water . . .

They started to pour the disinfectant into the bath and onto my hair as a shampoo. Next came the *Ajax* , which was scrubbed into the skin with the yard brush. If you thought you had any skin left after the Roman chariot, you knew now it was all gone after the scrubbing. The Human Wart, God love him, was fastidious in seeing me clean, paying special attention to my penis and genitals while Dickey-Bow, seemingly fascinated, stood writing notes and smiling at the wonder of it all.

Water . . . water . . . water . . . water . . .

The disinfectant was taking its toll on my stomach and I felt that at any minute now I would throw-up. That was when hands started pushing me further, down deeper, into the water and I knew I was going to die, not in a gun battle with the British or on a bombing mission in Belfast, but drowned in a fucking bath in Long Kesh. Yet, in my mind, I believed I could accurately form a picture of how the bath had been apportioned, where the screws had positioned themselves: an out-of-body experience.

Suddenly, the sound became peaceful, dissolving into an accommodating stillness, a degree of salvation.

I can remember being aware that I was now back in my cell, but how I got there was a mystery. It was near dark and the wing was quiet. I was aching all over. Only the smell of disinfectant and *Ajax* in my hair and pores told me it had all been for real. The only good thing to be had from it all was the next morning when JCB told me the news we had all waited and prayed for. Hippo, the man who would be here when no one else would, had squeaky-booted. Dickey-Bow had been the straw to break that particular camel.

72

13

John Wayne, where are you when we need you?

March 1979

"*Never find your delight in another's misfortune.*"
PUBLILIUS SYRUS

"*The fact that a person acted pursuant to order of his Government
or of a superior does not relieve him from responsibility under
international law.*"
THE NUREMBERG PRINCIPLES

Outside the cell's embrasure, crows had assembled, disturbing the
Sunday morning "peace". They had encircled a dead rat, not
believing their luck.

'Fuck off, ye bastards!' screamed someone who could no
longer bear the madness of the caw caw cawing.

Tranquillity spent, another morning in the Blocks had
begun.

An hour later, the hollow thud of doors being slammed into
their niches could be heard emitting prisoners to the canteen for
Mass.

I, along with a few others, had ceased attending since the
priest known as the Angel of Death, had made the remark that

cleanliness was next to godliness; a not so-subtle vilification of the protest by this Judas priest, minus the heavy metal. As the wing became sleep-inducing with the legato of responsorial psalms, I decided to go for a walk, pacing the liquorice-black floor, accumulating feet to yards, yards to miles in a going-nowhere wanderlust.

At the zoo, when I used to watch the beat-up lion pace. I thought it was following me, waiting to pounce and fell me with its great paws. Unfortunately, the reason was less imaginative: Depression. Pace pace pace . . . Burn the depression off, only to have it return more vengeful once the creature stopped walking. Occasionally it would leap at the wall, bouncing off it with the dead thud of a busted ball. Bewildered. Sad. Pathetic. Pace pace pace . . . The depression burnt my chest, forging an affinity between the lion and myself.

As I walked, the sky opened, revealing a delicious picture, a kaleidoscopic quilt of orange and blue bleeding into a vermilion peacock, proud in all its splendour. *A gull hung motionlessly on swirls of invisible beams, laughing.*

'Sam?' called JCB, from next door, his whispery voice barely audible. He had promised me a synopsis, a rough for "a book at bed-time", a cowboy book as pleaded by Cowboy, our foremost authority on the Wild West.

Cowboy loved cowboy books and always said that if they were good enough for Yeats, then they were certainly good enough for him. Cowboy was a legend, having escaped from British prisons at least twice, and shot at more times than Charles De Gaulle. Rumour had it that he had full size cowboy guns tattooed on either side of his body and that the Brits shot him, while he sunbathed, claiming the "guns" looked real!

'Yes, mate? What's happenin'?' I replied.

'Cowboy'll love this one. Of course, I don't expect verbatim, so I'm givin' you artistic freedom to embellish.'

I couldn't see him – this despite the fact that we had been "neighbours" for years in the Block – but I knew he was smiling. 'Go ahead, mate.'

'Okay.' He cleared his throat, drank a gulp of water, began. 'There's a black cowboy called White, and a white cowboy called Black . . .' He was laughing now, all paradox and irony.

A warm breeze played on my face, bringing with it forlorn memories of promises not quite kept. I could smell the sweaty attar of rotten apples and it made me think of school days and untouched, naked lunches housed secretly in desks. In the distance, I could hear a lawn mower drone across the expanse of grey brick and rusted wire. I could picture it slicing, shooting green needles skyward. Suddenly, it went quiet, leaving a steel period of nothing buzzing in my head. Not even this are we allowed, I thought, angrily. No outside sounds of normality. That, too, has become a luxury, a privilege.

' . . . and the stagecoach is carrying all this gold from Mister Silver's mine . . .'

I was grateful for JCB's interruption. His voice had a pleasant, sonorous sound and I found myself engrossed, drifting to the old Wild West.

I failed to detect the kiss of soft-shoe leather outside my cell . . .

'Anyway,' continued JCB, 'the gun-slinger has only one arm. His name is Jack Handy.' He was laughing at his own wit.

Failed to detect the slick movement of a key being inserted in a lock . . .

'Nancy Campbell, the can-can dancer, loves Mister Silver. Can-can. Campbell. Get it, Sam?' He was giggling.

Didn't feel the prickle of preying eyes on the back of my neck . . .

'The saloon owner is pissed because his girl – say gal, 'cause Cowboy's fussy about authenticity – his gal, Nancy, has her azure eyes on –'

Kabam!

I've experienced, like most people, various levels of pain, but I had never experienced anything like the pain of a devastating left-hook applied to my kidneys with such force that Ali or Foreman would have been proud. Ape Face had administered all 250 pounds of his prodigious matter to *that* punch, lifting me from the ground a good, two or three inches.

JCB, oblivious to what was happening next door, continued on with his book. 'Ya all dig deep in tham thar pockats.' He was now Bad Luck McCrae, the unluckiest robber this side o' the Mississippi. 'No fancy moves, or ya all be dead . . .'

'Think youse are all hard men, don't ye?' hissed Ape Face to my ear. 'Not too hard now.' He squeezed his knee against my windpipe, as I lay doubled-up on the ground, my skinny, naked frame about to be smashed.

'The other partner, Fargo, owns the only well for miles . . .' continued JCB, halting for me to capture his pun. When I failed to respond, he said, 'Fargo . . . wells. Get it, Sam? Wells Fargo . . .'

'See how easy it is?' said Ape Face. 'Snap yer wee neck without a peep. Easy, isn't it?'

There was little point in trying to answer. His knee crushing my throat made that futile. Anyway, I didn't want to embarrass myself by talking like a ventriloquist's dummy. From my periphery, Desperate Dan, the biggest screw in the world, stood, eerily silent, a grey shadow blending seamlessly into the sepia swirls and whirls of shit that adhered to the walls. His head touched the ceiling, such was his size. But he was the antithesis of Ape Face: stoic and taciturn.

Meanwhile, back at the ranch, JCB had become the persona of Bad Luck McCrae: 'Sheriff, if ya think fer one minute yar takin' ma back to that hole ya call a jail, then yar as stupid as a two-tailed dog . . .'

Satiated, Ape Face came to an end of his workout, his enormous chest heaving at the effort. He left the cell without another word, only the smell of sweat and fear remained.

'The two cowboys, Black and White, git on thar harses – say it just like that, Sam: *git on thar harses* – and ride into a blazing sunset of red,' said JCB with a pregnant pause, waiting for my opinion. What he got, instead, was a visit from Ape Face and Desperate Dan.

Kabam! Kabam! Kabam! went JCB's head against the wall, and for one terrible moment I thought he would come right through, saying: Guess Ape Face didn't like the ending! *Whack!*

Whack! Whack! It went on and on, a brutal madness. And may God forgive me, I was just glad it was no longer me.

About an hour later my cellmate returned from Mass, paced the floor angrily, then said, 'You'll never believe what I heard about that fuckin' girlfriend of mine. Remember I told you she went to Spain with her sisters?'

No, I didn't remember. Nor did I want to. I could barely breathe with pain and my kidneys were on fire. I wanted to cry.

'Well, apparently she didn't go with her sisters at all! No. I just heard from Hector that she . . .'

He rambled on for the next twenty minutes, cursing his girl – or ex-girl – then took a nap, snoring like a pig. It wasn't until later in the day he commented: 'You okay? You look a bit sick. Hey! Whaddya think about that girl of mine? Unfuckin-believable!'

My sentiments exactly, I thought, as Cowboy shouted out the window, 'Sam? JCB? All set for tonight, mates?'

There was little sympathy for either JCB or myself. Stop whining. Dry yer eyes. My rendering of JCB's book was a disaster. Most of the men fell asleep. And even JCB moaned at my terrible puns, which had replaced his. Though, to be honest, he told me later that most of his moans came from the beating.

'It wasn't that bad,' said my cellmate seeing my despondency. 'Could've been worse.'

The book? The beating? I didn't ask him to elaborate. Instead, I watched the night's sky, which was lit up with slivers of electricity. Lightning scintillated the dark, giving the cell a silver hue. Rain started to invade the glass-less window.

'Look at that fuckin' sky, will ye! It's on fire!' exclaimed my cellmate

We squeezed our faces tight against the concrete bars, preventing most of the cell becoming waterlogged and allowing ourselves a *de facto* "wash" which, technically, was cheating. The sky's canopy suddenly became raw, angry, unforgiving. It was the colour of chopped liver and purple ink set on fire, creating a circus; a carnival full of strange and beautiful creatures in gorgeous images of God's own manic zoo. Raindrops, the size of frogspawn, trickled down our receptive faces as the glare of lightning transformed us into oblique, grinning phantoms of the opera and my cellmate's greasy hair stuck to his forehead – as did mine – like a crown of hairy thorns. Beads of rain stained his face instead of blood.

Ach, God, You are true and wonderful, and thank You for this wet and beautiful night and washing some of this muck from our poor faces. But You don't mind, do You, if I don't fall to my knees in adoration?

As the pain in my kidneys shredded my insides, I asked God to allow the lightning to hit me, split me, engulf me with fire. I was wet enough. Good conductivity. Even my feet stood in small, vice-like puddles of rested water.

Go on. Do Your magic on me, God. Take me away from this madness. Hit me with one good bolt . . .

But He didn't. Instead, He let the rain mingle with my face and allowed me to remain a man among men. It was only then that I realised how sadistic He really was. He didn't send you to Hell; simply granted you memory so that you could torture yourself, over and over again.

14

Hospital, Tobacco-stuffing and Vietnam

April 1979

"Man grows wise against his will."

AESCHLYLUS

The beating from Ape Face had been beneficial. After weeks of urinating burgundy-coloured blood out the door of the cell, the "doctors" finally relented, sending me out to the military wing of Musgrave Park Hospital where I was quickly isolated in a room without a view, just in case I should contaminate some unfortunate being within the hospital.

The room was terrible: fresh linen, decent food, lovely-looking nurses, TV, and all the books and newspapers I could consume. I doubted if my Blanket metabolism could withstand such an assault, but decided to try and endure it for Mother Ireland. There was little conversation between the nurses and myself as they all came from loyalist areas, and weren't too shy in letting me know by their paradoxical silence.

After the operation on my kidneys, I was introduced to

Morpheus, the god of sleep. He came every night in the tube of a needle, carried by a fifteen-stone woman who could easily have beaten the best Russian wrestler. Each night she came, tossing me over like a rag doll, plunging the needle into my thigh, ignoring the raw stitches that snaked from my stomach to the top of my spine, lined like a map of Chile.

'This'll make ye feel better,' she grinned, ignoring my teeth-clenched moans. 'Be thankful it's morphine.' She did a wicked wink, and tossed me again. I waited for the Half-Nelson, but it failed to materialise. 'Good night,' she said, not meaning a word, as she flicked off the light leaving me to stare at *Vietnam: A Television History.*

My head was swirling. I could hear the gunships overhead and Tricky Dicky's static voice of no surrender – or was it Big Ian's? – somewhere from the *Fields of Fire.* As the pain eased, I floated to the ceiling in a haze of purple and blue, laughing. *Apocalypse Now* had nothing on me. Even in sleep I moved fraught with twitching nerves. In my mind I chased echoes forged in childhood; safe echoes of familiar voices, smells and laughter. Now the same thoughts brought me back, draining me, lonesome beyond redemption.

My recuperation was shortened by the tremendous capability of the "doctors" who, despite my protestations at the pain I was in, decided four days and *not* the expected four weeks were warranted. Being a Blanket Man had nothing to do with my aborted stay, of course, and Tricky Dicky still claimed innocence as I staggered from the room, in agony, handcuffed and flanked by four big peelers.

I moved with the pace of a snail, as I returned to the Block, crouched over like the Hunchback of Notre Dame, my stitches a corset covering my body, my knuckles almost trailing the ground as I walked back up the wing. A voice shouted 'Sam's back,' then a couple more joined in. Anyone else would have been asked for news, but the men knew better than to ask me. They still hadn't forgiven me for lying about Christmas '76.

'I suppose you don't have any snout with ye?' asked the solemn voice of Teapot, going through the motions, knowing it would be impossible for me to have any. He repeated the question and when I still hadn't answered a third time, he left the door, mumbling, 'Bastard. What a wanker.'

Even through my pain I had to grin at him. No, it wasn't good to be back, it was harder now that I had tasted what we had all been missing these last few years. But tonight would be different. Teapot would mumble an apology to me, as he and the rest of the lads would smoke their brains out, all thanks to a fifteen-stone woman whose bark turned out to be a lot worse than her bite, who had given me so much tobacco to take back with me – up my arse – that when I farted it smelt like Gallagher's cigarette factory.

I would relive the last few days over and over again in my head, sustaining myself with the unquenchable belief that at the end of all this madness, we could all go home again. Little did I know that none of us could ever, realistically, go home again. We had been kilned in a furnace. We had changed. Utterly, and forever. We would never be the same again.

The screws could – and did – smash bone and tear flesh. Our existence was minimalist in the extreme. We were zero and naked as womb departure. But what they could never do was to colonize our thoughts. They could never comprehend what made us tick for the simple reason that we were beyond what had come before, never to be matched. We were the Spartans. Fuck, we were better than the Spartans. We were the Blanket Men.

15

A Word in Your Ear

Much later in time

"*As the beatings continued, the screws systematically beat every prisoner the whole way down the wing. I remember the screws coming up my side of the cell. I was at the third cell from the bottom, and there was a man next-door to me called Sammy Millar – funny enough, he's a man I've never seen – though I would know his voice anywhere. I remember the screws opening his door, dragging him out and down the wing, kicking and beating him as they bounced him off the other cell doors. And when the screws were throwing him back into the other cell, I swear to this day, he must have bounced off the walls, because they hadn't even had his cell door closed when he was up at the window of his cell, screaming my name out, 'Massey! Massey!' at the top of his voice – Massey was a nickname the prisoners gave me after Massey Ferguson tractors. So, he's screaming out his window and I'm standing at my cell door, and I can't even speak at this stage because of the anxiety and the fear, I can't even swallow because I've no saliva left! Just as the screws open my door, Sammy's screaming my name out at the top of his voice, 'Massey! Massey!' And all of a sudden, all the fear and anxiety just swelled out of me, and I screamed, 'What the hell do ye want!' (Laughter from the interviewer and Massey). And I heard his voice come back to me saying, 'If you find an ear up there, will ye bring it back – it's mine!'* (More laughter.) *They've taken me out of my cell, booting and kicking me, and I'm laughing the whole way, I'm laughing the whole time the screws are doing this, and I'm not laughing because I think what the screws are doing to me is funny, I'm laughing at the sheer relief of it all because this man – just an ordinary guy, like myself, in the next cell to me – had managed to rise above all the fear and all the terror, and so I knew, when, after Sammy had said that on that day, the screws would not be able to break me, and I would be able to endure what was happening to me, and for every other prisoner coming after me in that wing, they too would be able to survive what was happening to them on that day, because on this occasion one of the prisoners had risen above the terror of it all and helped the rest of us to survive."*

MICHAEL FERGUSON, ex-POW.
Radio interview: *Ancient Circles*, USA.

16

Afternoon or, actually, in the morning

December 1979

"Sed quis custodient ipsos custodes?
(But who is to guard the guards themselves?)"

DECIMUS JUNIUS JUVENAL

The Brits and screws had upped the ante with the forced washing, wing shifts, mirror searches and beatings. They believed their methods were paying dividends and who could argue? Men were leaving the protest at an uncomfortable rate. We were always on the defensive, which meant victory was unattainable. New rules of engagement would have to be implemented to prevent the protest becoming an inescapable quagmire.

The morning-shift of screws entered the Block, unusually quiet, this particular morning and instead of the thunderous raps from their batons – which was their usual method of waking us – they merely opened the spy-flaps, looked in, then left mumbling. They were in an extremely sombre mood. We all realised that something had happened, but what?

It wasn't until "Charlie", the orderly, tapped my cell door, gently with his broom, that we found out.

'Did ye hear the news?' he whispered. An asinine question, really, considering he was our main – our only – source of news.

'No, Charlie. What was it?'

'The IRA shot a screw last night in his car,' he whispered, talking as if his life depended on it. If the screws caught him he'd be in trouble.

'Is he dead?' I asked.

'He better be. They're burying him tomorrow.' Quickly he moved away. Of all the days to be seen talking to us, this wasn't it.

The news of the dead screw was instantaneous. Everyone seemed to have heard it at the same time, whispering their opinion down at the pipes. But not all the opinions were the same.

'We're in for it now. Bet yer balls on it.'

'Dry yer eyes, will ye! Best thing that ever happened. Now they'll think twice about beatin' the crap out of us durin' the wing shifts.'

'It plays into their hands. Now they'll make martyrs out of the screws: "These poor men only doing their jobs". I can write the NIO press release better than the fuckin' NIO, for fuck sake!'

As far as I was concerned, shooting the screws couldn't come soon enough. My only wish was that our wing wasn't the next wing to be moved, but we were due a move in the next day or two and there was little point trying to escape the inevitable: the shift would be a nightmare. When they returned to give out "breakfast", they were whistling. The "grins" on their faces could cut glass. A pantomime was in progress: for heaven's sake whatever youse do don't let the Blanket Men see your emotions. Go about yer duty as normal. Pretence. Wear it like a mask.

As a "mark of respect" for their fallen comrade the screws "downed tools", announcing a three day "no work" period. No mail. No visits. No food parcels. No TV. No radio. Terrible. How would we survive this ordeal? We'd go mad without all of these. Unfortunately, for the screws, we weren't getting any of these anyway. They had taken away everything already. "How the fuck can we punish these bastards when we've nothing left to punish them with?" was the apparent remark from the governor who had "dreamed" up the mirror search as a way to break us.

As for ourselves, we got lucky – at least for three days. The screws refused to steam-hose any cells or "conduct" wing shifts as part of their protest – everyone now, it seemed, was protesting. And so we simply luxuriated in it all like kids on a picnic. No beating for three whole days . . . three days . . . three days . . .

We never stopped talking. We were on a high.

'Did I ever tell you that my da was a film star, Sam?' asked Joe.

'Catch yerself on! Even I'm takin' a reddner for ye with that one.'

'I'm serious! Do ye want to hear it or not?'

'Do I have a choice?' I asked.

'No. Put the blanket on your shoulders and get to the window.'

'You're crazy, standin' at the window on a night like this. It's ball-freezing,' said my cellmate who lay on his "mattress" in the foetus-position, shivering with the cold.

He was right. It was the coldest night ever recorded. White puffs of frosted air escaped from your mouth each time you spoke and the wind hurt your face, slicing it like a razor, making you wince. Outside, light as fluid as water seamed its way down the watchtower's facade illuminating it in an effulgent cascade of ocular rhinestones.

'Go ahead, Joe,' I said, braving it.

'Did ye ever see that film, *The Vikings*, with Kirk Douglas?'

'And Tony Curtis!' shouted Cowboy from his mattress, eavesdropping as usual.

'That's the one. My da and brother where in Wales doin' a bit of steel-erecting. Along comes this Yank askin' if anyone wants to earn a few extra quid. Naturally enough, everyone jumps at the chance for a few quid coupled with the chance of bein' in a movie with Kirk Douglas.'

'And Tony Curtis!' shouted Cowboy.

'Fuck Kirk Douglas and Tony Curtis!' someone shouted.

'We've a fuckin' wing-shift in a couple of days and with that screw buried, we'll all be fuckin' dead Vikings!'

Like all of us, the owner of the voice was on his nerves wondering what the screws had in store. We all knew it wouldn't be too pleasant.

'Whaddya mean fuck Kirk Douglas?' asked an indignant Cowboy.

Just as the conversation began to decompose, a shooting star lined the iron-blue night like a silver papilla chalking the sky and I wondered if it was an omen, or simply the blinking of my eye causing a brilliance gone forever?

'Make a wish,' someone shouted, proving it wasn't imaginary.

'It'll all be over tomorrow!' Derision.

'Some snout!' Laughter.

'A woman!' Yes! All in unison.

'John Wayne – nude!' shouted Cowboy.

'Gerry A and Martin McG forced to go through a wing shift before they could squeaky-boot!' Everyone laughing.

Quietness came as the icy wind took no prisoners. Snow began to fall in thick corollas, swirling tightly in a rage before pyramiding in tiny conics at the base of the wire. White rust clung to the wire, as if invaded by legions of sick frogs scaling for battle. Into our windowless cells came the wind, like a drunken banshee laced with evil. Her mocking howls reminded us just how lonely we had become.

'We're movin'!' screamed a voice from the top of the wing and a few of us laughed at that, too. They never moved at night. Security. Not enough screws on. Besides, they had yet to "clean" the wing opposite for us to move into.

It took us all by surprise. A first. Bodies that only minutes ago had started to "relax" for "sleep" were now rigid. Our minds and stomachs raced with cathartic jerks as we paced, wondering why a nocturnal manoeuvre.

Normally the intervals preceding the opening of a cell door lasted no more than 30 to 60 seconds: time enough for a prisoner to be moved to the ablutions area, searched then moved to a "clean" wing. Not this time, however. Three to four minutes were elapsing before each door was opened. In the distance we could hear the sound of tables being dragged across the Circle floor. Muffled screams and shouts were carried back making us pace faster, our stomachs churning with acid.

My cellmate and I just stared at each other like zombies. Each of us wanted to take a shit, bad.

Control your breathing. Don't let the fuckers see your fear. Steady . . . easy . . .

Getting closer. Two cells away. More screams. The freezing cold was irrelevant now. Fear was supreme.

They're next door!

God, I'm gonna shit my pants, except I don't have any to shit in.

The moon never looked colder or fuller. Not a cloud to diminish its supremacy, while speckles of stars winked Morse-code warnings all too late. Suddenly, the key was being placed in the cell door. It made me jump, a little. The door opened. No words exchanged. My cellmate went first. He preferred to get it over with.

I had done this so many times that my mind goes into automatic denial mode as I left the cell: *I'm walking in the park . . . at home watching* Top of the Pops *. . . It's Friday and I feel great 'cause I just got paid . . .*

The tableau of horror slapped me back to reality. Instead of the wash area the search was being conducted in the Circle. My next-door neighbour was being held upside down by his ankles by four screws. Six other screws surrounded them plus a notorious "white shirt" called Paddy Joe, all screaming obscenities at the naked, inverted prisoner. One of the screws was probing his anus while two other screws pulled apart his buttocks as wide as possible.

The park is packed . . . a group of children play cowboys and Indians . . . my brother Joe is waving at me . . .

The prisoner was then thrown on top of a table, the one the screws were using. It was covered in shit and blood. They grabbed his hair and smashed his face against the table's top. His nose broke easy; blood went everywhere.

My brother was waving at me . . . except it wasn't him, it was the screw in front indicating for me to move.

It was then that I made my decision. *Run! Run for all you're worth!*

The screws were immobilised with disbelief as I ran, running so fast I had to prevent myself slamming into a wall. The urine-covered floor was slick as oil on ice but my feet held well as I precariously raced for "home" pursued by a couple of screws who were within arm's length of catching me.

One of them kicked out at my feet narrowly missing. Instead, he lost his balance, slipped and slid, sending himself into the urine-covered floor. As I ran into the cell, a look of horror was on my cellmate's bloody face. He had heard the commotion and thought they were coming to do him again. His relief was short lived.

'Brace yourself,' I told him. 'They *are* comin' again!'

The screws were soaked in urine and sweat as they stood at the door panting and heaving like carnivorous greyhounds finally trapping their quarry.

I could only wait.

The first thing they tried was to pull me out of the cell where they could get a better go at me. But I held onto the pipes for all I was worth, thanking God that the screws had turned them off in winter, otherwise I would have had nothing to hold. Deep down I think my cellmate wanted to chop my fingers off, anything, just to get the screws out of the cell. But he held my head and neck – a bit *too* tightly, I thought later – forcing the screws to give up their tug-of-war with my legs and to settle for giving me a kicking instead.

It was all over in a matter of minutes.

'Did ye see him run!' said the urine-covered screw walking like John Wayne up the wing. 'Ha-ha! Think his arse was on fire! Ha-ha!'

'All that fuckin' runnin', replied the other. 'I could go for a nice pint now.'

Couldn't we all? I thought, as their voices faded . . .

In less than an hour it was all over. Inventory revealed broken noses, cracked ribs, teeth knocked out. Almost everyone had a black eye. I was "lucky". I escaped with a few forget-me-not bruises and a nail ripped from my toe after the chase. No one mentioned the anal search. We were too mortified. My cellmate refused to look at me. He knew what I had seen and blamed himself for what the screws did. We were "living" a parallel insanity between violent reality and an even more violent psychological madness.

It was fast approaching midnight and our soggy mattresses and blankets had yet to be thrown into the excrement-covered cells. To try and keep warm we jumped up and down, but the futility of this quickly became evident as the water and urine on the floor became ice, making our feet adhere to it. All joints in our bodies succumbed first as the drills of ice burrowed into the knees, then elbows, forcing us to kneel in mock adoration, then stand, anything to ease the pain of cold.

'How much longer do ye reckon before we get a blanket?' asked my cellmate through chattering teeth and bloody nose, now frozen.

I didn't want to talk. Every part of me was shivering.

'Have you gone deaf?' he asked.

'How the fuck would I know! I'm not a screw, am I?' As soon as I said it I regretted it, but I didn't apologise.

Like an invisible wrestler, the cold forced us onto the floor. Slowly, painfully . . .

The sound of wind is all we could hear. Tiny birds flew in our heads telling our brains that yes we could feel the cold and the pain and no amount of bluffing by us will change that. *Offer it up to God*, our Angel of Death was whispering. *Remember, I told you: Cleanliness is next to Godliness.*

If only we had him now, naked with his shit kicked in. See how much he believes in God . . .

I smelt Colditz even before he came to the window. The sweet sickly smell of marijuana had become his trademark and it could be smelt through the stench of shit and piss.

'Fine mess this is, wot, Millar? You people are a glutton for fackin' punishment.'

I strained to stand, thinking my knees would snap at any moment.

Colditz had his overcoat covering most of his face. His cap was pulled down. Only his nose and shadowed eyes were visible, as was the joint of marijuana in his mouth.

'Fackin' freezin', aint it?' he laughed, blowing out dove-grey smoke.

'When are we gettin' the blankets back?' I asked. 'It's been almost two hours. Men are freezin' to death.'

'Don't be tryin' that thick paddy act with me, Millar. Of course you're freezin' to fackin' death. That's the whole fackin' idea, aint it! I mean, you go and stiff one of their mates and expect kid-glove treatment? C'mon the fack! They're hopin' one or two of you facks will be as dead as their mate, come mornin'.'

Colditz still reminded me of Clint Eastwood even after all those years when I first saw him as I descended from the van that night in the yard. He always referred to the other screws as "they" rather than "we", as if deliberately distancing himself from them. The home-bred screws hated him almost as much as they hated us. Being English, they regarded him as a bounty hunter moving in on their territory and having dubious loyalties. They needn't have worried on that score. "I won't give you the Queen and country speech," he would say. "I don't believe in it. I'm here for the money. Pure and simple."

Before I could ask another question, he was gone, deep into the night.

A truculent wind was now gathering momentum. Small slivers of ice began to crystallise the dampness of the walls preventing us from leaning on it for support. At 3.00am the night watch clicked the key in the "time guard". It is repeated every hour on the hour. Still no blanket or "mattress".

Echoes. Childhood echoes. Dig deep. Find them, allow them to sustain you, balancing the madness with a perfect pinch of shaky sanity. You can do it. You know you can do it.

How the fuck can Kojak do that?

Do what, for fuck's sake?

You know. That thing with the match. How the fuck does he do it?

Are Sooty and Sweep real? Who is Doctor Who? How do Jacobs get the figs into figrolls? Are the Hulk's balls green?

4.00 am. Click! Still no blanket.

Now you know how meat feels in the deep freeze! *Serves youse fuckin' well! Gluttons for punishment . . .*

Gud lads, gud lads, those boys in the Kesh! said He Who Walks On Water. *Give me another Black Bush, Martin, me bucko!* screamed He Who Must Be Obeyed. *Let's have a nice warm drink fer them gud lads on a terrible night like this,* agreed The Great I Am. *Gud lads, Gud lads. Another whiskey for Mother Ireland . . .*

5.00 am. Click!

'God is dead: of His pity for man hath God died,' whispered Nietzsche, into my ear.

6.00 am. Click!

Fuck Mother Ireland, the Whore, and all who sail on her, She with her knickers exposed green, white and fucking orange . . .

7.00 am. Click!

'If I'd my way you fuckers would get nothin'!' said Ape Face, as he threw two damp blankets into the cell. His flaming red hair looked like it was about to ignite, such was his anger. 'Fuckers!' he reiterated as he slammed the cell door.

The blanket is absolutely useless now. We are beyond that stage. A flamethrower, perhaps, could help and knowing Ape Face he would be more than willing to use it. But despite it all, we knew we had beaten the Beast and everything it could throw at us.

'Can . . . can . . . can ye believe we . . . we . . . we survived that?' grinned my cellmate through chattering teeth and a busted nose, sounding like Marlyn Brando. 'I think we've all become *infuckingvincible*! Yes! *Yesssss!*'

There was no doubt in my mind that he was slowly losing it.

93

I simply looked on in horror, the soles of my feet glued to the frozen floor.

7.20 am. 'We're movin'!'

A sick joke? No. We *were* moving. *Again.* This time we weren't just moving to another wing. The vans coming into the yard told us it was another Block and this adventure would probably be as ghastly as the previous.

8.05 am. We arrived in the Block. A "welcoming committee" of screws greeted us with the customary kicks and punches which were impotent after last night's baptism of fire. The cells were wet with paint, such was their rush to move us. It wasn't long before the fumes caused headaches.

3.00 pm. Our "blankets" and "mattresses" were thrown in after seventeen hours of terror and record-breaking freezing weather. We had prevailed yet again despite the screws' proficiency to brutalise.

We have won. Unconquerable. Just like the fucking Spartans! We'll never be defeated.

17

The Angel of Death comes a strutting

June 1980

"Hell is paved with the skulls of priests."

ST JOHN CHRYSOSTOM

'Cowboy?' whispered the raspy voice of Seamus.

'What? Whaddya want, Seamus?' Cowboy's voice sounded forlorn, apathetic, as if preparing for sleep. He didn't want to be bothered. He knew Seamus didn't have a visit for at least three more weeks. Besides, he wasn't bringing back much – if any – snout, anyway, given that the screws had more or less effectively shut down all access to obtaining it on the visits.

Those who smoked found the lack of tobacco agonising and resorted to extreme measures. Some rolled the fluff they managed to pluck from their blanket onto bible pages and smoked these "holy smokers" only to throw-up an hour or two later. Others tried their hand at the skins sometimes left on baked potatoes with their jackets on (when the screws discovered this little trick they quickly put an end to baked potatoes). One man even claimed to be smoking the dried excrement as it flaked from the

95

wall. Two days later he squeaky-booted leaving us to ponder if the special "cigarettes" had influenced his decision and causing Finbar to comment, wryly, that he was either smoking shit or talking it.

'Cowboy. I can see a strutt just a couple of –'

'Where, Seamus?' Cowboy was now at the door, quick as a flash, his voice animated with newborn enthusiasm. 'Where, Seamus?' He sounded like a hunter about to capture his prey. "Strutt" was the slang given to a cigarette butt, sometimes – albeit rarely – discarded by a screw. A good-sized "strut" could make at least two, possibly three, Blanket cigarettes. To the smokers, it was worth its weight in gold. Cowboy, like the rest of the smokers, hadn't had tobacco for at least three months and was now looking upon the arrival of this "strutt" as nothing short of a miracle, a godsend and manna from Heaven.

'Down a foot from your door, Cowboy. Just where the joints meet.'

'Give me one minute to set up the apparatus, Seamus, mate.'

The "apparatus" being a long slender piece of toilet paper curved at the end in the shape of a hook, or more appropriately a question mark. It was always a question if it would bring home the bacon.

'Okay, mate. Go ahead,' said Cowboy sounding sixteen years old.

'A little to your left, Cowboy. Up a bit. More. To your right . . .' He was sounding like someone doing the Golden Shot as he now had the unenviable task of guiding Cowboy, whose vision was blocked, to capture the strutt.

'Can you push it out a wee bit more, Cowboy?' asked Seamus, nervously. Twenty minutes had elapsed with no sign of success. We could all hear Cowboy strain to control his temper. He was known for having little patience when he had the nicotine pangs.

'Screw on the air!' screamed the lookout from the top of the wing.

'*Fuck!*' hissed Cowboy, his frustration beginning to emerge.

The screw clicked the time-guard and proceeded back up the

wing only to stop, outside Cowboy's cell, to tie his lace. We could all picture Cowboy now, beads of sweat on his upper lip, praying to God not to let the screw see the strutt. A few seconds later, the screw moved on.

'Seamus? Did the fucker take it?' asked Cowboy, his lip bit off him.

'No. It's still there.'

We all breathed a sigh of relief not wanting to listen to Cowboy's death moan. It was like sitting on a bomb, waiting for it to be defused. For the next two hours no one dared to breathe a word as the Cowboy and Seamus Show continued, unabated with no success.

'Cowboy, you keep touching it but you're not pullin' it in.'

'Seamus,' Cowboy's voice quivered as he fought to control the emotion, which threatened to erupt. '*You're* the one guidin' *me*. Not vice fuckin' versa, *mate*.' He spat the last word out like an apple piece stuck in his throat.

Then it happened.

'Cowboy! You've got it! Take it *easy*. Slow . . . slow . . . bring it in. *Slow* . . .'

So much sweat was running down Cowboy's face he was having difficulty seeing clear. He was having double vision and could feel hot pain eat his chest. A heart attack? What a way to go, all for a strutt.

'Easy . . . that's right . . . almost there, Cowboy. Just a tiny bit more . . . got it!'

The ordeal was over. We cheered with relief as he trailed the captured strutt to his door. We could talk again without feeling the wrath of Cowboy. Or thought we could.

'Seamus! You stupid bastard! That was no strutt! It was only a piece of fuckin' paper! You need a pair of fuckin' glasses!'

Before Cowboy could abuse Seamus further, someone saved his skin by announcing the arrival of the Angel of Death coming up the yard. The Angel of Death wrapped the collar of his coat up to his neck. He had the flu and the night air nipped at any exposed skin.

'Angel of Death at this time of night! You know it's bad news,' said Finbar echoing everyone's thoughts.

'Maybe he's comin' in with pockets full of snout for us. Make up for all the years he's let us rot without as much as a butt,' said Cowboy not hiding his sarcasm.

No. We all knew it was to tell someone a family member had died. What else could it be?

As Death walked down the wing chatting with the screw we waited, holding our breaths, wondering.

'Millar. Priest here to see ye,' snarled Ape Face.

'Thank you, officer,' said Death, the look of disdain visible on his face as he entered my excrement-covered cell.

Cleanliness is next to Godliness . . .

'Sam, I've some bad news for you,' he said with his tepid voice and I knew it must be my father. 'Your mother died, two days ago, in Dublin.'

I was taken by surprise. I thought she had died a long time ago, when I was eleven, when she no longer wanted to know my math results.

'Did you say my mother?'

'Yes. Two days ago. I'm terribly sorry.'

I bet you are.

For the next minute or so nothing was said. He glanced about the cell with a mixture of fear and loathing. He couldn't wait to get out, back to the real world of a nice cosy home, a blazing fire and a large glass of brandy to chase away his flu and my stench.

'If there's anything I can do . . .' he was saying as he walked towards the door.

'Do you have any snout on ye?' I asked, not letting him escape.

'Snout? What's that?'

'Tobacco.' *As if you don't fucking know.*

'Oh. No, I don't . . . you know we can't bring anything like that in.' A watery grin appeared on his face and I wanted to slap it right back to where it had originated.

'How do you do it?' I asked.

'Do what?' he asked, turning to face me, wanting to leave.

'Live with your conscience. Doesn't the Church teach that conscience is the ultimate guide?'

'It teaches that your conscience should always be clear, in all matters, as mine is now.' He was warming to this.

'All these years you have watched as we have been tortured, degraded and humiliated. Not once have you tried to prevent it, and you're suppose to be a priest.'

He waved his hands in the air, a magician performing a trick. 'You don't have to live this. None of you do. You choose it. The onus is on you, not me or the Church which, people such as you conveniently use as a whipping boy.' He blew his nose. 'Do you know how often my non-Catholic friends ask me what in heaven's name is wrong with you people, forcing me to defend the indefensible?'

I didn't give a damn what he, his friends or the Church thought and told him so in no uncertain terms.

'Others have left the protest without any problems, why can't you?'

'*Many are called, but few are chosen,*' I replied.

His smile was pure evil as he shook his head. He sneezed, bringing the conversation to an end. As soon as Death left, Cowboy asked if there had been a miracle performed.

'What d'ye mean?'

'Did that *cunt* bring any snout?'

'No, mate. Just word that my mother has died.'

He was silent for a few seconds, then said, 'Ach, Sam . . . sorry for that big mouth of mine, mate. Didn't mean . . .'

'Don't worry 'bout it.' Besides, my mother's death was inconsequential and I had more pressing matters on my mind, like my own survival. Tomorrow we had a wing-shift to look forward to.

I would survive this wing-shift. And the next. And the next . . .

18

Jimmy Saville and Pan's People

Winter 1980

"A local thing called Christianity."

THOMAS HARDY

Rumours. A parched forest engulfed with flames of amber and copper. Copious. An unverified report circulated that a hunger strike was coming. No one – especially not us – wanted it, but it was coming just the same . . .

Outside my cell, raindrops the size of thumbs smashed the ground, causing leptons of dust to rise skywards.

'I'm afraid of no man,' boomed the voice, which we all knew to be that of the screw known as "Preacher". During wing shifts he would carry a large, heavy bible from which he would quote scripture. After each quote he would hit the naked prisoner's head with such force it caused vertigo.

'Lord, cleanse the sins –' *Whack! Whack! Whack!* 'from this sinner.' *Whack! Whack! Whack!* 'Let him see how much we love him. That we are –' *Whack! Whack! Whack!* 'doin' this from love, to save his soul.' *Whack! Whack! Whack!* Sometimes the blood would ooze from your ear or nose. 'Oh, thank you, Lord, for this great sign of cleansing blood.' Preacher would be soaked in perspiration as his eyes rolled in his head.

'What a bore,' said Finbar, loudly enough for Preacher to hear.

'Even though I walk in the valley of death . . .' Preacher was pacing the yard, allowing the rain to drench, soak right through to the skin.

'Ignore the bastard,' said JCB. 'All he wants is an audience.'

Preacher laughed. 'What I want is for one of youse brave men to come visit me when – *if* ye get out of here. Because I've just bought myself a beautiful Magnum .357 and I would just love to test it on one of yer heads. Not with whips, but with the tails of scorpions will I cleanse ye.'

An hour had passed and he still rambled on, singing loudly for all to hear.

'Shall we gather at the river –'

'Why don't you pack it in and stop behavin' like a wanker?' It was Colditz. We hadn't seen him in weeks and thought he had either been transferred or had left.

'Why don't ye mind yer own business and go back to England? No one wants yer sort over here, takin our jobs away from – *arrghhaa!*'

Colditz kneed Preacher in the balls, forcing him to drop before keeling over. A few seconds later he picked him up like a rag doll, placed the cap back on his head and by the scruff of the neck marched him into the Circle.

We learned later, from Charley the orderly, that after Colditz had thrown Preacher into the Circle he offered to fight any screw in the Block. His offer was declined, which didn't surprise us at all knowing the screws' aversion to one on one.

The hunger strike, started the month before, had reached a crucial stage by December with the health of the men quickly deteriorating, chief of whom was Sean McKenna who had been, by diagnosed the "doctors" in the block, as having only two days to live.

Those of us not on hunger strike were impotent in any action having been ordered to keep a cool head at all costs as any sign of frustration on our side would only be beneficial to the Brits and screws. This was probably the hardest of all orders to obey, knowing what our friends and comrades were enduring. Some of us were confident that even at this late stage something could be worked out without loss of life, and even the screws must have felt we might have the edge as some of them started to curry favour with us.

'I hope youse get all your demands,' lied the Human Wart who was as convincing as a Nazi at a bar mitzvah. 'We've all been put through tryin' times, but hopefully we're all the better for it and learn to tolerate each other.'

I wanted to puke at his toadying but on the other hand if he was frightened that we might win, then perhaps the screws had heard something that we hadn't.

'Is it Christmas *Top of the Pops*, or what, Sam?' laughed Finbar as the Human Wart walked despondently away leaving his liquorice footprints in the snow.

'I'd even listen to the fuckin' Queen, mate!' I replied. Pan's People floated in my head. I wondered if they had changed much? Pan's Pensioners now – not that that would make any difference! Outside the cells a white quietness had brought an artificial calm with it. Small birds made tiny indentations in the snow while the fat, diaphanous flakes threatened to cover them like tents.

'Governor on the air!' shouted a voice from the top of the wing.

A governor? At this time of night? What the hell was going on? Had the Human Wart heard something, after all? Not a word was said from either the governor or screws accompanying him as each door was opened, then slammed, and a document thrown in, haphazardly.

It was an "agreement" to end the hunger strike.

I scanned the pages as quickly as my nerves permitted and I

swear I heard Jimmy Saville introduce Christmas *Top of the Pops*. He was smoking the biggest cigar in the world and surrounded by Pan's People: "Well gals and guys, this week's number one is the Blanket Men and . . ."

I then re-read the document as meticulously as possible not wanting to miss anything of importance in its 48 pages.

As it turned out, it contained very little substance. It was a masterpiece of detrimental ambiguity, full of alternative interpretations which managed to give with one hand while taking with the other, a spider's web of ambiguous semantics of maybes, perhaps, and time-will-tells. There was no way we could settle for this. All the years of torture and torment flushed down the shitter for an inimical "agreement" that wasn't even worth the paper it was printed on.

Jimmy Saville quickly faded to black. As did Pan's People. I thought I could smell their perfume and it made me want to cry.

Maybe next Christmas . . .

19

Hope

Spring 1981

*"As a child I was very aware of being an inferior class. As an adult,
I certainly was in a situation where I could easily have picked
up a gun . . . I grew up with guys who went on hunger
strike and they experienced some things in Belfast that
drove them to starve their bodies for 70 days."*
LIAM NEESON, *Actor*

We knew we had lost the impetus generated by the first hunger
strike as the second one commenced in March. This time the
strategy would be different: volunteers would join the hunger
strike periodically instead of en masse as the former one. We also
acquiesced to the ending of the "no wash" part of our protest in
the hope of maximising the plight of the men on hunger strike.

In all honesty, it was a great relief to us all to be able to wash
again. Our hair, which hadn't been washed or cut in years,
stretched down our backs, greasy and tangled like oily dock
ropes; our teeth, which last saw a tooth brush many years ago,
amazingly, were unaffected, largely in part to the screws refusing
to give us sugar as part of their punishment towards us.

Ironically, had they done so, they would no doubt have inflicted far greater pain via toothaches.

Our first shower in years! God, was it sweet! I will never forget the first hot sprays hitting me with the propulsive ferocity of porcupine quills, or the intoxicating aroma of shampoo and soap making my nostrils flare with snobbish delight, loving the decadence of it all as I watched years of dirt fall from my –

'For fuck's sake, will ye hurry the fuck up! You're gonna waste the water. The rest of us haven't had a shower in years, either,' complained the voice behind me. He was small, dark, and his body was covered in scars from gunshot wounds. I didn't recognise him, but he knew me. 'We've been next door to each other four years and you don't even know me?'

All these years never knowing what he looked like, with only his voice to interpret an image, Cowboy was nothing I had envisaged – and it showed on my face.

'And you don't look like anything I imagined, either!' he laughed, reading my mind.

The rumours of him having guns tattooed to his sides were, sorry to say, unfounded. One of the screws watching us laughed an artificial laugh, hoping to join in the conversation.

'What's so funny?' asked Cowboy in an icy tone, freezing the screw to the spot.

'Nothin' . . .' The screw's face turned crimson, then pale as Cowboy's upper lip curled in distaste.

The screws were nervous, now that we were out of the cells, and with good reason. Payback could come at any second, and they knew it. In their minds we were mad men, lions waiting to pounce, or insuperable Gothic creatures devoid of all things human. The Creature they had created in their own minds, their own propaganda, was now on the loose and as far as we were concerned we would not discourage that mindset.

Cleaning our teeth was the next ordeal as the rough toothbrushes made unfamiliar strokes in our mouths, turning the sinks crimson from our raw gums, transforming us into feasting vampires.

And then to my hair. I sat in a chair as the "barber" hacked at its waist length, making my head feel lighter with each touch. And even though it was a great relief to feel the cold air on my neck again, a sudden burst of nostalgia swept over me as I watched the years of hair being brushed away. An old friend was now gone. But there was more and I could no longer put off the inevitable which I had been dreading. The barber clipped my facial hair as close as possible, leaving me to remove the stubborn shadow with a plastic razor. Small nails of hair give way, leaving my exposed skin screaming with pain as I constantly sliced my face, shaving blind.

It had been more than four years since I last saw myself and my vanity refused to allow me a look in the mirror knowing it would be a stranger staring back, an old battered stranger who would question the sanity of it all.

Yet, you are perpetually conscious, as you sit in the "comfort" and darkness of your cell, of the man a few feet from you who is slowly and painfully dying. You have prayed so hard that the blue of your mind becomes an accusing leather screen of condign phosphor questioning your very existence: Why are you not on hunger strike, suffering with the rest?

And the more you scream for it to leave you alone, the more it torments, until you finally tell it you lack the courage, that you could not go without food for a few days, let alone weeks; that you have read books on the suffering the body and mind must endure as the skin shrinks to fit the perfect skeleton with its bones as brittle as baked chalk; that you shudder at the thoughts of migraines so violent they bite through your skull, piercing your eyes. Then come the blackouts, blindness and coma. Finally, death.

I shuddered in the darkness, a coward hiding from myself, as each day brought the hunger strikers closer to death. The shrill voice of Thatcher squealed like fingernails clawing a blackboard.

The screws, for their part, placed great plates full of Irish stew outside the cell of each hunger striker in a sick and feeble torture to entice them to eat. The aroma filled each cell in an appetising

107

mist, which competed against the natural groans of an empty stomach. They then fanned the mist into the cell just to make sure each hunger striker got the message. This was always followed with a screw's loud voice: "Good man! That's the way! Get tucked in. There's more where that came from." The fact that each hunger striker refused to even acknowledge these pathetic manoeuvres sent the screws into a rage culminating in empty lockers being carried ghoulishly by them with the words that it wouldn't be long before we're burying you in this.

Despite this provocation we remained disciplined and reversed the psychology by letting the screws know that they would be the next to go should any of the men die. Then the strangest of things happened. Something so perfectly timed it made you wonder about fate, and perhaps – *just perhaps* – there might be a God, after all.

When Frank Maguire, MP for Fermanagh/Tyrone, died it came as a shock to all the POWs. He had been a staunch supporter and we lost not just a friend but a voice that had consistently highlighted the ill treatment meted out to us by the Brits and screws. His death brought our morale down another notch. It was the lowest we had ever reached.

Then, just as in life, Frank once again helped us out.

'Bobby should run for Frank's vacated seat,' suggested someone whose arse was obviously out the window. A ludicrous suggestion. Hadn't we discouraged our own people from participating in any elections run by the Brits? And how could we compete against such a well-oiled propaganda machine? Plus, there was always the trap-fall that if Bobby did stand and received a low number of votes it would hand the Brits a big stick to beat us with. They would proclaim the low vote proved the prisoners had no support and that they had been right all along.

But there was no alternative . . .

20

Tragedy

Tuesday, 5 May 1981

"Our torments also may in length of time
Become our elements."

MILTON, *Paradise Lost*

The days prior to the election became nerve-wracking. The Brits tried desperately to have Bobby's name removed from the ballot paper. The Catholic Church, through their priests, informed us that: "No one would vote for Bobby Sands." It was truly comforting to know that the Brits and Church were soiling the same pair of pants.

If we could only get a respectable portion of the votes cast, that in itself would be a significant victory for us.

Quietness enveloped the Blocks as we waited on the result from our clandestine radio, which had been smuggled in on a visit. The OC forewarned us that under no circumstance were we to give any impression of knowing the result for fear of losing the radio, which he kept for news bulletins. His orders were that, irrespective of the outcome, bite your tongue.

And we probably would have if not for the fact that not only did

109

Bobby do well, he topped the poll, becoming the new MP for Fermanagh/Tyrone.

We screamed, we cried, we banged the doors until we could bang no more. We had won. We were floating and nothing on this earth could bring us down. It was all over bar the shouting. We hugged each other. No one would have to die. We could live like human beings again.

The Human Wart looked suicidal. The Preacher was speechless. The Volunteer could barely conceal his grin. Every thing was falling into place.

'The light is at the end of the tunnel, Finbar. Can you believe it after all these years?' asked JCB who was ecstatic, giggling like a school kid. 'I could be home this time next year.'

'A *light* at the end of the tunnel, JCB.?' said Finbar sarcastically. 'The tunnel hasn't even been built yet for any light to emerge.'

'It's over, Finbar. Admit it, mate,' I said, coming to JCB's defence. 'Even fuckin' Thatcher isn't devious enough to allow an elected MP to die. So lighten up. Don't put a damper on it.'

He was silent for a moment, then asked: 'How long've ye been on the Blanket?'

'You know the answer to that,' I said. 'Same as yourself. Over four years. Why?'

'Oh, just thought the way you were talkin' it was only four days. You know the Brits as well as I do, what they're capable of.'

I can't let him get to me. He's simply winding me up . . .

'Okay, Finbar. Whatever ye say. You win.'

The tragedy being, he was right all along.

The Brits contemptuously dismissed the result, claiming it didn't change a thing. And in a last ditch effort to save face – its own, of course – the Church sent in a confederacy of dunces to "negotiate" an end to the hunger strike. They explained what we "might" get, "probably" could get but never what we *would* get. All they produced was a rehash of the document that ended the first hunger strike in such acrimonious ambiguity. They were not in the slightest bit embarrassed by their mendacity. Perhaps, had they advanced such "concern" years ago we would not have been in the dire straits now facing us. It was all too little too late.

It was early Tuesday morning when a small tapping sound could be heard coming down the pipe. It sounded like a heart beat. We were not unprepared for what it meant . . . but it still came as a shock when the news of Bobby's death filtered through.

21

Catch 22

Winter 1982

*"We are not saints, but we have kept our appointment.
How many people can boast of that?"*

BECKETT, *Waiting for Godot*

'It's difficult getting used to wearing shoes again, after all these years, isn't it Sam?' asked Finbar, answering his own question.

We were walking at a steady pace around the yard trying to break-in our shoes, which felt like planks of wood, clogs with tiny nails in them. Our feet seemed to balloon the further we walked.

Months had now passed since the ending of the hunger strike, which had taken the lives of ten men. The Brits had conceded some basic rights to us: we wore our own clothes instead of prison garb; we had access to newspapers, books and writing material and we could now take an hour of exercise, walking the yard. But the crux – not doing prison work – still remained.

Clouds rolled in releasing small gumdrops that tasted like new leather on my tongue; an addictive percussion after all these years

113

of drought. Men ran for shelter but I could only stare at my cell window and picture my face, a silent scream, squeezed between the bars, year after year. It was horrible to assimilate, but it still burns in my head, branding for ever the enduring chill of an unassailable belief in a moment that time could not conquer.

Rumours. Chassis without foundation. Prisoners thrive on them. We heard so many over the years you'd think we'd be immune to them. But no, not us. Our first response was always: is that genuine? That'd be brill. Are ye sure, now? No fuckin' about?

And we always fell for it, even when we knew how impossible it sounded, just like me telling everyone it would all be over by Christmas all those years ago. So this latest one was no exception, plus it was feasible.

After the hunger strike ended, part of the "concessions" made to us was the implementation of lost remission. It all sounded good in theory except it, like all British agreements, had a Catch 22. To be granted the remission we would have to do prison work. After three months of towing the line, lost remission would be restored. In my own case, for example, if I were to work for three months I would subsequently be released at the end of three months instead of the two-and-a-half years, which remained, on my illegal sentence.

It was tempting, of course, and the Brits knew this. It was the old divide and conquer trick. But I took the view that if I had not come on the Blanket in the first place I would have been home almost three years ago. And not forgetting: no welcoming committee in the reception; no nakedness, degradation, humiliation; no strip searching, anal-probing mirror searches; no wing shifts, forced washing, horrendous beatings.

Fuck it, I thought. *Two-and-a-half to go. No problem.*

Days, weeks, months and years of more wing-shifts, more beatings. Deep in my heart I knew I would be "free" some day. I dreamt constantly of it, night and day, like an adventure game, clutching it in my fists, burning it in my conscience for all time, hiding it beneath my tongue like Sunday-morning Mass.

Little did I know then, what an adventure I was in for when, years later, freedom would eventually come.

22

The real Great Escape
(minus Steve McQueen)

25 September 1983

"Chance and uncertainty are two of the most common and most important elements in warfare."

CLAUSEWITZ

"A week before the date there were still six men protesting and who refused to end it. They were all serving long sentences and saw the protest as the only way of expressing themselves effectively. It was a big step for them to end it."

DEREK DUNNE, *Out Of The Maze*

'Why the hell are youse continuing with this protest?'

The question the screws, the Brits and the Church had asked all these years was now being asked, ironically, by an unlikely source: The OC of the H Blocks. Veins protruded from his forehead as his face alternated from crimson to purple.

'You're gonna have a heart attack if you don't calm down,' advised Blute whose enormous bulk dwarfed the moaning chair he sat on.

Months had now passed since the official protest had ended

leaving five others and myself on a *de facto* protest of our own.

'The Movement should be priority in your actions,' continued the OC, ignoring Blute's advice. 'Not some emotional – no matter how well intended – protest that can only help fuel dissension when what we need most is to be able to move as one.' He sucked in his breath then released it slowly. He wasn't having the desired effect he had hoped for. 'This has been a traumatic protest for us all. Everyone suffered. The lads who died were all friends of ours. But we've got to build on that – and quickly. We need complete unity on this and I'm askin' youse to reconsider and do what's best. Even if humble pie has to be swallowed . . .'

No one was listening any longer. We had heard it all before, weekly at first, now daily. Our minds were made up. Our volition was solid. We weren't for turning. No matter what. The OC gazed out the window, shook his head in bewilderment then sat down, warily. He was drained, as if arguing with us had become too much.

'Okay,' he said, more to himself than us. 'Only two people in the Block know what I'm about to tell youse, and God help any of youse if ye open yer mouths.' He leaned forward from the chair and whispered so low I could barely hear.

The greatest escape in Irish history was coming, like an unstoppable train of steel and courage. No one could stop it, its determination, its destination. No one. Not the Brits, not the screws. It was then that the six of us made the decision: we would be more than proud to facilitate it . . .

Our day had come. The Circle was a scene of organised chaos. Prisoners – those going on the escape – ran in all directions, some in the uniforms of screws who were now tied up and bundled in one room. Outside the control-room, the body of a screw lay like a beached whale with blood oozing from a head wound. He had refused to hand over the keys when asked to do so by a volunteer. His brave or foolish action rewarded him with the inevitable. A group of prisoners surrounded him, offering words of encouragement that he wasn't going to die, as they attempted to stance the flow of blood.

I was angry that they would be concerned about any screw after what we had been through. But my initial thoughts changed as I realised it could be the Volunteer or some other screw who had helped us in the past. As I edged closer, the remorse in me quickly changed to euphoria. It was none other than the Human Wart.

The eidetic images of his hangman's noose tied to the penis, then pulled; his grubby sausage-like fingers probing rectums of naked men; his urinating into the mouths of sleeping prisoners would haunt me forever. No, I decided, if there truly was a God, then the Human Wart should survive. But only as a vegetable, locked in his cocoon of perversity. *Quid pro quo* had been a long time coming, but now that it had arrived I would savour it for as long as possible. Not since Fletcher Christian beat the fuck out of Captain Blight with the cat-o'-nine-tails had justice been so sweet. No "man" had it coming to him like the Human Wart, and it almost made me believe in God again. (Unfortunately, the Human Wart *would* survive and receive one of the highest medals for bravery from his Queen only to be charged, years later, for sexually molesting his own nephews and nieces. Of course, not one prisoner was surprised by this turn of events, and we doubted if any of the screws were either. They had known it for years.)

Everything, seemingly, was going like clockwork. All the main goals in the Block had been achieved. All that remained was the arrival of the Happy Wagon. It wouldn't be long . . .

'It's coming! The Happy Wagon's comin'!' shouted a volunteer.

'Get this mess cleaned – pronto!' ordered the OC. 'Youse two. Help the MO move the Wart. The rest of you men go about your business as screws. Don't fuck up.'

The last three words were a command as well as a plea. Everything was riding on normality, or the semblance of it. The driver of the Happy Wagon nodded to the "screw" at the gate as it opened, allowing him access. Nothing was out of place. Perfect. Come into my parlour, said the spider to the fly . . .

'See what happens to heroes?' said the volunteer to the driver, gun at head.

He had walked into the nightmare that all screws dread: the one where prisoners have taken over, holding hostages. This was worse than a nightmare. It was real, and the fact that a fellow guard lay dying or dead made it more tangible. The driver simply nodded. He felt faint. He needed to go to the toilet. Had he ever given the fingers to these men? Would they blame him for the crap that lousy cook called grub? He was only the driver, surely they understood that? *I always did my best to make sure the crap was warm. That bastard of a cook! He's the one who should be here, not me. It wasn't fair! Why did it have to be me, dear God?*

'You're gonna drive us through each gate, nice and calm. Do you understand?'

He nodded. His tongue had disappeared. He needed a shit.

'We have a hand-grenade, as well as guns. Every man here is a lifer and has sweet fuck all to lose. Try anything stupid and we all go up together. Understand?'

Oh, God! A fuckin' hand-grenade! I'm dead. These are maniacs. That fuckin' cook!

'Okay, okay! You can stop nodding yer head. We get the picture.'

The driver couldn't stop nodding, and who could blame him? I probably would have nodded just as vigorously, under the same circumstances. Perhaps even more so. But everything now hinged on fear being the spur. Had enough of it been put into him, or would he try at the last minute to be another Human Wart? It was all academic now as prisoners – some attired as screws – piled into the Happy Wagon. As the van disappeared slowly down the yard with its precious cargo on board, I wondered if it, at last, would live up to its name.

The propulsion of events, coupled with the fact that at any minute screws and armed Brits could come storming through the doors, was a great incentive to complete as quickly as possible our scorched-earth policy. Everything possible was burnt: photos, files, cell cards. Anything to cause confusion.

I couldn't resist the urge to look in at the screws who were tied and stripped to their under-wear, huddled together, fearful for their lives. Our fear had lasted years. Theirs only minutes. I felt cheated that their punishment should be so light and wanted to rectify it. I could so easily have set fire to the room and let God deal with it. The innocent would survive while the guilty perished.

Small petals of smoke rose from the smouldering documents as the Human Wart's blood congealed into a wine-coloured stain shaped like a question mark, but all I wondered was how far the lads had got, what must be going through their heads as they stopped at each gate? How on earth could they get through one gate, let alone sixteen?

About an hour later, the radio supplied the answer: *"And just to repeat our earlier headline. News of a massive attempted escape from the Maze (*Long Kesh) *is coming in. Details are still sketchy, but a number of men have been caught . . ."*

I was devastated. All captured. I felt sick. I cursed God. Could He not grant us one break, after all these fucking years. What kind of a God would –

' *. . . a significant number still at large."*

God forgive me! I knew You were really on our side.

It was instantaneous. The entire Block burst into one volcanic our-time-has-come-at-fucking-last scream of jubilation. Doors rattled like thunder, furniture banged off walls. The hair on my head stood up, fired with electricity, and I swear my feet floated from the ground. I stared out the window, watching my smile reflect back at me. We had done the impossible. Escaped from the unassailable fortress so loved and boasted of by Thatcher. This was the best revenge. There would be a lot of sick people tonight.

Then they came. They converged like insects covering the entire yard: screws and the notorious RUC, angry but fearful. Prisoners had guns. Must be careful. They were mad enough without guns . . .

I was amazed at my own calm. I wanted them to come, see

what could never be defeated, and see the face of the Blanket Men, *unfuckingconquered*.

The governor was reeling, staggering like a drunk as he entered the Circle, gun in hand. He could not comprehend the anarchy that greeted him; of his men tied and stripped to their underwear, of a wounded screw and documents turned to ash and congeries.

'Bastards! Someone will pay for this!'

'What do you reckon, Sam? The news says a couple of screws have been stiffed,' said Pat.

'We can only hope it's true, mate,' I replied.

Doors began to open. A governor, accompanied by two POs, a screw and two RUC members, was doing a quick head count, desperately trying to find out who was gone, who remained. The little bonfires had done the trick. It would take them a while to determine the names of the escapees. The longer the better.

'Are you fuckin' deaf, Millar? I said move it!' screamed the screw.

I eased myself slowly off the bed, and as casually as possible walked towards the Circle which was now a shadowy vignette of smoke and blood, screws and cops, all sombre, like Orangemen on the Twelfth.

'Take off your shoes!' snarled a screw.

'You take them off.'

With the help of a few others, he did. Next came my jeans, my shirt. Other prisoners were going through the same routine. Eventually, we were frog-marched out the door and down the yard. The tiny stones cutting my feet made me think of Bangor beach. Instead of crying gulls, I could hear barking in the distance.

As I entered the gate of the other Block I could see the dogs, lined in a perfect flank, straining angrily on their handler's chains. We were forced to walk through, dogs snapping inches from our skin. The cold numbed the first nip but the second and third started to hit home. Then came the bites, making me scream, hating myself for it. The dogs were now in a frenzy, almost uncontrollable. They bit, snapped and ripped the skin with impunity.

'Bastard! *He kicked the dog*,' screamed a screw. Someone had committed sacrilege. The horror of it! 'Kicking a defenceless creature,' screamed the screws and cops as they kicked the shit out of the semi-naked man. 'That'll teach 'im, the fucker!'

"*An utterly fearless man*," said Melville in *Moby Dick*, "*is a far more dangerous comrade than a coward*." I could only agree with his sentiment as the prisoner continued to ward off the dogs and screws with impotent, shoeless kicks. Each time he went down he came straight back up.

No one escaped the dogs.

The next day, reports filtered in of how many men had made it to freedom, how many captured. The prison came to a standstill as the Brits conducted an inquiry into how the impossible became possible. Things would never be the same. We knew it. The screws knew it.

The escape had brought us all the added benefit of no-work being the norm. We could no longer be punished for refusing what was no longer on offer, and within a couple of months I found myself in a van heading to the Reception, heading home. It was *deja vu* in reverse. It had been a long and arduous journey, authentic faith tested but still unconquerable in its frightening belief.

My father and brother greeted me at the gate. It had been years since I last saw them. My father said nothing, simply shook my hand and smiled. He left the words to my older brother, Danny.

'Welcome home, kid.'

23

The Casino

July 1984

*"All who have been famous for their genius . . . have
been inclined to insanity."*

ARISTOTLE

Cobalt smoke drifted upwards, spiralled before dissipating into
the high-rise ceiling. Down below me, people clustered around
each table trying to match luck against skill, skill against luck.
Thousands of dollars exchanged hands.

I watched, fascinated by the dealers' prowess of boxer-speed
coupled with arithmetical perfection. In Belfast, we called it
"21", or "pontoon". Here – I was now living in Queens, the
largest of the five boroughs that make up New York, and with
over100 ethnic groups settled there making it the most ethnically
diverse as well – they called it "blackjack".

The card tables were half-moon shaped, covered with lush
green and large enough to seat seven customers. There were ten
tables going full speed. Behind the seated customers stood more
customers waiting for a seat or "jockey-betting", placing their
bets beside those of the seated customers.

Except for the *oohs* and *ahhs* of victory and defeat blackjack is a quiet and unnerving game with most communication done by a slight movement of the finger or hand. A finger motion asks for another card, while a slicing motion means the customer will stay with what he/she has. These rules are strictly adhered to and once the dealer has released a card from the "shoe" it can't be returned. Therefore, a customer must be wary of getting an itch at the wrong time or waving to a fellow player. An unwanted card is the usual punishment.

The "casinos" were known as "after-hours joints" in New York City. They were mainly large houses converted and styled to resemble Atlantic City casinos, albeit on a much smaller scale. What they lacked in size they more than made up for in their cosiness and chic, although that was only partly the reason for their popularity.

The chief reason was taxes. In New York the casinos don't tax winnings. Not through benevolence, but because all casinos in New York are "illegal", with only one concern: the visits from officers of the "Public Morals", a gung-ho group of sledgehammer-carrying cops whose job it is to close them down or, at the very least, the ones refusing to give them a bribe. These cops always intensified their raids whenever elections were due, to make themselves look good for the local politicians. They would disguise themselves as business people, out-of-towners or use any camouflage that would blend in, before raiding the clubs, usually between the hours of 8.00 and 11.00 pm, and would leave their calling card in the form of smashed tables, bottles and wall fixtures. What they were really after was quite simple: the same as ourselves – the money.

'Tell us where it's located and there'll be no smashing, just confiscating.' His name was Murphy and he looked every part of it. He was in charge of his PMS and thrived on the vandalism of it.

The owner of the casino hated the PMS and his policy towards them was simple: *Not a cent. Even if they demolish the place, not a cent.*

When Murphy was told that we hadn't a clue what he was talking about he would work himself into a frenzy by turning into a modern day Thor, his sledge-hammer knocking out walls, splitting card tables in half. But no matter how much damage they inflicted they could never find the money. All that was left for their anger was to arrest and then place us in the local lock-up for a night or two, until a judge had fined us – usually a couple of hundred dollars each – and admonished us not to break the law again.

The casinos operated seven days a week, 24 hours a day. Food and liquor were provided free to customers, as was transportation to those who wished it. The card dealers came from all walks of life and various countries such as Korea, Puerto Rico and Canada. When I first started, only a couple were from Ireland. But that would all change drastically, in the months ahead.

The owner of the casino was an Irish-American by the name of Mac, a self-made millionaire whose family came from Tyrone. He had done time in prison for killing a man and was a one-time boss of the Irish Mob that controlled the Bronx and lower Manhattan. An unassuming and soft-spoken man, he was rarely seen in the casino except at Christmas to thank all the dealers and hand them an envelope containing a monetary gift.

Mac's overseer was a man named Ronnie Gibbons, from Liverpool. He was an ex-boxer who fancied himself with his fists and brain. A copy of Marcus Aurelius' *Meditations* was never out of his reach and he was forever quoting the stoic philosopher. Ronnie had first, accidentally, bumped into Mac at a prestigious health club in Manhattan, where he did a regular workout on the punch bag and ropes. Mac was apparently impressed by what he saw.

'I could use someone like you for my club,' he said, handing Ronnie a business card. 'Give me a call sometime.'

Normally, Ronnie would have torn the card up. He was self-employed at the time and loathed the thought of working for someone. "As a slave", he called it. But something told him to

125

pocket the card with grace, as he was well aware of whom he had spoken to. Ronnie regarded himself as the *Ragged-Trousered Philanthropist*, a modern-day Robin Hood who believed you should take from the rich and give to the poor. Sometimes when that philosophy became a bit muddled he found it hard to distinguish the poor from himself.

When he first started in the casino he became not only bouncer – which was what Mac had wanted him for – but jack-of-all-trades. If a bathroom needed cleaning and the janitor hadn't shown up, Ronnie would quickly get to work on it, leaving it spotless. A dead bulb needed replacing? Ronnie was there, stepladder in hand. If a customer called for a drink while the regular barman was busy? Hey presto, Ronnie with a tray full of drinks! There he was again, helping a customer on with her coat. What a guy.

At least that's what Mac was thinking as Ronnie worked his omnipresence to perfection, fooling everyone except Barney Jameson, Mac's overseer at the time.

'There's somethin' not right 'bout that guy,' complained Jameson to Mac's father, John, as they both counted the winnings from the 4.00 to 12.00 shift. 'And that phoney accent of his drives me nuts.'

'He doesn't drink,' said John, beating down his second large whiskey of the day. 'Never trusted a man who didn't drink. Like the Pope havin' sex. Just not right.'

'Listen, both of ya. Ronnie's here to stay,' said Mac as he double-checked his father's figures on the payout cards. 'He's got lots of potential – especially with his fists. He could become a good asset for the House.'

The two words Jameson *didn't* want to hear: potential and asset.

'Still don't trust a man who doesn't drink,' mumbled Mac's father.

A few months later, fate dealt Ronnie a winning hand in the form

126

of an attempted robbery. The robber, a young man in his teens, was knocked unconscious by Ronnie's quick reflexes and thinking.

'Can I pick a winner or not?' smiled Mac, at hearing the news.

A week later, despite the protest of Jameson, Ronnie was elevated to the position of manager where he quickly made his presence felt. He overhauled security to prevent a re-occurrence of walk-in robbers; he checked, then double-checked expenses so that every dollar was accounted for. This caused the animosity to grow between him and Jameson.

'We've been paying out too much for liquor,' said Ronnie at a meeting of managers. 'The House doesn't consume half of what we're being charged.' Ronnie spread the receipts on the small oval table in front of Mac.

Jameson's brother-in-law supplied the liquor and Jameson quickly rushed to his defence. 'The House gets a good deal from the supplier. And what's all this "we" business? Anyone would think you owned the place instead of Mac.' It made Jameson sound defensive and he realised it, too late.

'I'm talking collectively,' explained Ronnie in a calm voice. 'The profit and longevity of the House should . . . must come first.'

Mac watched amused. A wise owl knowing that sooner or later it would come down to this: two roosters fighting for their share of the farmyard.

'What's your association with Mike Bloom?' asked Ronnie. He had moved close to Jameson.

'Whaddya mean *association*? He's my brother-in law, as Mac knows and everyone knows. Whaddya tryin' ta say, son?' hissed Jameson.

'I'm saying perhaps your in-law is faulty with his figures. It can happen. He probably didn't mean anything by it . . . Just carelessness perhaps. I'm sure he'd like to rectify his mistake, given the chance.'

'Just whaddya talkin' 'bout? Whaddya tryin' ta say?'

'I estimate his *mistake* has cost the House about five grand over the last year alone, and I haven't even checked the receipts for the year before. Who knows what the final tally will be.'

'Mac?' said Jameson, incredulously. 'Can ya believe this punk? Insultin' my brother-in-law who is more than good to the House with his prices.'

Mac said nothing, only watched, fascinated by the silence in the room. Each manager – there were eight in all – wished he was someplace else. Not because of the humiliation of Jameson, but because each wondered if he was next to be scrutinized. Quickly each went over past deeds, not liking what he remembered.

Ronnie hit Jameson full force in the face, knocking him out.

'Tiny! Come up here, please,' shouted Ronnie.

'Yea?' asked Tiny the enormous bouncer, entering the room.

'Throw this piece of shit in the dumpster outside.'

'Huh?'

'He's not allowed near the casino – ever. Okay?'

With Jameson gone, it was left to Mac's father to sum it all up. 'Never trusted that man Jameson from the day I met him, Ronnie. Drank too much for my liking,' he said, his hand catching another large whiskey. 'Never trust a man who drinks too much.'

Ronnie simply smiled. Mac senior would be well worth the watching.

'Where da foick is Nicky, that damn *com-u-nest*!' screamed Tommy Mullan as he grabbed another tray of chips from the office. 'We're bein' moidered by those Chinks and Jews and that little boistard is still missin'!'

Nicky was the best dealer the casino had. He had lightning-fast fingers and mind, a great entertainer. He was the only one the customers never got angry with. He was from Romania and always carried a small pistol beneath his armpit.

Tommy Mullan's anger was another matter. His violent life began as his mother's ended – during parturition. "An angry, ugly baby", quipped the nurse who would rather have seen baby die over mother. By the age of eighteen he had seen the inside of Attica, Sing Sing and Green Haven. He tried his hand as a heavy for the Irish mob in Boston where he was shot twice in the face, losing an eye in the process: "Really annoyin'. Like havin' a golf ball for an Adam's apple". Spotted by Mac as a diamond-in-the-rough, he was hired as bouncer/doorman, bringing with him the acumen of a street survivor with an indispensable loyalty that bordered on fanaticism. If Doc – another one of the pit-bosses – was suspicious of foreigners, Tommy was suspicious of everyone, including Doc whom he suspected of pocketing more than wages and tips.

'Take it easy, Tommy,' advised Susan, the assistant manager. 'You'll have a heart attack. Nicky'll be here ASAP.'

'Don't talk shit, woman! We're almost out of black chips. It's n-r-key out there! Foickin' little com-u-nest.'

'Here, honey,' said Maria, a bartender, holding a glass of *Johnny Walker Black* out to him as he passed closer to the bar.

Tommy hesitated, weighing the consequences of more whiskey in such a volatile situation, and then quickly disposed of it down his throat. He hated seeing good whiskey go to waste. He hated seeing good whiskey go *anywhere* except down his throat. 'That hit the spot, Maria. But no more. This damn ulcer's killin' me.'

'I told you to stop feeding him drink,' hissed Doc to Maria as Tommy entered the fray in the centre of the room.

'He's the boss. No? I do as *he* says. Not you,' replied Maria, dismissing the glaring Doc with a toss of her hair.

He was too. Despite Doc being the designated pit-boss, Tommy was Mac's right-hand man and the *de facto* boss. Rarely did they work the same shift, but when they did it was Gunpowder and Spark with the inevitable explosion.

'All these spic dealers Mac hired aren't doing much good,' said Doc to Susan. 'They're getting paid twice as much as the other dealers, and for what? So they can give the chips away twice as fast! If I had my way –'

'Well ya doint, do ya?' said Tommy, standing menacingly behind Doc. 'It's Mac's call, and he'll hire and fire anyone he wants.'

'I'm telling you those spics are detrimental to the House. It's madness having them here.'

'End of discussion. Understand? If ya doint like it git another job. That can be arranged.'

Tommy waved for me to come down from the mezzanine and take Table 4. The exit sign was beaming, making me hesitate. This was my last chance to escape. I had been dreading this moment. My initiation into the world of blackjack was about to begin.

We had been taught at the dealer school that we were mere robots, card-dealing machines: *Show no emotions. It is not your money. Don't take victory or defeat personal. When a customer wins you congratulate; when they lose you commiserate. Our one cardinal rule is fraternizing. Do not do it. Caught fraternizing with a customer and you are out – no questions asked, no excuse accepted.* I took a deep breath as I walked to the table. No more school. This was the real thing.

'I'll spot ya, kid.' Winked Tommy. 'We're down eight g,' he whispered, pretending to scratch his nose. 'I've a feelin' you're gonna be one of our lucky dealers, kid.'

Just what I didn't want to hear. There is a myth amongst pit-bosses of "hot" and "cold" dealers, of dealers who carry some special talisman with them. It's nonsense, but unfortunately for me Tommy was a firm believer in it. It was going to take more than having a lucky shamrock shoved up my arse to save this Titanic table and the thought of being down eight grand was not going to help. I felt all eyes on me as I tried to shuffle the cards exactly as I was taught at the school. But they felt like rounds of bread in my clumsy fingers and I dropped some on the floor, much to the delight of the customers who started laughing and hurling abuse at me. I began to perspire.

'Don't let dem bother ya, kid,' encouraged Tommy. 'We'll wipe those doirty grins off der gubs in a wee while.' If he had had a gun in his hand there is no doubt he would have shot someone. Every few minutes, he would force his dentures out on to the edge of his tongue, scrutinizing them. It was a disgusting habit.

To my right sat Victor, an old hand from Atlantic City. He was the perfect spotter and had told me the spotter is the most important person at the table.

'A good spotter will nick any potential problems in the bud before they get out of hand. He must be assertive at all times. An honest mistake can make a dealer – or customer – look bad, so the onus is on the spotter to defuse the situation as quickly and diplomatically as possible without anyone losing face or being called a cheat. Also, watch out for distractions. Dames with their tits hangin' out all over the place; coffee being spilled on the table . . . Even pricks fakin' heart attacks. They'll try every trick in the book, these people. But just keep your eyes on the table. Nice and simple, and you'll do just fine.'

It was like having an older brother watching my back.

Ten to twelve decks of cards are used in each game. At the card school they teach you how to shuffle as a butterfly of quietness and perfection. I was making a complete mockery of all I had been taught. Once shuffled, you hold the decks in one hand stretched towards the customer, while your other holds a "cut card" – a clear piece of card-shaped plastic – which you offer to enable the customer to cut the block of cards with. The entire block is then placed in the "shoe" – a clear plastic housing – that holds the block in place, snugly, until they are removed one at a time at the speed of light.

Unfortunately for me, my light had yet to be lit.

'Oh, a virgin? So nervous, little boy. We not hurt.' She was a Korean woman, as were the others at my table. They were all dressed identically in dark suits and red polo sweaters. They chain-smoked, blowing what they inhaled into my face, stinging my eyes. 'You bring us luck, we tip big,' she smiled, not friendly, just business.

'I'll try,' I croaked, my voice rusted with fear.

'Bad luck, we cut off balls,' said the smallest of the coterie. They thought that great.

'Ignore 'em, Sam,' advised Victor. 'They're only trying to fuck with your head.'

I had been warned about the Korean gamblers. They are very passionate about gambling, almost religious. If they smell weakness in a dealer they would have no qualms about going for the kill. The cards refused to come out. I had packed them in too tight.

Victor leaned over, flicking the cards, loosening them. 'Nice and easy does it, Sam. Take your time.'

'C'mon! C'mon! You too fuckin' *slow!*' All the Korean women were screaming.

Slowly but surely I began. As each game progressed, my confidence became stronger. After four games, some of the chips began to accumulate back in the tray.

'He no good! Get new dealer,' they shouted. 'He deal as old man deals – fuckin' *slooow!*'

I had been on the table for almost an hour but found it invigorating. I was getting a buzz, a high.

'Would ya like some refreshments, Samuel, me bucko?' asked Tommy, all smiles, elevating me from kid to first name term.

With all the chips back in the tray, the customers now had to buy them back if they wanted to continue. The Korean women quickly removed $100 bills from their handbags and placed them in front of me. I fan-tailed the money in front of Tommy and Victor to verify the amount before signing my name on the pay-card, and then showed it to both men before pushing the bills down into the cash box, which was attached to each table, with the aid of a narrow plunger.

At any given time the manager can look at the pay-card and know exactly how much each cash box contains. Normally, when it reaches a couple of thousand dollars the manager removes the box, replacing it with an empty one. This is done to deter would-be robbers and to prevent the cops getting any of it during a raid. The money is then counted in the safety of the office and in the presence of Mac or his father, just in case someone should have sticky fingers. After that, if the money isn't "sent home", it is hidden in an intricate labyrinth of hide-holes and false props placed strategically throughout the club. Something as innocuous as a *Maxwell House* jar could contain hundreds, if not thousands, of dollars. Bronx Tommy had become mesmerized by the reversal of fortune. His glass eye stared at the ceiling and I thought I saw a tear.

'Enough! We move,' said the Korean boss-lady. The troop of women pushed themselves away from the table.

'Well done, Samuel me bucko. Take a long break. Ya deserve it,' said Tommy, carrying the security box to the office.

'Not as bad as you thought?' asked Victor as he lit a foul smelling cigar.

'No. To be honest, I was enjoying myself and hated seeing them quit.'

'Ha! Enjoy it while you can. Cards are as fickle as women and cats. No loyalty, Sam. They'll bite the first chance they get.'

As I left the table for refreshment, Doc the pit-boss, followed me.

'I've been watching you, Sam,' said Doc, who had the equanimity of an undertaker and was perpetually attired in dark three-piece suits that perfectly reflected his sombre mood. We stood at the bar and he towered over me like a vulture studying carrion. 'You're becoming involved with the clientele. Feeling for them. In any other profession, that would be admirable. Here, it could mean the kiss of death. Don't think for one minute that they feel sorry for us when they win . . .They don't! That's the mutual understanding we have. Understand?'

Before I could answer, Maria, the Puerto Rican barmaid, asked, 'Can I get you somethin', honey?'

'Let me have a *Coke*, please, Maria,' I answered.

'Bottle or powder?' she laughed, opening the fridge.

Maria was a beautiful, sybaritic woman addicted to gold that adorned a good portion of her exposed skin. People she liked, she called honey. Those she didn't, she said: "You. What can I get *you?*" Which is exactly what she said to Doc as she poured my *Coke*.

'Water,' replied Doc, not hiding his xenophobic disdain.

Doc was suspicious of all foreigners – including Maria and myself – and was fluent in racist epithets. Everyone was a "chink", "nigger", or a "spic". Behind my back he called me a "mick", which didn't bother me in the least. I'd been called worse in Belfast. He had once seen Maria reading a copy of Jorge Castaneda's

Companero, the classic on the life and death of Che. He went ballistic, calling her a "commie bitch". The beautiful woman only smiled, incensing him further.

Maria poured the water into a tiny whiskey glass – no ice – and left it perilously at the edge of the counter.

'As I was saying, Sam. Feelings in this business can kill you quicker than a card shark with a photographic memory.' He glanced dubiously at the water as if suspecting Maria of "spiking" it. 'Physiognomy. Know what that means?'

Hadn't a clue. No doubt I was about to find out as he gave me what passed for a smile, hurting his face in the process.

'It means "facial appearance as a reflection of inner character".' He paused for effect but only received a loud fart from a drunken customer on his way to the toilet. It didn't help that the customer was a Russian immigrant. Doc glared, shaking his head. 'One look at your face and I can read it like a book. So can they,' he gestured towards the tables. 'Especially the chinks, who will prey on any sympathy you show towards them. They perceive it as weakness.' He stopped grinning. 'As do I.'

'Some more *Coke*, honey?' asked Maria.

'No thanks, Maria,' I replied, and away she went, back to *Days of Our Lives*, ignoring Doc who was becoming agitated at the interruptions.

'I wish Mac would get rid of her. All she does is watch soaps, all day long. A waste of the House's money,' grumbled Doc, pushing the untouched glass away. 'Yes, the chinks and the rest of the scum can lose the business that took their parents 20 years to build. So what? That's not our problem. We don't put a gun to their heads. Do we? No. We don't. So remember that when you go home tonight.'

I nodded. He walked away.

'Don't let him bother you, honey,' advised Maria. 'He thinks he's better than the rest of us, that his shit don't stink, that his mother – if he ever had one – didn't fuck to have him. Huh!' She leaned on the counter and whispered. 'C'mere. Let me tell you somethin' 'bout him.'

I leaned closer. A brandy and chocolate aroma, mixed with *Chanel*, rose from her.

'All the time I bin here, he niver make a pass at me. Know why, honey?'

'No.'

'He's a *comepollas*,' she hissed through white and gold teeth, her eyes gleaming.

'A what?'

'A homo, honey. A fuckin' faggot. Know? A first class *cock-sucker*, honey. Know?'

'Oh.'

'Yes, honey! With George the wrestler.'

'The bouncer who works the midnight? That's a strange combination, Maria. Are you sure?'

'Am I sure! Sure I'm sure. You think all I watch are soaps all day? I *know*. Just don't drop any chips in front of him, honey!' she laughed, all the way back to *Days of Our Lives*.

24

A Meeting of Minds
(or minders)

September 1984

"There's no such thing as a free lunch."

ANONYMOUS

I had now been with the casino for about two months. The pay was good, and I looked forward to each day meeting all the different characters. This particular day was chilly, even with the sun creating long shadows, as I made my way down 18th Street towards the casino's location. I couldn't help but notice the large limo parked outside, chauffeured by a very attractive black woman. As I passed, the window slowly opened.

' 'Ello, mate. 'Op in.' Ronnie was grinning.

'Where'd you steal this from?' I inquired.

'Don't be a twat. I bought it, yesterday, from an up-and-comin' young black singer in New Jersey called Whitney Houston. Listen, I've some serious business I need to discuss with you and the other Irish lads. I'm takin' you all out for some grub tonight, over to *Milano's*. Tell the rest of 'em I'll pick 'em up 'bout 8.00 pm.'

'What's it all about?'

'Next month we'll be openin' another casino and I want you to be a manager.'

There had been talk of Mac opening another casino, this time on the West Side. 'What kind of nonsense are ye talkin'?' I asked. 'I'm lucky being able to deal!'

'Well, if things work the way I believe they will, you'll be one of the main people in charge of 'em. But don't say a fuckin' word yet. Understand?'

I thought he was full of shit, but nodded. 'No problem. See ye tonight.'

That night, we arrived at the restaurant, which was well known for its outrageous prices and "celebrity" customers.

'Don't be put off by those prices,' Ronnie insisted, as if reading all our minds. 'The House is footin' the bill, so just get tucked in.'

We did, knowing we were unlikely be in a place like this again.

Afterwards, waiting for dessert, he said, 'Right. Down to brass tacks.' He was pulling out a notepad and pen. 'You're all as ambitious as me, and in about four weeks you will all be given the opportunity to realise those ambitions.' He glanced at every one of us. 'Everyone here will be given managerial positions as soon as the new casino opens. I want you all to get stuck in, be assertive in everything you do.'

We were all smiling. This was music to our ears.

'The casino at *18th* is not doin' half as well as it should and could. Too many old timers as managers and all bloody foreigners.'

We laughed at that one, being all Irish and illegal immigrants.

'But that's all goin' to change and everyone here will help implement the new policy. I want to open a chain of casinos, just like *MacDonald's*.'

'Will we be selling Happy Meals as well?' I asked, smiling.

'If that's what it takes to fill the casino, we'll do it. I've *carte blanche* from our Mac, but we've got to be careful how we handle the wops. Personally, I don't give a toss 'bout 'em, but Mac's the boss and he doesn't want to step on too many toes at once.'

'But what about the present managers? Aren't they gonna be pissed off about all this – us takin' their jobs?' asked one of the others.

'That's where you lot come in, isn't it? Let them know who the boss is. If they don't comply, break a leg.'

A couple laughed, thinking he was joking. They didn't know him well enough, yet.

It was obvious he was using us for his own ends. I wondered if he thought we were just dumb micks who could be climbed on to built his empire, his Napoleonic dreams.

As the evening progressed, the sombre talk lightened. Everyone was filled with the thoughts of "running the show" and how they would be the best managers Mac had ever seen. I wondered how long it would last and how many bridges we had left – not to cross – to burn before it all came tumbling down.

'Right. Be back in a sec,' said Ronnie as he left to make a phone call. 'Order some more dessert then we'll be on our way.'

It was five minutes later when we all heard the tapping at the window. There, with his pugilist nose squeezed tight against the pane, was Ronnie. His half-moon grin and joker eyes told us the worse: he had done a bunk, blew without paying the bill, leaving us in the lurch. A miniature stampede ensued as we fled for the door leaving the bill cemented in the waiter's hand.

By the time we caught up to him in the limo, tears were rolling down his face. He thought it all great stuff, getting one over on the restaurant and us. 'The looks on your faces!' he repeated, over and over again.

And this was the man who was planning on building an empire.

25

Brothers and Sisters,
thicker than . . .

January 1985

"The only thing that can destroy a family business is the family."

BRONX TOMMY

Clouds, the colour of battle-ship grey, began to disperse, revealing a curtain of gorgeous indigo sky. Overhead, the Roosevelt Island cable car moved effortlessly, following me back to Manhattan. Inside the 'car a little girl waved. I waved back and she slapped the window with her mittens, laughing.

Ronnie had asked me to meet him outside the Metropolitan Museum of Art on the Upper East Side before we took a taxi down to the proposed location of the new casino. This one, appropriately enough for his aspirations, was situated behind the Empire State Building and would be opened with a bit more flair than usual. I felt that such a high profile was obviously going to cause problems, but Ronnie believed otherwise.

'This is how it should be,' he said. 'Bang-smack in the middle of Mid-Town with all those Jap tourists with big bucks and big buck teeth!'

141

He was now wearing *Brooks Brothers* clothing, but he was still the Ragged-Trousered Philanthropist. He handed a homeless man a couple of dollars but not before "enlightening" him with a few quotes from Marcus Aurelius. I'm sure the man wanted to hand him the money back, wondering if it was worth listening to all this ranting and raving for two bucks.

A year had now passed since he had become the main man and things were going fairly well. His plan of easing out all the old timers had almost been completed. Most of the Irish dealers were now managers or pit bosses and Mac had faded into the background, spending more time away from the casinos. Having achieved this control Ronnie started to introduce family members to the trade. It made little difference if they knew nothing about the casinos or the meaning of blackjack. To Ronnie, blood was thicker than water and they now had a job, irrespective of what the consequences might be.

A woman joined us.

'Sam. This is my little sister Rita. She's goin' to get stuck in with the rest of us.'

We were standing outside a large house whose large floors could easily be converted.

"Ello, Sam. Heard a lot of good things 'bout you,' she said.

She had a pixie face, short hair and tomboy demeanour. Her eyes were sharp, weighing you up as soon as they tasted you. 'Hello, Rita. Didn't even know Ronnie had a sister.'

'You know Ronnie by now, Sam. Business first; family last.'

If only that had been true, perhaps things would have been different.

'Let's head in,' said Ronnie, opening the door of the large brownstone. 'Think about it! Three floors of blackjack. It'll be the biggest in the city, mate.'

It was impressive. Each floor was the size of a miniature ballroom. I already had it peopled in my head.

'How long before it'll be ready?' asked Rita, trying to give the impression that she didn't know, as if Ronnie wouldn't confide in her.

She was well worth the watching.

'Soon. I'm negotiating with the landlord to get the price down.' Ronnie slapped the paint dust from his hands. He hated getting his hands dirty. Something I should have remembered later but didn't, until it was too late.

'I've a new position for you, Sam.'

'Oh? And what's that?' *And what's that smell?* I thought.

'Box manager.' He watched to see my reaction.

'You're busting my balls, right?'

'No. It's yours if you want it.'

'But what about Mac's da? That's his job. You can't fire him. That's crazy.'

'I can fire *anyone*. But I'm not goin' to fire 'im. Just give 'im a job where he can't be tempted by money.'

Money had been going missing from the House. It could only have been one of three people: Mac, his father or Ronnie. Being the box manager meant I would have access to all the money coming in and out of the casinos. Only Ronnie and Mac would have the same access. But with Mac taking a back seat it actually meant only Ronnie and myself.

That's when the thoughts came into my mind: What if it isn't Mac's father? What if it's Ronnie? What if he's setting me up for a fall? 'I'll have to think about it,' was all I said, surprising him.

'Okay. But I need to know soon. This could be lucrative for you, so don't let it slip through your hands.'

We went back outside to the chill emerging from the East River.

'I'm famished,' said Ronnie. 'Let's get somethin' to eat.'

'No thanks. I haven't forgotten the last time we went for a meal.'

He laughed. 'Okay. See you in the mornin'.'

'Good bye, Sam. See you soon,' said Rita, a crocodile in preparation.

26

Have you ever ridden a Harley D? Me neither!

June 1985

"Millar's sense of humour was darkened by eight years in the H-Blocks, and he had the air of one who felt he had given all that the cause could require."

NEW YORK DAILY NEWS

'Can you ride a motorbike?' asked Ronnie, a grin on his face.

'Yes. Why?'

'I've got one for ya.'

I didn't believe him, and he knew it.

'No, seriously. I've got it outside. All the money we'll save on taxi fares, getting you to and from the clubs, will pay for it in no time.' His beeper sounded. 'C'mon. Let's go outside, see if you can handle it.'

A motorbike! I tried to remain calm but the thought of riding up and down Manhattan on a big Harley D was just too much. I was going to be the next Peter Fonda, straddled on all that hot chrome and leather. My own "hog". My own –

'What the fuck is that?' Reality hit me.

'Your bike, mate. Like it?'

It was a scooter. A "mope-head". One of those little things ridden by midgets in the circus. It was depressing just to look at. 'Is this a joke, or what?'

'This'll be marvellous for zipping in and out of the traffic, mate. You'll be the envy of all who spot you,' enthused Ronnie. The scary thing about it was that he was deadly serious. 'No more hassle about parking meters. You'll be able to bring it right into the club –'

'No! N fucking O! You can stick that bike right up your arse. I don't care if you give me more money, the answer is still the same. No. No. No.' As always, I had my principles . . .

It was terrifying, riding in and out of traffic on the bike – especially near the cabs. They were like sharks, missing me by inches, laughing. Still, I had to admit, it saved searching for cabs, plus I was able to "zip" in and out of traffic with ease. The raise in my daily wage helped, as well.

No sooner had I arrived at *32nd* when a call from *82nd* came in, telling me they had too much money in the place. I hopped on the bike again and headed there. The Iranian was losing everything but the oil rigs.

'I can't believe he's still here,' I said to Chris, the day manager, as I emptied two cash boxes.

'Two days non-stop. Doesn't even go to the bathroom. One minute he's down 60g, the next he's Lazarus. Go figure,' she replied.

A commotion at the front door made me turn just in time to see Rocky, our bouncer/doorman stagger in, his face covered in blood.

'Nobody move!' screamed the Puerto Rican, sawn-off shotgun in hand. 'Everybody hit the back wall . . . Now!'

Behind him came two more, each armed with a rifle, each disguised as pizza-delivery men. Everything went silent, except for Rocky who was groaning, holding his bloody nose. Their faces weren't masked which meant they either didn't care, or they

146

knew no one was going to be alive to identify them. Another ominous sign came next.

'Who is the box-boss. We know he's here. We even know his name is Sam.'

I could feel the blood drain from my face.

'Which of you is Sam?' he repeated oh so calmly.

I remembered the part in Spartacus when the Romans have him and his men captured and offer them a deal: *Give us Spartacus and we'll send you back to the salt mines, your lives spared.* Kirk is about to step forward, admit who he is when suddenly one of his men stands up, proclaiming "I'm Spartacus" but really saying *I'm fucking Spartacus, you Roman bastard!* Then the next man stands, and the next, all claiming to be Spartacus. It brought tears to my eyes, that part, but as I looked about the casino I realised there was little chance of any of my co-workers standing, shouting, *I'm Sam, you bastards! You'll get no money here!* Instead, the opposite would probably happen: "*He's Sam, the mick bastard, over there beside the fridge. Kill 'im!*"

To my surprise, no one said a word. But I knew we all feared the worse.

'Okay. Play tough. Everyone! On the floor! Now!'

It was a race to see who could hit the floor first. I think I won.

'Take off your pants! Ladies, you included.'

We did as ordered. I debated with myself about handing over the keys. If I did, what was to stop them shooting us, anyway? Could I stall for time, hoping someone had seen something, alerting the cops? In all honesty, I knew I would never hand over the keys. The Belfast stubbornness started to boil in me and if it meant everyone in the room being shot – myself included – then fuck it. No keys.

'Don't make us angry. Okay? We get the money, we leave. Simple. We don't? Well –'

He aimed his weapon towards the ceiling and fired. The blast brought some of the ceiling down, snowing us with plaster. Each of us jerked our legs involuntarily, wondering what was coming next.

Those shots saved all our lives. Someone had called the cops and within minutes they arrived, screaming through a bull-horn for everyone to come out, and quickly. During the confusion, the would-be robbers escaped out the back grill, using a key that was known to only a few.

We all walked out, minus our pants, into the Sunday morning sun. It felt great. We were alive. And even when the cops lined *us* up instead of the robbers, and allowed a local photographer to take our photo, no one complained. We were just glad it was over without anyone seriously hurt.

The front page of the New York tabloid carried the photo of us lined up outside the casino. Its headline said it all: *Dealers caught with their pants down.*

'What the hell happened?' asked Ronnie.

'We got hit. That's what fuckin' happened!'

'Calm down, mate. Calm down.'

'Someone could've been fuckin' killed. They knew my name and the way out. So don't tell me to calm fuckin' down. You tell me how they knew everythin'.'

'I don't know, mate, but we'll soon find out. Three spics? Right? Okay. I'll sort it out.'

'You couldn't sort a box of Liquorice All Sorts out. Every thing's crumbling all about ye and ye don't even see it.'

'It's only a robbery. No one's hurt.'

'Some one *could've* been killed. Don't you understand? It's not just the robbery, but a million wee things starting to accumulate. And your family's part of the problem.'

'My family? What do you mean?' His voice was soft, as if he had just been shot in the back.

'First your sister and brother. Then your bloody uncles and cousins.'

'If you can't take care of family –'

I cut him off. 'Look, Ronnie. Rita installed those *Joker Poker* machines. She gets all the profit – none to the casino. Same as the cig machines. Then there's her *girl*friend. She hires her as manager. Manager of what? The only time she shows up is at the end of a shift to collect her and Rita's wages! She's walkin' on everyone's toes, makin' enemies. I even heard a couple threaten to kick her in the dick.' It felt good, getting all this off my chest. Like confession on a wet Saturday afternoon.

'Kick her in the dick?' He was mortified. 'She's not her *girlfriend*. At least not in the way you're implying,' he said indignantly.

'There's more,' I said, placing my hand inside my coat pocket and pulling out an envelope.

'What's the problem now?' he asked fearfully, probably thinking the envelope contained explicit photos.

'The "master" drop cards. They're out of sequence. Major problem.'

'What? How the . . .' He picked up the cards and checked. Then double-checked.

'Only four people have access to these,' I said. 'Myself, Mac, you . . . and Rita.'

'I think I'm going to have a heart attack, mate.' He wasn't joking. 'Between kicks in the dick, then this.' He tapped the cards with his fingers.

'If Mac found out about this . . .' I left him with that kind thought as I walked out.

The next day we went for coffee. He had a plan. Another one. Ronnie *always* had a plan.

'First. The *Joker Poker* and cig machines now belong to the casino. Okay?'

I nodded.

'All my cousins are out. Okay?'

I said nothing.

'Rita's, er, friend? No longer on the payroll.'

'And Rita?' I asked. 'And the two missing drop cards?'

'We don't know if it is Rita. It could have been an honest mistake on someone's part.'

'You don't believe that. Neither do I. You're thinking with your heart, not your head. What would happen if Mac found out? Bet your balls it never happened when he was running the show.'

'What can I do? She's my kid sister –'

'– who's screwing us! Get rid of her, or at least demote her where she won't be in a position to do it again.'

'That's a tough order, mate. Let me talk to her.'

'For all our sakes, do more than that.'

He never did, of course. He believed blood was thicker than water, even if it was contaminated. I knew it was only a matter of time before we were all out of a job.

27

Dodgy characters and a Danish

July 1986

"The almighty dollar is the only object of worship."

ANONYMOUS

The next casino opened with a flourish; the best food, wine and entertainment. Exotic flowers and plants swamped the place. A new dress code was introduced for all dealers. Gone were the coloured shirts and ties loved by the Hispanic dealers. In their place came the conservative white shirt and black bow tie. No more drinking while on duty. And no more loitering on the premises after work.

Outside 32nd Street, our bouncer, Mike, said hello as he let me in. Mike had replaced Tiny who had just died a week earlier after a massive heart attack brought on by an overdose of cocaine. Bob Seger's "Main Street" was playing as I entered.

Our clientele came from all walks of life. High rollers and low lifers, judges and crooks, or crooks and crooks, as Victor would say. There were "actors" and hookers (the best tippers); brokers from Wall Street (the cheapest tippers); Arabs and Hasidic rabbis

151

from Brooklyn; a famous ballerina, Raging Bull and a Norman Rockwell grandmother called Anne.

Some customers who gambled a significant amount of money had access to our "blue" book, granting them credit of up to $5,000 dollars. Anne was in the "blue" book but was having trouble paying back what she owed. I was given the unenviable task of getting it back and hated the thought.

I waited until she had finished her daily ritual at our buffet table: black sweet coffee, a Danish thick with figs and a glass of brandy to "wash down" the after-taste of the coffee.

'Good mornin', Anne. How are ye this mornin'?' I asked pouring myself a coffee, praying Stanley the Dentist didn't spy me.

'Top o' the morning, Sam,' she smiled. 'These Danish are lovely and fresh. Where do you get them? I've tried searching –'

'Could I talk to you, Anne, for a minute, in the office?'

Reluctantly, she entered the room. 'What's this about?' she asked as she sat down.

'I really hate to bring this to your attention, Anne, but we're tryin' to curtail a lot of the expense and recover some of the outstanding debt owed to us. Unfortunately, you're near the top of the list.'

She looked slightly embarrassed. 'I know, Sam. Usually I'm good at paying my bills, but the last month has been tough with my husband passing-away.' She rested the coffee on the table and brushed away the crumbs on her calico dress that depicted tiny birds in flight.

I hated myself. 'I'm sorry, Anne. I didn't know about your husband. You should've told us. We'd have tried to help you out.'

'Pride, Sam. When you get to my age you try and keep as much dignity as possible. I'm sorry about all this, but I promise you on my dead husband's grave that I will have cleared *all* my debt by the weekend.' Her lipstick left a half-moon on the paper cup.

'You don't have to clear it all –'

She held up her hand. 'This weekend. The club's been more than good to me. Oh! I almost forgot.' She reached down into her straw basket. 'This is for your daughter. It's her birthday tomorrow. Right?'

'Anne, you've really got to stop buyin' gifts for everyone. You'd have cleared your debt by now.'

She always knew whose birthday it was, and always bought them something. It was sad watching her leave. A lonely old lady whose only enjoyment in life was this casino. I cursed Ronnie for putting me on the spot and vowed that from now on he could do his own dirty work. That was when Stanley the Dentist spotted me holding Anne's half-eaten Danish.

'I've told you about that coffee, Sam. May as well paint your teeth – oh, no. Not a Danish?'

There were plenty of perks to be got in the casino, provided you knew how to go about getting them. I thought I'd landed on a gold filling mine when Stanley offered to do my dental work free of charge. Little did I realize what a pain in the arse he'd become. He was the worse tipper and most boring blackjack player in the world.

'May as well just go out there and suck on one of those jackhammers. That's how beneficial they are . . .'

He went on and on, just like one of his drills, only finally grinding to halt when I threw the Danish and coffee in the bin.

'So, she fucked us then?' said Ronnie a week later when Anne had become a no-show. 'You fell for all that shit from her, didn't you?'

'What did ye want me to do? Get Mike to work her over a bit? Make her hand over her wedding ring? She just buried her husband, for fuck sake. She'll be back.'

Just then the news on Channel Two came on, announcing, "A 70-year-old woman was arrested at an upstate retirement home, earlier this evening, when she tried to kidnap her husband – under gun point – from the grounds of the home. Police said the woman tried to abduct her husband, who suffers from Alzheimer's . . ."

'I don't believe this,' said Ronnie, staring incredulously at the screen, watching Anne being placed handcuffed, in a cop car.

This was our grandmother? Our bearer of gifts? She of the $6,200 debt?

As the story unfolded, we learned that Anne's husband was not dead but, in fact, had been convalescing at the private home. Anne, fearful that her in-laws were trying to get their hands on her husband's insurance money, kidnapped him, pre-emptive, before "they could". It was sad to witness the anguish on her face as she was led away. But her look of anguish wasn't half as bad as Ronnie's.

'I told you not to trust *anyone*. Now do you understand?' he said. 'That old bastard could've held us up at gunpoint. We'd never have lived it down. Who's next on the list?' he asked, checking the blue book. 'I hope it isn't her sister. She's probably got a machine-gun under her knickers.'

The casino was packed and for the next hour solid I did nothing but empty cash boxes. The Russians were screaming and being as obnoxious as usual. The Koreans were unusually subdued as their luck was going belly-up. Only Stanley the Dentist seemed to be winning as black chips piled up in front of his grinning face.

'Sam!' he shouted, then winked at me, then his chips.

I did a thumbs-up. 'Good man, Stanley! Win a million!' *ye cheap fuckin' prick.*

'Great, mate, eh?' said Ronnie, scanning the tables. 'Full to the brim. Just like a nice cup of tea.'

'Yes. Brilliant,' I replied. 'Who knows, if this keeps up, I might just get an increase in my wage?'

He didn't want to hear that so he left to converse with the customers, bowing like an idiot at the Korean table. He'd been watching too many kung fu movies. Still, he was happy as a lark. Everything was going well for him. June would see another casino opening.

Then it all started to go terribly wrong. Having started with a bang in January, the casino had collapsed financially by March pulling the others down with it. Their strength, paradoxically, was their downfall. Ronnie had become complacent, believing they could run themselves. The nepotism he had promised to eradicate still prevailed, eating away, like rust. He had tried to turn the casinos into a family business, not realising that the only thing that can destroy a family business is the family and the final nail in their coffin came when one of the unused casinos – where we stored back-up blackjack tables – was burglarised. The thieves made off with a few thousand dollars and a small cache of guns that was kept beneath floorboards – just in case –. That was bad enough but it also happened that Rita and her *girl*friend – who stayed there free of charge – were discovered by the intruders and forced to strip before being tied-up.

Some people believed Rita had stepped on the wrong toes and got what she deserved. I told her to look on the bright side: neither of them had been hurt. And wasn't it fortunate that Ronnie and myself had discovered them, and not Bronx-Tommy or Doc? Just like Queen Victoria – she wasn't amused.

The collapse came as no surprise to anyone except Ronnie. Even so, he remained philosophical about it: easy come, easy go. Besides, he told me, another plan was in the making. Someone "bigger" than Johnny Mac was going to bankroll his next project. A new, bigger and better casino was in the making. He had learned from his mistakes – no more family. He would watch over *every* transaction, dotting and crossing. He would live in the new casino so that, if a problem arose, he would be on it like a fly on shit. In the meantime, would I mind if he stayed with me for a while? Just until he got the okay from this new, "bigger" partner of his.

'I haven't a bean, mate,' he said. 'But as soon as this big deal is finalised, I'll pay you back . . .'

I wanted to say yes, but couldn't. Should have said no, but wouldn't. Let me see, was all I could promise. I'd let him know in a day or two. I wanted to ask him where was the family blood now? Not one of them had offered him help . . .

28

Beer, Hotdogs and Money

August 1986

"Be careful what you wish for . . ."
CHINESE PROVERB

That summer, as in all previous summers, I went upstate to Rochester. It was always good to get out of the city for a while and much of my time was spent meeting old friends and going to the many picnics – beer drinking gatherings.

'How's everything going down there?' asked Tom, a retired cop and friend.

'Could be better . . .'

'What's the problem? You don't seem yourself.'

An idea had been germinating in my head for the last few months, an idea so audacious I knew I would have to tread very carefully. 'I've been havin' problems in the casino.'

'What kind of problems?'

Tom looked upon me as a son. When I first arrived in America, he helped me get a place to stay. If I was short of money, he was the one I asked.

'Those Italian pricks down in New York are tryin' to put the squeeze on me,' I lied. 'Keep lookin' for more protection money.' That lie couldn't be further from the truth. The fact was that the Italians never fucked with the Irish. They knew better.

'I don't like you being down there. They're all crazy. I wish I could get you a job with me, working as a security guard at *Brink's*.'

I started laughing. 'That would solve all my problems. I'd rob the fuckin' place and open my own casino!'

Tom looked at me strangely and I knew I had insulted him. As a New York cop, he was highly respected both by colleagues and the community, which he served. He was an ah-shucks-Jimmy-Stewart kind of a guy who did everything by the book.

'It's just the beer, Tom,' I assured him, none too convincingly. I had already "visited" the *Brink's* depot, when Tom took me over for a "tour" when the other guards were gone for the day. I had been amazed at the lack of serious security in the place, and this was highlighted by one or two stories of how a pizza deliveryman had simply walked straight into the place without being stopped. He had found the security door to be wide-open and to his amazement piles of money sat unguarded in corners, waiting to be placed in the massive vaults – when the guards found time, after the baseball game! But the most glaring lapse had to be when a guard would run out to one of the local stores, leaving the doors ajar using nothing sturdier than a pencil! Millions guarded by a pencil! Their laziness turned this transgression habitual and there was no doubt in my mind that the money was there for the taking.

Tom's reaction had told me what I had wanted to know: there was no way he would go along with my mad idea. And so I quickly put it out of my head. For the moment . . .

Upon my return to the city, I stared searching for a job, taking anything available and finally ending up as a doorman in Park Avenue. Four months had passed and Ronnie was still in my apartment, driving my wife crazy with his daily recitals of Marcus Aurelius. I knew it was time for him to go when he borrowed the complete works of Socrates from the library. Enough was enough.

'Look, mate. You're gonna have to find some place to live. I hate havin' to say this, but you're drivin' us all nuts.'

He only laughed, annoying me further. 'Don't worry, mate. I'm meeting that new partner of mine tomorrow night. You'll be able to tell those rich wankers in Park Avenue to stick their job.'

Two weeks later he was still sleeping on the floor of our apartment. Socrates was replaced by Homer, and my wife was threatening to go back to Belfast if I didn't get Ronnie out of there.

'Sorry, mate,' I said, helping him into the elevator with his sole suitcase.

'Don't worry, mate. I'm seeing that new partner . . .'

I watched as the elevator door closed over, drowning out his words but no sooner had I waved a joyful good-bye when the phone rang. Something told me it was Ronnie, probably in the telephone box across the street, begging for one last week.

Don't answer it. Let it ring.

But it wasn't Ronnie. It was Marco, a former bouncer at the casino. He had served time in the US Army and was a veteran from the Gulf war.

'Listen. About that other thing . . .' he cryptically began.

'Yes?'

'No problem.'

'Can you come next week, with me?' I asked.

'No problem . . .'

When I met him, he was smiling, his hand outstretched as if greeting me for the first time in years.

'Don't say a word in the car,' I said, a plastic grin still on my face. 'It's bugged.'

We drove down Lake Avenue towards the beach in silence. On

reaching it I parked the car, removed a few *Buds* from the back seat and as soon as we were far enough away from the car, I came straight to the point. 'How'd you like to make some serious money?'

It was late evening but the heat was still horrendous. Mosquitoes bit my ears as I watched calmness come to splintered waves.

'How serious?' he asked, taking a slug of *Bud*.

'Maybe a million.'

The *Bud* hit the back of his throat, making him cough. 'Are you shittin' me?' he asked.

I knelt on the sand and, with my finger, started to draw. Before long, I had sketched the rough layout of a bird's-eye view of a building, a collage of rectangles and squares. I didn't speak. Even when the waves slowly crept in, erasing my work, I said nothing, waiting for it to disappear.

'Let's go,' I said, eventually, brushing the sand from my jeans.

We walked along the beach, whispering in each other ears, like lovers on a first date. An old lady walked by, exercising her dog, shaking her head with disgust.

As it turned out, I *was* shittin' him. It was more than a million. A lot more . . .

29

The Whale Hunter

August 1986

"The unexamined life is not worth living."

SOCRATES

It was hot and sticky when I returned to New York on a Sunday afternoon; stained shirts and biting underwear; 90° in the shade and rising. A record was in the making. They said this muggy, claustrophobic weather made New Yorkers strange. Sometimes it made them do strange things.

I was feeling isolated for the first time since my arrival in the city. Most, if not all, the Belfast lads had returned home. The casino had been their only source of income so most had decided to get out while they still had a few bob in their pocket. I couldn't blame them. I would have probably followed them had it not been for the schizophrenic thoughts of breaking into *Brink's*, wondering if I could really get away with something so audacious, so dangerous and live to tell the tale.

Above me, the sun floated on a ghostly haze as I entered the

161

narrow street, which was a conglomerate of amorphous homeless people covered in liquid shadows, their slim belongings nipping at their feet. An old, dilapidated church was now their home.

'Yer axin' fer trouble, pal,' said a deli worker, watching me walk towards them. 'Moiderin' moither foickers, dem. Tha woist.' He pointed accusingly at the homeless as he denuded a tiny runway of *Juicy Fruit* and popped it in his mouth. His jawbones ballooned nervously, as he chewed, like Norman Bates in *Psycho*.

I nodded, but otherwise ignored him. As one who had traversed the streets of Belfast, New York, or its people, held little fear for me.

The abysmal conditions of the homeless, in this the richest city in he world, never fails to shock. Their accretion is cultivated by an obscene dichotomy where, a few streets away on Park Avenue, the affluent feed and pamper their pets with apathy. Worlds overlapping; rarely touching.

At one time these people were the salt of the earth, pillars of society. Now they were the dregs, witnessed but unseen, screaming apocalyptic profanities in splenetic asperity. One man, his left leg truncated at the knee, was ensconced in a dilapidated wheelchair. Older than his years, his face sagged, as if the dogs of poverty and depression had stolen every bone from it, highlighting tiny dark webs which etched his eyes.

Near the end of the street, a bulging garbage bag lay gutted, revealing a desiccated sanitary towel, which protruded from it like a bloody tongue panting in the heat. The mist oozing from the bag was stomach-churning to most passers-by. Not me. I'd encountered – lived in – worse.

As I side-stepped the bag, a man covered in a Paisley-print shroud bumped me, mumbling: 'Dirty my skin with bruises, punk? Ya betta kill me – cuz I'm cumin' fer ya! See? *See?* Whaddya hear, whaddya *sssayyyyy?*' He stuck out his tongue, which was carpeted in baked bean sauce and sores.

'Leave the man alone, Jo Jo,' said the one in the wheelchair. 'He done you no harm, no way.'

162

Jo Jo glared at me, then his friend, before walking backwards into the shadows.

'He don't mean no harm, really. Just suspicious of folk.'

I didn't know if I should get out of the street as quickly as possible, say my thank you and be gone. Instead, I opted to put my hand in my pocket for some change.

'Don't do that. Don't insult us.'

My face reddened.

'Sorry . . .'

'No need for that. Your face already done apologized.' He laughed, galvanizing his entire body into coughs and shakes. 'Don't laugh enough. Out of practice.'

'You don't sound like a New Yorker,' I said.

'Neither do you, if you don't mind me sayin'.' The coughing didn't come this time, only the smile. 'Ah come from Tennessee, if a man can say he came from some place. Ah write, mostly, but do can-gatherin' to survive. You?'

'I'm from Belfast. I work in a casino . . . when it's not being shut down by the cops, that is.'

'Well, Ah learned somethin' today. I didn't ever know that New York had casinos. Must put that in my writin'.'

'They're illegal,' I explained.

'Nothin' wrong with that. Hell, being homeless in this city is illegal if you were dumb enough to listen to the Mayor!' He pushed his wheelchair up to me. In his lap rested a bag of empty cans. 'Belfast? That's a tough ol' place. All that killin'. Sheer crazy.'

Now it was my turn to laugh. There were more people killed in New York on any given weekend than there were in a year in Belfast. It seems everyone creates bigger monster so as to diminish their own.

'Must be tough,' he repeated, wondering.

'Not as tough as trying to survive in a wheelchair in New York,' I said.

'Could be worse. Wheels could be gone.' He smiled, not meaning it. 'Ah'm not a regular at this can-gatherin', you know, but it's part of a strange adventure Ah fell into since comin' to New York City from Tennessee this last Christmas time.' He searched his pockets for something, found it and lit it up before inhaling it, deep down into his lungs. 'Ah did have a better Saturday myself on account of the eight bucks plus Ah got for the cans and an idea came to me that same mornin'.' He blew a small amount of smoke into the air, as if not wanting to waste any. 'Usually Ah get just enough cans for cigarettes and coffee so Ah can set some time aside and look over the ideas and writin' that Ah've been workin' on for going on eleven years now. In all that time Ah've travelled all over America, truck-ridin'. Ah rode all across the edge of Canada on freight-trains and went painting on a ship out of Montreal that took me to Hamburg in Germany. That was when Ah lost my legs, on board a rusted old whaler. A message from God not to hunt His creatures without feeling His wrath.'

I thought he was going to tell me he had lost his legs in Vietnam, and in a perverse way I thought the truth more fascinating, almost romantic. I was late for Ronnie, now, but I no longer cared. Along the avenue people were waving down air-conditioned cabs to avoid the oppressive air. The cabs' skin shimmered nervously, like stranded salmon – all silvery and scaly.

'Ah spent almost eight years in Dublin City in Ireland,' he continued, 'and travelled all up and down over there lookin' into the folk-music traditions that together with the Blues and Baptist gospel singin' was the roots of our country and Rock'n'Roll music. Then living as hard and rough as Ah mostly did got me interested in the people at the bottom of society and in all the strange wanderin' homeless ones who live on the streets of cities and out in the hobo-jungles. Living with these people and watching them has taught me many ways to survive and a whole heck of a lot besides about society. Then my Grandpappy, who half-raised me, was a reading man. He got thousands of books, all kinds bought out of the moonshine he makes and sells. He planted some seeds got given to him by a biker club from Philadelphia. They come down every year on their 'cycles to collect the weed and bring him a two-pound sack of speed from the "crack-capital".'

Jo Jo mumbled, somewhere in the shadows. I wondered if he was searching for a knife.

'He's a readin' man, my Grandpappy, so Ah also have a deep interest in mechanics, electronics, science, inventions and technological innovations. He's all but disowned me now because of the way Ah've been livin' and my areas of inquiry. He and Ah've had a feud goin' on because he never did tell me who my Daddy was or how he came by me for certain. He tells me versions until Ah don't know who to believe.'

He inhaled once more on the butt and it disappeared between his finger and thumb. There was a smell of skin burning in the air.

'Ah got a draft-version of my book just about hammered together usin' a lot of songs Ah'd written, when it all got burned in a fire in west Philadelphia, October last. This, along with every other thing in the world Ah had and carried. Guitar, too. A beat-up and beautiful old guitar that almost broke my old darn heart. Ah did go back to Tennessee then, but Ah could not stay and listen to Grandpappy telling me "Told you so! Temptin' fate". He's retirin' and wants me to stay there and learn "the mixture", the moonshine, and tend him 'cause he's old. Hell Ah will if he'll last, but Ah gotta burnin' to do my own work. Besides, he could buy himself a nice old lady nurse if he really wanted.'

He spun the wheel-chair in a semi-circle, faced the sun, then said, 'Say, Ah'm sorry. Ah guess Ah just had to open up to someone. Ah can tolerate hunger; but silence has always been a mean torture for me.'

I said nothing, fearing I would ruin the stillness of time. Even the old church seemed to be swelling in the heat, listening, casting shadows further down the street. Long gone were its begging tongues and burning candles, but somehow it still infused the imagination with vitalized, agonizing-angels with alibi faces all majestically attuned to a vivid tapestry.

'Ah know you gotta go, but Ah may as well finish what Ah started. Ah decided to take my own final challenge of this journey. . .

To come to New York City with no money or nothin' and see if Ah could make it through the winter and find the people that live so hard all the time and learn their way and see what songs and ideas this gave me. Ah've done this now and it was pure hell mostly because of the attitudes of 'normal folk' and because of the hopelessness felt on the streets. Now Ah've emotional scars and a bunch of new songs and ideas, but Ah've gotta get above this condition to get a little distance, if Ah'm to write about it or try to help these people. And Ah hope then to find a business manager so Ah can sell some of the material.'

The silence of the street became eerily beautiful. Like a symphony performed by ghosts of fallen warriors, you could fall right into it and be carried away, for ever and ever. He had talked for an hour but it seemed barely a minute. An hour ago I had been wrapped in self-pity, now it was gone. He was telling me, a stranger, his life story of family intrigue and dirty dealing, of the rusted hopes of life's oppressive deepness and the unassailable belief that acuity of hindsight conquers all the dark guilt that clings stubbornly to our souls.   .

I wanted to tell him of a life I once knew, of madness, brutality and death, where auricular whispers recruit the emotions, destroying them forever.

I wanted to tell him what it's like to hurt until you feel so empty and so full that the only possible release is death, making you afraid of your own emotions.

But before I could answer, an allegoric rain was upon us, stinging. Potholes became pregnant with it, gurgled as they choked on it. A troop of yellow cabs navigated the slick, aqueous streets while the homeless squeezed their backs tight against the church walls, preventing most of their belongings becoming waterlogged. The cabs drenched me with their power of indifference for I, also, had become invisible, a nothing.

Overhead a tribe of starlings flew for shelter, screaming like their cousins in Long Kesh. I turned to say goodbye, but he was gone – they all were.

'Hey!' shouted the deli worker, wiping his massive hands on a powdered apron. 'Ya really shouldn't be down here on yer own. Dem scum moither foickers wud cut yer throat and think nothin' of it. Go on, now! I'll watch yer back.'

For respite, I quickly entered the Strand Bookstore on Broadway where I browsed through its army of new and used books.

No sooner had I touched a book titled *Silver's Goldmine*, than latent memories flooded back to me. Memories as redolent as perfume on a lover's skin. It made me think of JCB, his head banging off a cave wall, pounded by Neanderthals with night-sticks. It was selfish, I know, but I was glad I was here, no longer there.

The deli worker was still at the back door, shaking his head in disbelief, obviously thinking of how lucky I was to have got out of there with my life still intact. In a way, I *was* lucky. Lucky to have met a man whose name was unknown but who put things, for me, in their perspective and suddenly my isolation in the great city was no longer complete. I was free again, and I knew exactly what I would do if – *when* – the time came to enter a heavily armed building without first knocking for permission to come in.

It was only a matter of time. And *timing* . . .

30

A Telling of Truth

December 1987

"A coward turns away but a brave man's choice is danger."
EURIPIDES

Things progressed slowly. I still took whatever jobs I could find, while Ronnie opened a tiny store in Soho selling silk scarves and ties. The rent was $8,000 a month, but he wasn't paying a penny. The landlord had fallen for his golden gift of the gab, just like scores before him. So there he was, in the glass showroom, sandwiched between art dealers and high-priced restaurants, his tiny stock of fake designer labels resting on cardboard boxes.

And as for Marco, all he could do was keep thinking about all that money. It was driving him mad, but there was nothing either of us could do until we found a suitable third man – if ever.

I was beginning to doubt if another person could be found and in desperation I put forward the only name open to me.

'We need a van,' I told him as I fingered some of his wares. 'One that can be hidden until everything is ironed out.' I already had a car hidden away, but was finding it impossible to get my hands on a van. I told Ronnie as little as possible, allowing him to only whiff the potential. The less he knew, the better. I hadn't yet said it was an armoured-car depot. I didn't think he was ready for that just yet.

'No problem, mate. Know just the place.'

"Just the place" was a car showroom on the West Side. We went straight up the stairs where new vans were being displayed.

'I hope you're not thinkin' of stealin' one of those?' I said, hoping he wasn't, knowing he was.

Before he could answer, a young black salesman approached us.

'Hello, my good man,' said Ronnie, hamming it, his broad Liverpool accent gone, replaced by the Don of Oxford. 'I'm looking for a new van. Would you be so kind as to show me what is available?' He looked the part with his three-piece suit and gold-rimmed glasses, an empty leather briefcase tucked under his arm.

'Certainly, sir. Our latest models are on the second floor. If you'd just follow me . . .'

For the next hour, the salesman did a tour of the best they had in stock. I stayed in the background while Ronnie opened up the engine, pretending to have a clue how it worked. Every time the salesman opened his mouth, Ronnie would simply reply, "Now, that is really lovely. I'm very impressed, my good man". Before we left, he shook the demented man's hands, telling him that he *certainly* would be visiting again and what an asset the man was to the company. Oh, and have you ever read Marcus Aurelius? No? You really must . . .

'That was a waste of fuckin' time,' I said when we reached the corner of the street. 'What was all that nonsense about, pretending to buy a van? Surely you know someone up in Harlem who could get one for us?'

Ronnie's estranged wife lived in Harlem and he knew a couple of second-hand car dealers from it. He just smiled and winked.

'What's this then, mate?' He tapped a key on my nose. I could still smell the newness of the metal. 'While you were hidin', I was watching. I couldn't believe they just left the keys dangling on a hook, askin' to be pinched. Probably an insurance scam. Bet that's what it is. Be back in a tick.'

Without hesitation, away he went, back to the showroom. Less than ten minutes later he pulled up alongside me, his face beaming like the red paint from the new van.

'What are you waiting for? 'Op in.'

The confidence he had shown in obtaining the van strengthened my belief in him. But did he have the "bottle" for it – as he liked to say? We would soon find out.

We walked over to Washington Square. Dark clouds appeared from nowhere as we stood in the doorway of Edgar Allan Poe's old lodgings.

'Bet this place could tell a story or two,' said Ronnie, peering in the window. 'A lot of nutcases hang out here at night hoping to see Poe's ghost. Probably the reason there is so much killing in this city.'

Before he became *too* morbid, I decided it was time to tell him what exactly was in store should he decide to come on board. It was then that the rain came down in great buckets, making us run for the shelter of a small café. I should have seen the rain as an omen, but didn't.

'You'll probably have to smack one or two of the guards with that knock-out punch you have,' I said, sipping a cup of coffee, watching his reaction. 'If that fails . . .'

He had a grin on his face but his eyes contradicted it. 'Yeah,' he said, eventually. 'We got to do what we got to do. The old one-two should do the trick.' He stood up from the table and with everyone in the café watching, he started doing the Ali shuffle, followed by upper cuts and left and right jabs aimed at an invisible opponent.

Everyone in the place was in stitches, except me. 'Will you sit the fuck down?'

He eventually did, but not before the grand finale of a Michael Jackson Moon Walk.

'Shouldn't really be any problems, though. Wee buns,' I said, blowing gently on the hot coffee.

'No problem,' he agreed. 'Wee buns.'

It was then, just as the richness of the coffee flooded my mouth, that I knew we had problems. Big-as-a-house problems.

We left for Rochester, two days later, early in the morning, when darkness still held the upper hand. We had a long eight-hour drive in front of us and the sooner we started, the better. I drove in front, in the car, guiding Ronnie behind me in the van. A large falling of snow was forecast and we knew we'd have to make good time or risk the possibility of being stranded, somewhere upstate.

We headed out of Manhattan via the snowy expanse of Park Avenue, which was interrupted by soldier-like Christmas trees positioned along its entirety. Each tree was heavily garnished with fairy lights that glowed eerily like mermaids and iridescent insects in the night. My eyes flickered to the trees outside each building, their cambric branches of lighting streaks were heavy with snow and looked precariously close to snapping, falling on people below. The wind was starting up again, swirling scuffs of white snow into tumbleweeds with flakes the size of butterflies, all the while skidding off the frozen East river, wickedly hunting down victims. Cars, debilitated, were caked in ice like displays in a fishmonger's. Bing Crosby was on the radio and Santa was everywhere, *yo ho hoing*.

We kept strictly within the speed limit despite the teasing vastness of the New York thruway, which just cried out to be tested. I just hoped Ronnie wouldn't give in to its challenge, knowing that New York State cops would be all over us in seconds.

Everything was going fine until halfway through the journey when I happened to glance in my mirror, just in time to see Ronnie exit the thruway. He had taken the wrong exit.

Fuck! I couldn't get off the thruway until the next exit which was about 30 miles away. I banged the steering wheel with my fist, calling him all the stupid bastards under the sun. All he had to do was follow me, but as usual he couldn't do something simple, everything had to be complicated in his book. By the time I got off the thruway and backtracked the 30 odd miles he was nowhere to be seen.

I didn't realise it then, but that's what he intended . . .

The plan was cancelled. I returned to New York with barely enough money to pay for the petrol and tollbooths, seething with rage, angry at putting my trust in Ronnie when I should have known better.

A few days later I went to meet him, to tell him what I thought of him. I took the subway in and couldn't take my eyes off the doe-eyed waif from a poster advertising *Les Miserables* on Broadway. A local wit had scrawled: *Do I look miserable?* Answer: *More or less.* My sentiments exactly, I thought, as I stepped from the train and headed towards his shop.

'You're one gutless bastard,' I said, entering the shop, loud enough for two customers to hear me. I wanted to wreck the place, throw his dubious wares out into the street, followed by him.

'Calm down, mate,' he replied, quickly easing the two customers out the door, telling them I was a great kidder. Ha! Ha! Ha!

'*Calm down?* You gutless bastard. That's all you are. A typical fuckin' gutless Brit.

He took exception to being called a Brit and requested that I withdraw the offensive remark. I refused.

'I know how it must look, mate. But the truth is that I got confused with the length of time on the road and all that snow. It was blinding me. I thought I saw your car pull off at that exit and followed you. As God is my witness, I couldn't believe it wasn't you. Finally, I got back on the thruway and managed to make my way up to Rochester. But you weren't there, mate.'

The last sentence was an accusation and his face had the anguish of a betrayed dog, deserted by its owner. Had he gone to

Rochester? Obviously, there was no way of clarifying this or his indecisiveness. Was that what he was betting on?

'It's all academic now, anyway,' I said. 'It's finished. The opportunity will never come again. We fucked it up.'

'Don't say that, mate. We'll think it out better the next time. We rushed it. It would have been a disaster if we'd –'

'*Don't*. Okay? Don't say another *fuckin'* word. Understand?'

He didn't and I left, never looking back at him, the moth who simply wanted to boast of touching the flame without being burnt, to be guilty by association.

31

Showtime!

5 January 1993

"We must always hold the possibility of disaster in mind."
SENECA

"Hollywood couldn't have done it better."
NEW YORK'S *IRISH VOICE*

"Security guards told the police that they were surprised by assailants, who had somehow evaded the sophisticated security system. They could not say how many robbers there were . . ."

NEW YORK TIMES, FRONT PAGE

370 South Avenue is a red-cement block building housed in a desolate industrial area close to Interstate Highway 490. It is the sort of building you never give a second glance. No one could imagine this one-storey, prosaic building being an Aladdin's cave or the *Brink's Incorporated* armoured car cash depository.

That was the whole point.

Brink's Incorporated, established in 1859, is the oldest and largest security transportation company in the world with 160

175

branch operations in the US, 40 in Canada and affiliates in 50 countries around the globe. It has a nice neat history, and I was hoping to become part of it. I was hoping we would have got it done before Christmas. Instead, it was now 5 January 1993, five days before my birthday. The time was shortly after 4.00 pm. By 7.00 pm it would be the best or worst birthday I ever had.

Over the years the plans had changed drastically. No more excuses. Deep down I knew it was total madness, but it had become a monkey on my back – *no, a fucking great big hairy ape* – a Siren calling me, teasing me with untold wealth. Whatever happened from here on in, there would be no turning back, for either Marco or myself.

The first thing we needed to do was find a parking spot as close to the building as possible without being in the "eye" of any cameras in the area. I was becoming frantic. What little space there was had been allocated to the few homes in the area, leaving just one side of a narrow street available for parking. The problem with this was that the van would have to be moved before the designated time that the local "alternate side of the street" law came into effect. I knew we couldn't afford to get a parking ticket, which might come back to haunt us later. With no other choice, I parked the van in the company of trees that lined the street, and prayed no one would be looking out their window on a freezing night like this.

Most of the money would be coming down from the Federal Reserve Bank in Buffalo to be distributed locally in cash machines. The last armoured car from the Federal Reserve Bank in Buffalo had just made its stop at *Brink's*. I could see it pull in as I walked briskly towards the building.

The freezing, wet weather was perfect for our hooded jackets and balaclavas, allowing us to blend in with the few people heading home. We were all duplicates, as if we had purchased our clothes from the same Army 'N' Navy Store in Brooklyn. The approaching dark brought tiny bats of trepidation scurrying about in my stomach as the chalky headlights of 490's traffic lit up the *Brink's* depot. A voice in my head tried to reason with me, asking what the hell I was doing here. But I already had the answer to that. I had a million of them

Reaching the car park of *Brink's*, Marco quickly slid into Tom's tiny car, which was placed between two elephantine armoured cars. I had spotted his car from the highway, and smiled. Tom kept it in the same spot as he had done, each working day. I was banking on another of his habits: he normally left the doors to his car unlocked, as did most people upstate. Marco squeezed himself into the back of it, and hid in its shadows, while I watched from a safe distance, communicating with a walky-talky. I knew when the last truck would leave, but more importantly I knew that the guards always sent someone out, just to make sure the grounds were clear before they commenced their work of placing money in the vaults. If I spotted the guard coming out, I would radio to Marco to take him just as he was about to re-enter the building.

Timing was crucial. We both had to instil confidence in each other. He depended on me getting it right at the correct moment, and I depended on him carrying it out to the letter. One slip-up, and we were both finished and penniless, with only prison as our reward. Get it right, and we would both be laughing, all the way to the bank or, as in this case, all the way to the *Brink's* . . .

'*The last truck is leaving*,' I whispered into the walky-talky.

Marco didn't answer, so I whispered it again. '*The truck is pulling out.*'

Then came his sarcastic reply. '*Darn it, I know. I'm right beside it.*'

The truck moved out slowly and I knew that within the next few minutes a guard would appear.

'*Someone's comin' out,*' I whispered into the walky-talky. The icy wind was cutting the face off me, and I was finding it difficult to hear Marco's reply, '*Can you hear me? Someone's out, lookin' about.*'

The guard went to the side of the building and then, to my horror, walked gingerly towards Tom's car. From my distance, I couldn't make out what he was up to. His hand seemed to go to

177

his hip. Had he seen something? Heard my voice from Marco's walky-talky and gone to investigate? Was his hand going to a gun on his hip? For a heart-stopping moment, the guard stopped beside Tom's car. I wondered if Marco had heard my instructions? I couldn't communicate, fearing the guard would hear the muffled static.

I was conscious of only two sounds as I stood in the dark, the wind whistling up my arse: my heartbeat, and the chime of a clock in my head warning that time was ticking away. I had to move the van in 20 minutes, or risk the possibility of getting a parking ticket. Worse, it might be towed. Now *that* would be fun.

Nothing was moving at the *Brink's*. The guard seemed to be peering into the car. It was then that I made the reckless decision to walk towards the depository, to take the guard before he captured Marco.

I walked calmly, but briskly. The guard still hadn't moved. His back was to me. Ten seconds and I would have him.

I needn't have worried. Marco was also moving, slowly easing himself from the car. 'Don't raise yer hands, pal,' he softly commanded, pointing his gun at the shocked guard. 'Keep them in your pocket. No heroics. Understand?'

The guard nodded.

'Now, turn around, nice and slow, pal. We're all going to visit the rest of your pals in there, like one big happy family. Behave, and all this will be over before you even know it. Understand.

'Sure,' said the guard, turning to face me.

It was Tom. I felt like shit because I knew he was probably frightened. I could do nothing to reassure him, so I said nothing, wondering if he knew it was me.

A few seconds later we were "in like Flynn", entering through the door, which was still ajar, stopping only when I signalled. Somewhere in the dark, voices spoke, as if from a great distance, thinning themselves out into hums. I glanced at my watch. We had less than eight minutes to secure the building, disarm the rest of the guards, and for me to return to the van and drive it in all nice and casual.

I placed my finger to my mouth. Someone was approaching. A door opened. In my mind I could picture the guard staring down the dark where we stood, smelling something wrong, his hand on his gun. Would he fire first, ask later? Was this the one who was trigger-happy, as reported by Tom, laughingly one night, over a couple of beers? The one who boasted of hoping some "motherfucker" would be stupid enough to rob the place while he was on duty: "Ha! I'd shoot that mother in the balls first, watch him scream in agony. Then – *kabam!* Right in the fuckin' head"?

Kabam, a sound from another time, another place.

My hand went instinctively from my balls to my face. I tried not to think about it, fearing it would cloud my judgement, but no matter how hard I tried, I couldn't erase the picture of my face, a bloody pulp, splattered all over the walls.

The footsteps echoed back from whence they came and I exhaled out my mouth and arse as Marco tapped on my shoulder indicating to move. Two minutes gone, and Tom was secure. We placed him in the back, away from the rest, before we made the perilous journey up the stairs.

One flight of stairs later, and the light from the room stung our eyes. We had made it to the most sensitive part of the plan: the "Trap", the command centre that monitored all the cameras that are festooned throughout the building. One of the many locked cabinets in the "Trap" housed video recorders to record all the activity in and around the vaults where the cash is handled: cash-counting machines, offices and garage.

From their own TV monitors, I sat and watched as the guards went about their duty, guns on their hips. One was in a vault. I could just about make him out. Another was stacking moneybags. I scanned the room with the remote, a voyeur, zooming in and out, familiarizing myself as best I could with the little time left. An empty *Coke* can lay squashed beneath a counting table; a newspaper sat on top like a table-covering, as if they were expecting someone for supper.

Mustn't disappoint, I thought.

Suddenly, my eyes caught the open cupboard with its family of evil-looking shotguns, lurking inside, waiting and hoping. *Bastards. Bet you'd love to shoot the arse off me.* The metal stared back. Helpless for now . . .

I could even see the irregular sepia rings from the guards' coffee cups staining yesterday's newspapers. I had suddenly become an editor. This time tomorrow they would all be reading about themselves. We all would. Marco leaned over my shoulder, pointing at the guard in the vault.

'I'll take him,' I whispered and I knew in my heart it would be dodgy because it was Trigger Happy.

Just my luck, I thought, knowing any noise and the alarms would sound. For a second, the dread of the automatic door shutting, trapping me, entered my mind. Worse, old Trigger Happy getting the draw on me, shooting me in the balls, laughing his own off, shouting: "Motherfucker! Got ya! *Ka-fuckin'-bam!*". I shivered, but quickly pulled the balaclava over my face. It was *Showtime*. Or shit time, depending on the outcome.

Within seconds, I was behind the guard in the vault. I had been so slyly successful, it was necessary for me to cough, just to make my presence felt. Initially, he turned to me smiling, believing it a prank, then staggered back in disbelief as I pointed my gun at him. His hand hovered menacingly over his own.

I covered my heavy Belfast accent with the worst Russian one ever heard. 'Don't even think about it,' I hissed, my nerves racing.

But he was thinking about it. All those fucking John Wayne and Gary Cooper movies raced in old Trigger Happy's head. We'd all be dead in a minute because of the Duke and *High Noon*. A single bead of sweat rested on his left eyebrow like a rabbit's head peering nervously over a hedge, searching for the hound. Slowly it trickled down, leaving a transparent trail behind.

He was going to do it! The crazy bastard was going to go out in a blaze of fuckin' glory, taking me and everyone else with him. I pulled the hammer back on my own gun and it sounded like someone opening a rusted can of beer. I expected the trigger to fall off and land at our feet. But it was that sound that snapped Trigger Happy back to the real world; a sound I'd be eternally grateful for.

'Get fuckin' down!'

He did, and I quickly removed his gun, frisking him, knowing he was the type who probably concealed a gun between his cheeks. With plastic 'cuffs used by the cops for crowd control, I secured his wrists.

Marco's guard had more sense, dropping his gun and belt to the floor immediately. Everyone – the other guards included, it seemed – was relieved when Trigger Happy was secure. It wasn't his money, anyway. *Brink's Inc.* paid these men the minimum wage expecting them to lay down their life to safeguard their stock.

Three minutes. That's all it took. It was frightening, the ease. As I left the building to bring the van inside, a feeling crept over me. I had been disappointed. It was all anti-climatic. Three years in the planning and it was all over in three minutes. For some reason, I was the one who felt robbed . . .

With adrenaline rushing through us, we became supermen. Mountains of money disappeared in front of our eyes as we heaved it into sacks. Every now and then we stopped and grinned at each other. I was so happy I wanted to hug myself, give myself a big kiss. It would transpire later that we had lifted almost 1,200lbs of paperweight in less than fifteen minutes. A Guinness record! Each 100lb of paper represented, roughly, $1,000,000. I don't care what anyone says, there's a hell of a lot to be said for incentives.

Just as things were going so well the sound of someone banging on the front door made us freeze, not daring to breathe. Perhaps it had just been the winter wind playing havoc with our nerves, winding us up? When it banged again we both knew the truth. I placed my finger to my mouth and quickly, but quietly, took the stairs to the security room two by two. In a second I had the cameras scanning the exterior of the building.

I couldn't believe it. Outside, a lone black man stood, banging on the steel door. Every now and then he seemed to be glancing over his shoulder at someone, waiting in the dark. Had someone seen something suspicious? What if there *were* more than one, waiting to rush us? Could it be an off-duty cop, coming to check? Could it be fucking robbers, coming to rob us? All was possible in that moment of madness.

Whatever was racing through our minds, we knew we would have to go down and find out what he wanted. The longer we stalled, the more suspicious he – they? – would become. As Marco walked slowly to the door, I stood in the shadows, directly behind, a guard's automatic shotgun ready in my hands. Marco took a deep breath before speaking through the security vent.

'Yea? What's the problem, pal?'

The man seemed as nervous as us. 'I'm very sorry . . . but we're lost. We're trying to get back on the highway . . .'

It turned out to be nothing more sinister than a black man lost in a strange town. His wife and kids sat in a car on the side of the road, terror on their faces, probably thinking about some KKK nutcase coming along in the dead of night. As the car disappeared down 490, we sat down against the wall, not saying a word, both knowing each other's thoughts. I laughed. So did Marco. We couldn't stop, giggling and biting our lips, tears rolling down our guilty faces.

With the van now packed to capacity, I jumped in, started the engine. Thunderbirds are go! It sputtered, sending dark smoke into the air, then shook like a spacecraft ready for take-off. It shook and it shook, but refused to move. We had put too much money in. The engine was burning up and the building was black with smoke, everyone was coughing. It conked out.

Marco was upstairs, removing the videotapes, hindering the cops as much as possible.

I tried the ignition key again. Nothing. Just as I was about to get out, Marco jumped in beside me, not wanting to say a word, in case that word caused panic. A phone call could come in at any minute. Perhaps someone had seen all the smoke, or something suspicious. He was first to move, opening up the engine, checking if it could be fixed.

Something told me it couldn't.

'Get some of the bags out,' he hissed.

In less than a minute we removed about one third of the bags. The adrenaline was fading fast and my muscles began to ache.

'Try it again.'

I wanted to remove the mask. The sweat and smoke were stinging my eyes, making it difficult to see. Instead, I tried the engine, pumping the gas pedal, praying to God, knowing He wouldn't approve of this. The van sounded a splutter of relief, coughed then roared. I was sagging and drained with exhaustion. If it stalled again, that would be the end.

The massive doors of the garage slowly – *too slowly* – opened, introducing the night sky. It was the most beautiful sight I had ever seen. It made little difference that we left over $3,000 000 behind in one of the biggest robberies in US history, I was simply glad to be out of there, taking in that cold night air. The mask was off and I was breathing again.

In the back of the van lay a grand total of almost $8,000 000; $5,500 000 in 20s and the rest in mixed denomination bills. Not bad for an hour's work for a "kid" from Belfast. Unfortunately for Tom, he was sitting on top of the bags as Marco had insisted on taking him with us, in the hope that the rest of the guards wouldn't do something stupid. I felt bad. He lay there like a piece of meat in an abattoir. I justified everything by telling myself that I would take care of him, later, financially. He would no longer have to work for *Brink's*. Besides, we would drop him off in a while none the worse for the wear.

Less than twenty minutes later, the van pulled into the garage of a prominent New York State lawyer, a cousin of Marco's. Quickly and quietly we unloaded the sacks, placing them behind a false wall that blended perfectly into props scattered throughout. The temptation to keep just a little of my cut for the journey home was overwhelming, but thankfully the cooler head of Marco prevailed. 'Don't be stupid. What if you're stopped?'

Before departing into the night's darkness, I glanced at the lit-up dining room where the lawyer was entertaining some friends. I swore he winked at me, raising his glass in a toast, a smile so innocent it was believable.

Marco departed in a car – his cousin's, presumably – and I took command of the van. We would meet, in about a month, all going well. And as I drove back on the eight-hour journey to New York, a billboard greeted me asking if I had enjoyed my stay in Rochester and if I would be coming back? I smiled at the woman and winked and said *hell, you betcha I enjoyed it, but don't be offended if ya don't all see me again.*

It had all gone according to plan: beautiful in its perfection. A pity the van had been so small, but that's the way it goes. Couldn't complain. No one hurt. No one caught. Perfect.

My arse! Twenty minutes later I turned on the radio, and soon realised the "perfect" crime had been perfect for only about the same amount of time. The guard – Trigger Happy, the one I re-cuffed – had managed to wriggle free to raise the alarm. Police helicopters were already in the air, searching for us. The radio mentioned a van. They even knew the colour! *Fuck!*

Had it not been raining, perhaps I wouldn't have left the tire mark behind that stuck out like a black, sore thumbprint on the pale floor of the *Brink's* depot. But that was all in hindsight. Spilt milk. And as the New York State thruway started to congest with police cars something in my stomach told me I wouldn't be making it home, after all. The thruway would be cordoned off at each exit, guarded by trigger-happy police only too willing to burn the barrel off their guns as they used me for target practice.

Each time the headlights from a car followed behind me, my stomach heaved. I tried to listen to the news and for the helicopters overhead, at the same time, all the while trying to keep my speed at exactly 55mph. A couple of times I thought I heard someone in the back of the van. The robbery was now headlines on every radio station I tuned to. A van, grey in colour, was described as the getaway vehicle with two, possibly three men inside. All armed, all extremely dangerous. Proceed with extreme caution. Repeat: *all armed and extremely dangerous.*

The fuckers were setting me up to be massacred. I could picture the steroid-bloated cops, all grinning, lurking behind their cars, lights and sirens all turned off, smelling me coming a mile away. *Fox News* or even *Hard Copy* would interview them all, afterwards, each claiming to have fired the fatal shots that left half my brains scattered across the New York State Line. They'd be heroes, and get a few spoken lines on *Cops*. They had it made.

Twice I had to stop at a filling station for petrol and each time I thought that this is where it all would end. Would I burst into flames, or would they wait until I was about to re-enter the van? No. It would be the flames. Give me a taste of what was waiting for me at the end of the Big Journey.

Seven hours later, as I slowly came to a halt at the tollbooth, ticket in my hand, I was certain – *here* is *definitely* where it ends. The bastards probably wouldn't even give me a chance to surrender.

'You have a nice day,' said the smiling lady at the booth, as she handed me change from a twenty.

It was then – looking at her beautiful, but dead smile – that I knew everything was going to be just fine.

'Thank you. I'll do my best,' I replied as the van lurched forward towards the early morning sun just coming into view over Manhattan.

With a bit of luck, I'd be home soon. In an hour I'd be back in work at Park Avenue. A perfect alibi. You simply can't beat the "perfect" plan. It works every time . . .

32

Room for Heroes

June 1993

> *"An elegant sufficiency, content,*
> *Retirement, rural quiet, friendship, books."*
>
> JAMES THOMSON, *Scottish Poet*

I had noticed the store with its "For Rent or Sale" sign on a couple of occasions as I drove by dropping my kids off at school. It was a perfect location for what I had in mind and was situated in an upper-middle-class area with the idyllic neighbourhood of Greeks, Italians and Irish, a community of hard-working people who had tremendous pride in where they lived. Yet, some negative points could be drawn from the exterior: it looked quite small and had enormous rusted locks – four in number – each the size of a coconut studded to its metallic skin. I wondered if this was a gauge of crime in the area or simply an over-cautious owner? A swath of dry vegetation led straight up the building's side like a seven o'clock shadow.

'I've seen you a couple of times looking at the store. Are you interested in it?' The man asking the questions was slim built, tall with red hair. There was no doubt about the Irish in his freckled face dotted like rusty nail-heads.

I was caught off guard by his sudden appearance. 'I'm just looking, at the minute. I'm thinkin' about opening a store in the neighbourhood, but –'

Before I could finish, he had my elbow and was fumbling for his keys. Within a minute the locks fell to the ground and the shutters clanged open. I was quickly ushered inside.

'Terry O'Neil.' He put out his hand and I shook it. 'Has every little thing you would need. Bathroom in the back, plenty of storage in the next room . . . and there's a great restaurant down the street. What kind of store are you opening?' he asked, continuing before I could answer. 'You can even see the Empire State Building lit up at night, all red white and blue. It's great to look at.'

'Yes, I know. I see it every night from my own apartment,' I said, deflating his swelling pride-filled face.

'Oh . . .'

It all sounded rather cosy but the truth was being stretched, slightly. It was a bare, skeletal box devoid of even a single redeeming factor, wounded from a sad case of self-abuse and neglect with odds and ends, snarled in a confused state of disarray, scattered haphazardly on the floor. It looked completely uninviting. Granny paint was wrinkling and wires hung nervously from exposed lights turned gangrene-yellow because of all the carcasses of rotting insects attached to them. Even the dust looked menacing. I thought about my allergies and asthma. It reeked of strangled cigarettes. The air conditioning wasn't functioning properly either.

Terry read the reluctance on my face perfectly. The store's ten months of emptiness had started to eat at him – or at least his bank balance – and there was no way he could countenance further reductions brought about by this ugly duckling. Outside, vast slabs of trees circled the back of the shop, suffocating in their closeness.

'We could chop them down,' said Terry, worried. 'It would

bring in better light, expose – *reveal* – the store's hidden vastness. To be totally honest, I was just saying to my wife, the other day, that those trees seem to –'

'No, I think they're great.'

' – do wonders for the store,' he smiled, not missing a beat.

'My father had a tree, just like that one, in his back garden.' I pointed to the tree in question, its bark splintered by squirrel teeth. 'He was great at stuff like that. Won prizes and got himself on the front page of the *Irish News* . . . our local newspaper in Belfast.' I was blabbering like a fool. 'But they made him leave his trees and garden behind when we moved. Said they wanted to build a ring-road . . .'

I thought I witnessed a tear in Terry's eye. Probably from all the cobwebs dangling from the ceiling, covered in dust.

'Shameful,' he said, shaking his head in disbelief. 'I don't understand people. Some of these trees have been here hundreds of years. They were here before us, and will be here after us.'

He sounded like a page from *National Geographic*, or Thoreau. I didn't want to remind him that only a few minutes ago he wanted to coat them all in concrete. I didn't tell him how much I initially hated the trees in my father's garden, how he made me stand guard, after school, on a coal heap in the garden fearful that neighbourhood kids would steal the apples before he had the chance to sell them to the greengrocer. I was to stand-watch for the first thieving head that popped up over that wall and was to let them have it with all those lumps of coal at my feet.

'Coffee?' asked Terry, breaking my thoughts. 'Rossalina's Restaurant makes the best coffee on the planet, and as for their Italian food . . .' His eyes went to heaven, indicating high praise. 'They do deliveries, also, seven days a week.'

'You don't happen to own it, as well?' I smiled, but deadly serious.

'No, but we've been friends for years. They're great people. Did I tell you they do a special each Tuesday and Thursday?'

'White with one sugar, Terry, please . . .'

He quickly left, promising to be back in ten minutes, returning in less than five. We stood outside drinking the coffee while listening to a neighbour's barely perceptible sprinkler spit on a lawn covered with wilted daisies and bored weeds. Sparrows and magpies swooped and darted between scattered bushes while a fountain of pigeons squirted skywards destroying the beauty of perfect blue. I watched as they transformed themselves into dragonflies before disappearing into shapes the size of rice beads.

'There's a lot of work here, Terry,' I said. 'I don't really know if I want to spend the money and time involved.'

He nodded. 'Of course there is, but you see the potential in it. Don't you?' He was grinning. He thought he had won.

He had. Almost. 'Well, I've two other premises to look at. One tomorrow, the other on –'

'Look no further. Two months free rent, plus I personally will take care of all the electrical work and odds and ends.' He put out his hand for the gentleman's agreement.

'*Three* months? Sounds very generous, Terry.'

His hand was slightly twitching as it moved towards mine, reluctantly, in slow motion. He shook it – a bit too tightly – and for the first time since our meeting asked my name.

'Patrick.'

'Beautiful name,' said Terry, not wanting to know the rest of it.

That's the way all deals should be done, I thought, as we reached the outside of the shop, wishing each other a good day in the balmy heat. A handshake, no questions asked, no implications for either party should things turn dark and nasty. I committed the day to memory, hoarding every single word and touch for a time when life would no longer seem so wonderful and calm. A perpetual moment, never spoiled by its disastrous conclusion . . .

Eagerly I commenced work on the store, the very next day, scrubbing it from top to bottom while buckets of white paint set patiently in the yard, ready for their call to do battle.

As Jai Park – a Korean sign maker and old customer from the casino – set about outlining his plans for the store's exterior, my mind set about furnishing the interior and I vowed to myself that this would be no ordinary comic store.

If you build it, they will come . . .

People *would* come, from miles away; kids would torture their parents or guardians to bring them. Once I had the little kid, I would capture the bigger kid – the father, the dweller of retro – mesmerizing him with the comics from his childhood, winking at him as he pretended to browse, inviting his defence, "For the kid, actually. I'm just looking".

No need for embarrassment, I would assure him. *Look at me, the biggest kid on the block. And how about that* Spiderman *Number 5, eh? As close as near-mint condition you'll ever see. Bet you've never seen a copy as clean as that?* I would say, easing it from the wall, gently, as if it were an Old Master, or a stick of dynamite.

He would tell me then that, in fact, he had seen a copy as clean and bright as this one and that was the day he tried to coax his old man for ten cents, begging, pleading for one more hand-out, because he's just got to have *this* copy to keep his collection fluent.

Did you get it? I would ask, knowing the answer, knowing how his defeated and devastated face would have looked that bright Saturday afternoon.

"Na," he would answer, "ten cents was a lot of money to my father who had better things to do than encourage my daydreams of flying and lifting cars with one hand." He would then grin, embarrassed.

I wanted to be the Hulk, I'd confide in him, unlocking a key in my head that a good psychiatrist would kill to obtain. He would smile with relief at our shared dark secret.

I would not tell him that I wanted to be the Hulk so as to kill my father, smashing a building over his head as he screamed at me, blaming me for his wife walking out that door, all those years ago. No, I would not want to lose my first customer, so I'd smile right back at him, letting him know that I knew his real reason for wanting the "super powers" and why his father refused to give him the ten cents on that beautiful Saturday afternoon and that it is hard – real hard – to obtain money from the dead. I can see his eyes, ready for popping, anticipating, and the tongue licking. Just at that point it would be the time for me to introduce him to the *Mylar* experience. *Wait until I show him my Fantastic Four Number 1. He'll shit his pants then die of a heart attack.*

The comics – the expensive ones – are secured in an archival storage *Mylar*, keeping grubby-fingers from destroying the irreplaceable. It gives the comic a false liquid gleam, as if it has just left the publisher's ink. Normal plastics, vinyl, and other storage materials slowly oxidize releasing harmful acids, which slowly eat paper alive. *Mylar* is a storage material specifically developed for the long-term storage of historically important documents such as the Declaration of Independence and the Magna Carta. Used by leading museums worldwide it is considered completely impregnable for up to 400 years. I doubt if I'll be about to contradict their claim.

Once he saw the *Mylar*, he would know were speaking serious money. A mortgage might have to be gambled on; the kids' college days look doomed. Fuck, he might have to rob a *Brink's* armoured car . . . and suddenly he'd be transported back to his first meeting with Peter Parker, Bruce Wayne, Clark Kent et al because the moment he'd touched the comic, he'd be mine, everlastingly trapped in *Spiderman's* web.

My love for and addiction to American comics could be blamed squarely on my father. It was he, after all, who had started me on the carousel by introducing me to the wonders of *Marvel* and *DC* at the early age of seven, bringing back bundles of them from his trips to New York as a merchant seaman. The writers and artists had a profound impact on my youth, employing a dazzling range of storytelling devices. I learned more

192

about the world of words from Stan Lee, Jack Kirby, Neal Adams, Jim Steranko and Steve Ditko – the unchallenged masters – than I ever did from any combination of teachers with angry leather straps and angrier leather faces. Graphic artists like Robert Crumb and Art Spiegelman filled an even greater need in me, later.

'The name? You're sure?' asked Jai, clicking his fingers in my face, rousing me from my childhood trance. 'No going back.'

I had pondered over the name for the store for days. The obvious came to mind. *Heroes and Villains?* I'd be asking for trouble with that one. *Dragon Slayer?* Would that scare people away? *Hulk's Kingdom?* No, *Marvel* would have me in court quicker than Clark Kent removing his shirt in a telephone booth. Finally, I opted for the more cryptic *KAC Comics*. The initials stood for each of my kids: Kelly, Ashley and Corey.

Tomorrow would bring the big day. I was nervous and excited. What if it was a complete flop? What if no one came? What if . . .

But I believed, deep in my heart, that they would come, eventually and I would be watching the kids faces light up, their images travelling in a universal language of silence, where necessity of words is irrelevant, remembering my own tiny face in the wee shop on the Duncairn Gardens as I pleaded with the woman to hold on to *X-Men #14* for me, promising her I would have her three pence in a week, and here is my bus money and school-dinner money as a down payment and commitment of trust. I tell her she can even hold on to the comic until I come up with the goods. Does she not realise that the comics are the only things keeping me sane in a house gone mad? All I ask is that she put the comic under the counter, away from greedy prying eyes, away from someone who would have the audacity to take what rightfully belonged to me. She is amazed by my passion and tells me she will hold it for three days. I'm devastated because I know I will never get my hands on that sort of money in the time allocated. And then it becomes so clear it frightens me. I will be able to get it! Why didn't I think of this before? Tomorrow is the day I bring the rent for my father's house up to be paid on the Antrim Road at the wee corner business. It's simple. I'll sign the wee orange book. I can master the signature on it perfectly. My father will never know and I'll have enough money to buy as many comics as I can carry. Fuck! Why didn't I think of this before? It's perfect and the great thing about it is that I will be able to do it every week, for the rest of my life. I'm gonna be rich . . .

Terry popped in on his way home, to wish me all the best for tomorrow. 'I'll be honest, Patrick. When you told me you were opening a comic book store I thought, bang goes my rent. But now . . . I'm not so sure. It almost makes me wish to be a kid again.' He glanced from wall to wall. Not an inch of space to be seen as comics cover every spot. 'God, you must have hundreds of 'em.' Then he spotted the price on some of them. 'You're kiddin'. Right?'

'No,' I smiled. 'And believe it or not, those are great prices.'

'300 bucks for a *Batman* comic?'

'That's cheap. Look behind you, at the one in the glass case.'

He read the price out loud, then whispered it to himself, like a Gregorian chant. 'I don't believe this. And people actually pay that sort of money?'

'Gladly.'

He was caught by the beauty of it all. He remembered his *Green Lantern* comics and, regretfully, asked me how much they would fetch if he still had them. When I told him he became quite despondent.

'Don't worry, Terry, you're not the only one who destroyed or lost his collection. If no one lost their comics, these comics would not be as valuable and as sought after as they are. The *Wall Street Journal* stated what all enthusiasts already knew: that gold-and-silver-age comics appreciate in value quicker than real estate.' He didn't want to hear that. 'Perhaps you should come into partnership with me? Sell me the store?' I smiled.

He left, no longer wanting to hear me. He mumbled

something about *Green Lantern* and thought he could still have a couple of copies in the loft or perhaps the basement.

The door chime alerted me to someone entering and I turned to see my first customers come through the door. They were not what I expected.

'How's it goin'?' I asked, nervously. My stomach froze. Not because they were my first real customers, but because of their uniforms: New York's finest, all blue, different shades. They said nothing and I felt that at any minute I was going to be arrested for the *Brink's*.

''Long you open, pal?' asked the smallest of the two giants who's at least 6 foot 2 from his knees.

'Tomorrow's the openin'. You're my first customers,' I smiled, even though I know how scary it must have looked.

'Nice place. Great collection,' said Giant Number One, while Giant Number Two appeared to be looking down the hallway, suspiciously.

'Got a bathroom down there? Too much coffee.' He smiled and I was thinking how to say no.

Above the cupboard in the toilet was a grip-bag containing single dollar-bills. Over 20,000 of them! From the *Brink's*. I should have burnt them while I had the chance, but I couldn't stomach good money going to waste. Now I was paying for my greed.

'It's . . . a bit small. I doubt if you'd be able to squeeze past those mountains of boxes down there with all the comics in them.' My smile started to fade. It looked very suspicious, my smile, and I hated it for trying to get me caught.

'Ha! Don't worry. I've been in tighter spots,' he said, manoeuvring his bulk nimbly for such a giant.

So have I, pal, I thought as he sucked in his breath, winking at me, his frame slowly edging through the barrier of boxes, victoriously.

'Don't forget to wash your hands, Jimmy,' shouted Giant Number Two. 'Never washes his hands, that guy,' he said, apologetically to me. 'So, where ya from? Just moved into Queens?'

Think very carefully. 'No, I used to live up at Jackson Heights for years.'

He nodded. 'Gettin' dangerous, that place. Lots of drug dealers. It's the cocaine capital of America . . .'

What he conveniently erased is that it was also the most ethnically diverse neighbourhood in New York. It is home to approximately 100,000 people whose famous residents at one time included members of the big swing bands that dominated the music scene in the '30s and early '40s, including Benny Goodman, Woody Herman, and Glenn Miller.

Giant Number One seemed to be taking an awful long time.

'Where you from? Ireland?' he asked, knowing the answer. What he wanted me to tell him is exactly *whereabouts* in Ireland.

'Yes. But I've been here a good ten years,' I said, trying desperately to avoid the trap.

'Still got the brogue, though,' he continued.

'That's right. Proud of it.' Careful, I thought. Don't get too defensive. He's only being friendly. Or is he? Where the fuck is that other big bastard? Fallen through to the East River?

'Jimmy's people are from Ireland. Isn't that right, Jimmy,' he says to Giant Number One who, thankfully, reappeared a bit thinner than when he went on his excursion.

'Cork. Great people. The best county in Ireland, I believe.'

'I'm from Antrim. The real best one.' Had he spotted the bag? Did he open it? Don't be stupid. You'd be 'cuffed by now.

'Jimmy Coogan.' He put out his hand and I shook it. I wondered if he'd washed his hands. 'This is Tommy Johnson.' I shook his hand, also. 'I've a lot of friends who collect comics, over at Rikers Island.'

'Rikers Island Penitentiary?' I queried, dreading the answer.

'Don't worry. They're guards – not prisoners.' They both laughed. So did I. Rikers Island Penitentiary is New York's largest and most violent prison, where ten jails sprawl across an area half the size of Central Park. I'd seen it from a safe distance. Hopefully, it would stay that way.

'That's great. I'm sure I could work out a special deal for

them,' I replied, hating the thought, but thinking ahead. One never knows . . .

'That's nice of you, pal. I'll let them know. Anyway, we've got to run, but don't you be worryin' about this store. We'll be passin' every now and then. Let the bad guys know we're here.' He smiled and his teeth were scary-white.

I closed the door, wondering what I had let myself in for as I turned off all the lights – except for the neon superheroes flashing in the darkness. I doubted if I would be able to sleep that night and promised myself to get up very early the next morning and make sure every tiny detail was "perfect".

Tiny stars cloud the sky above me and the darkness feels vast and heavy as the bottle-green ford conveniently parks beside an umbrella of trees. Faint headlights danced with the darkness, guiding moths to the ugly bug ball. I was sure it was the same one I had noticed the preceding evening, but when an old man emerged from it, bent and grey, I laughed at myself for such foolishness.

'Drive carefully,' he said to the driver, as the car slowly edged away from him.

He looked straight at me, but through me, and suddenly my skin began to tingle, just like Spiderman's. *You've got to get out a bit more*, I advised myself. *A lot more . . .*

33

The Rat

8 July 1993

"It appears to be one of the biggest robberies in U.S. history."
NEW YORK TIMES, FRONT PAGE

"We are offering $300,000 reward for information leading to the suspects."
BRINK'S INC.

"Gentlemen, in this business, you're only as good as your rats."
U.S. LAW ENFORCEMENT ACADEMY

'FBI. Agent Fuentes speaking. How may I help?'

A few moments of silence seeped in, making the pause seem longer. It was as if the person at the other end of the phone was having second thoughts, weighing up an action he might, in time, come to regret. Being the "professional", Fuentes detected the hesitancy and quickly moved.

'Would you prefer to speak to one of our female agents?' He didn't know if the person at the other end was male or female. This would grant them a possible option, helping to overcome any last minute doubts.

'*I need to . . .*' *A cough, a clearing of the throat, not the conscience.*

Again the silence, but at least he now knew it was a male. '*Yes, sir. Just take your time. I'm sitting right here.*'
Easy. Don't rush him. But something in the FBI man's stomach told him that this could be the call they'd all been waiting on. They knew he was out there. The local rumours had mentioned a grudge. This could be him.

'*I need to speak to Agent Stith . . . the one in charge of the Brink's case.*'

Had to be him! The caller's voice still held the telltale twang of Belfast, only partially eroded by years in America. '*Agent Stith isn't available at this moment, sir. But I can put you through –*'

No! No one else. I'll try and call at the same time tomorrow . . . perhaps.'

'*Sir, if you would just –*'

Damn! Hung up! Fuentes cursed himself, wondering if he had frightened him away. He wondered what Stith would say. They were all under pressure. Damn! Almost . . .

The FBI man needn't have worried. The caller would be back. Back with a vengeance!

'*There is danger to wearing a wire. There is nothing cool about it, the way Hollywood have you believe. I don't wish to scare you off . . . just prepare you in case . . .*'

The man sitting opposite the FBI agent nodded. He was determined to go along with this, despite the burning in his heart, making it pump even faster. '*I've thought long and hard about it,*' *he replied, softly, almost a whisper.* '*What they did to my brother . . .*'

The FBI man knew all about the man's brother. He had read the file more than once. A robbery gone wrong, said the report. Off the record said: revenge, a love triangle turned sour. Whatever the answer, it had produced their only solid lead. And with all the pressure they were under, the agent was almost grateful it had happened, in a perverse sort of way, of course.

'Okay, then. Your first stop will be Molly Malone's on Tuesday night. Our sources tell us there is a good possibility he will be there, probably with his girlfriend.'

'That's no problem. I used to be a regular there.'

'Don't get complacent, please. This guy is dangerous as well as smart. We believe he has killed at least two other persons, apart from your brother. Don't take any chances. He already knows you hate him and will certainly feel wary if you try to have a conversation with him.'

'Oh, I'm well aware of that. Believe me. But I'm hoping the Jenny Light will make him a bit more cocky than usual, especially when we're taking a piss together, just like old buddies.' The man tried a smile, but his mouth had gone dry and tight.

'Don't forget,' the agent reassured. 'We'll only be a few yards away at most. Don't get macho. Understand?'

The man nodded before standing to go.

'We appreciate all you've done for us,' said the agent, opening the door.

'Let's hope it works and we get this bastard. That's all I want.'

My sentiments exactly, thought the agent, closing the door. *Tuesday night would tell . . .*

34

Money? Don't mention
that word to me

July 1993

"Money is like muck, not good except it be spread."
BACON

*"We are now offering $500,000 for information to
help solve the robbery."*
BRINK'S INC.

Money, money everywhere, and not a drop to spend. I couldn't touch it with a barge pole, and it was killing me. Every time I went to the garage to check on it, I realised how a conformed alcoholic must feel each time he passed a bar. The smell of the money was making me sick. It was laughing at me, all those 100s, 50s and 20s. George Washington's false teeth almost came flying out, he was laughing so much.

Things couldn't get worse, I thought, answering my mobile phone. I called it the "bad news phone" because only three people knew the number, knowing only to use it in the event of something dire happening.

'Hello?'

'I'm gonna ask ya a question, then call ya back in two minutes. What did Danny G's father own? Think about it. When I call ya back, *don't* say the answer. Understand?'

Before I could reply, he hung up.

My mind raced. Who the fuck was Danny G, never mind his father and what did he own? The more I tried to figure it out, the more my brain froze. Less than a minute and he'd be calling me back. I hadn't a clue. Then it hit me. Danny G was an old friend of the caller. We had met only a couple of times. He had always fancied himself as a bit of a singer, but until the big day arrived, he'd have to content himself with working in his father's tire depot. But what did that have to do with me?

The phone rang again.

'Hello?'

'Do you remember?'

'Yes . . . at least I think so.'

'Good. Get rid of 'em immediately, but prudently. The vultures are on to you.'

The phone went dead. Its click made my stomach churn. I looked out the window of the comic-book store, and glanced up and down the street. I felt like closing the store and making a run for the Mexican border. They were on to me! Fuckers! How? I didn't want to believe it, but my source was impeccable.

I should've got rid of the van from the very beginning. No, I should never have used it in the first place. Being so cocky was now going to be my downfall. Keeping it, I had tried to make things look as normal as possible. Still driving the same old piece of shit wouldn't bring undue attention to myself, I had reasoned. Now it was coming back to haunt me. The fucker. I began to pluck at straws. It was only the tires he had hinted at, not the van. Perhaps I still had a chance.

They could be anywhere, the Feds. Every tree hid one. The old lady with the limp, coming towards me, was probably one. I wanted to knock her flying, test the fake cane that balanced her, watch her comrades come rushing to her aid, guns blazing. I closed the store and brought the van to a Greek friend who owned a filling station. He asked no questions as to why would I want to replace practically new tires. He simply replaced them, putting the old ones in the back of the van.

I drove miles, trying to think where I could dump them, watching my mirror, waiting for the sirens. Eventually, I stopped at a *MacDonald's* and after a cup of coffee, felt better, calmer, despite the caffeine.

The calmness lasted until I took one of the papers from a bunch on the counter. That morning's *New York Times* carried an article about the robbery, claiming the Feds had a new lead. I left the restaurant, more depressed than ever. My stomach told me something was going to happen, probably today, something beyond my control.

Just as I was about to start the van, I noticed the dumpster. I couldn't believe my luck. It sat with its jaws wide open, in an adjacent car park, a group of trees camouflaging it, filled with all sorts of crap, but more than enough room for the tires. Perfect.

As I drove away, I took a last glance back, just to make sure. Nothing. I admonished myself for becoming paranoid, for giving the Feds too much credit. They hadn't a clue. Would never have a clue, the fuckers, and for the first time in hours I relaxed, smiling to myself.

Had I looked back, just one more teeny-weeny time, I would have crapped my pants to see the two grinning agents placing the tires in the back of their van.

Marco and I had agreed to meet at La Guardia Airport, close to where the planes took off. This would drown out any potential listening devices, or so we hoped. We set the date, 27 February, through a code we had developed prior to the robbery. Of course the Feds had long deciphered our code and knew every move we made. They had placed their agents in and around the airport days prior to the arranged rendezvous. Little did we know that we were walking into a trap. The Feds, who had been biting their nails to nab us, now would have the irrefutable evidence they had so patiently awaited: the two of us together for a photo opportunity.

That morning, as we all drove to the spot, each of us could hear the sound of an explosion. It was near noon and I could see ribbons of smoke snaking into the air. A gas explosion, I thought, turning the radio on, listening to the Stones singing, "You can't always get what you want". I made a left, towards Astoria Boulevard. The airport was in sight. I'd be there in a couple of minutes, unknowingly into the open arms of the FBI.

Suddenly, the music was interrupted by a voice saying that unconfirmed reports were coming in of a massive explosion at the World Trade Centre, of people being killed and injured.

People were stopping their cars, in disbelief, not fathoming such an act on American soil. The terrible irony of the explosion was that it had saved our necks – albeit for then – as every agent on the East Coast had been pulled off their designated case, making the explosion their number-one priority, trying to find the perpetrators.

As I pulled into the airport, the New York Feds were pulling out, cursing their luck.

As days turned to weeks and no arrests, my confidence grew. I had only one problem, a problem I never believed I would ever have: Money. Too much of it . . .

All this money, and no place to hide it. I kept the entire cut in the back of my van, bags of it, shrouded by a few oily blankets, passed each day by numerous residents who came to pick up their own cars or trucks from the private underground car park. Each morning I awoke, wondering if the van's contents remained intact, grateful the van looked like shit, low on the list of car thieves.

But enough was enough. Sooner or later someone would come across it, probably by accident and either steal it or call in the Feds. It was time for me to come in from the cold. Someone would have to be told: someone whom I could trust. After much deliberation, one name came to the fore – Father Pat.

I first met Pat when a friend of mine asked me to drop him off at his home, in the lower east side of Manhattan. His brother-in-law had gone missing and he wanted to know if Pat could help. I was extremely cold towards him, initially, as my experience of priests in Long Kesh had made me very cynical and gave rise to a nasty taste in my mouth every time I met one. Pat, I found out, slept in an old cupboard and was constantly answering the phone and door from people needing his help. At first, I thought it was a con he was pulling, but as I got to know him over the following weeks I began to develop a grudging respect. His lifestyle was austere, to say the least, and was in sharp contrast to the lifestyle of priests I had known in Ireland.

Occasionally, I would drop in with material I picked up from work at Park Avenue: paint, cement, furniture and household goods. Whatever the rich threw out, he knew a hundred people who could use it. His motto was simple: *Pray for the dead; but fight like hell for the living!* Eventually, we became friends.

I approached him, not knowing if he would refuse, or simply condemn me, telling me never to blacken his door again.

'If someone had a good bit of money, and wanted it kept safe, what would be the best way of goin' about it?' I asked, matter-of-factly.

He was having a light lunch, as was his norm. I was sipping tea.

'Oh, there are hundreds of ways, I suppose,' he said, uninterested. He had just got off the phone, and the call seemed to have bothered him.

'It's just the money I'm makin' in the casino. I'd hate to be arrested by the INS (Immigration), and have them confiscate it.'

'I don't think they have the power to confiscate your money, even if you are here illegally.' He picked at some tired lettuce before pushing the plate away. 'I have to go out. I shouldn't be long. Want to wait?'

'No, I've got to be going myself,' I said, knowing Pat's

"shouldn't be long" could turn into hours. Besides, my money was parked outside his door and this wasn't the best of neighbourhoods. Even a shitty van covered in oily rags would disappear, if you didn't keep an eye on it.

'I'll try and find out some more about the INS,' he replied, seeing the look on my face as the black homeless man glanced in the back of my van.

'Get the hell away from that van!' I shouted at the bewildered man, regretting it instantly.

Pat was a well-known advocate for the homeless, and he wasn't one bit amused at my attitude.

'I've been on edge lately,' I mumbled, as way of an apology.

He simply nodded and got in the car, disappearing out of sight. I thought about giving the black homeless man a few bucks, but he had also, strangely, disappeared.

It's funny how you remember the important things when it's too late . . .

Over the next few days I was relentless in my single pursuit of finding a safe haven for the money. Pat was still top of the list, but if I couldn't persuade him – and soon – I'd be in trouble. I'd give him one more try. If his answer was no, then an old friend would have to be brought in. This might cause problems later, but I needed a fix, short-term or permanent was irrelevant. I needed it *now*.

Pat was also relentless, but more in his quest to alleviate the suffering of the destitute roaming the streets of the lower East Side. I knew if he had one weakness, it was the poor and their impoverished existence. I began to play on it.

'If a person had the right sort of money, he could do an awful lot of good for the homeless in this place, couldn't he?'

He had three old suits in his hands, which he quickly stuffed into a bag. Two shirts, a scattering of ties, and a pair of boots that had seen better days followed them. Eventually they would become a welcomed gift for someone in Alphabet City or Hell's Kitchen. He continued packing clothes away, ignoring me.

I wanted to scream it out, hit him on the head with a big bag of money, instead I simply said, 'Pat. I need your help.'

He stopped packing, straightened his back and planted himself in the chair at the window. He could see my van across the street and said, 'You better be careful. They'll be giving out tickets in twenty minutes.'

A parking ticket was the least of my problems, this time. 'I've got some . . . money. I need a safe place to keep it – maybe for quite a while.'

He stared back at the van and I wondered if he knew already. 'The casino?'

For a second, I didn't realise what he meant. Then it came to me. Pat still thought I worked in the casino, transporting money across the city for Johnny Mac. 'Well . . . I wouldn't say it was the casino –'

He cut me off with a wave of his hand. He didn't want to know my business. 'How much needs to be looked after?'

'I don't really know just yet.'

'Give me a figure. A few hundred? A thousand?'

'I really don't know. I haven't counted it yet.'

He laughed at that. 'Haven't *counted* it? It sounds like a fairly large sum. Why not?'

'I've been . . . busy,' I mumbled. 'But I need your help. Desperately.'

He scratched his beard, then said: 'Let's have some tea.'

It was the first time I had ever known Pat to be speechless. It took a while for him to find his voice.

'Where . . . where in God's name did you get this? Is this all casino money?' He was looking into the bags beneath the oily rags. The quiver in his voice told me he might have a heart attack. What a headline: *Dead priest found on stolen loot.*

'I can't tell you where it came from – not yet, maybe later, maybe never. But you've got to give me your word that you'll never breathe a word about this, no matter what you decide.'

He didn't answer. Instead, he quickly covered the money, his face full of panic. 'We've got to get this out of sight. Have you been driving all this time – no. No time for questions. Hurry up!'

A few minutes later, the van was parked in a secured garage. And as the steel shutters closed, for the first time in days, I felt my body tumble into relaxation.

'Where did it come from?' asked Pat as we sat down to tea, alone in his study. A small, cheeky mouse ran across the floor, stopping at my feet, staring up, as if it, also, needed an answer.

'I can't tell you. It's for your own safety, Pat. Best you don't know.'

Minutes elapsed in semi-silence with only the squeak of a hungry mouse being heard. I wondered what was going through his mind, if he was thinking of turning his back on me while the going was good. The silence was terrible, heavy.

'Okay. It's safe at the minute, but we'll have to come up with something more permanent. Give me a day or two. Okay?'

Take a year. I was sick of it. 'That'll be great, Pat, but when you call me, don't say anything on the phone. It could be bugged.'

He raised an eyebrow, but remained silent as he walked me to the door, watching me stroll toward First Avenue for a taxi. It wasn't until later – when it was all too late – that he mentioned the black man following me up the street. He was sure he had seen him some place before, but just like me, he couldn't quite put his finger on it at the time.

Eventually, Pat came up with an apartment to store the money in. It was 330 First Avenue, apartment 10D. The impression he had given me was that a friend who was no longer in the country had rented the apartment to him.

It was a rent-controlled apartment, a "gold mine" in tight-spaced New York. It had the tired, dusty look of the uninhabited. A few posters lined the walls; a family of dried-out plants sat withered in each room mingling with records and books: lots of books. All I needed was the music of *The Odd Couple* to be playing. It was obvious the place hadn't been lived in for ages.

We went outside to bring in the bags of money. Just as I turned the corridor, a man was waiting at the elevator door as if waiting for it to open. He was a black man. That was unusual as the apartment complex was exclusively "white". As I walked towards the lift, he opened the door, smiling.

'Which floor?' he asked, holding the door.

Suddenly, my Belfast wariness kicked in. He was dressed rough, almost homeless in his attire, but the manicured fingernails gleaming like mother-of-pearl, contradicted. Also, no black man worth his salt in New York would open the door for a white man, allowing him to enter first. It would be tantamount to being an Uncle Tom. My suspicion heightened. I had seen this man before, but couldn't put my finger on where.

'No thanks,' I said, hoping my face didn't say too much. 'I've other stuff I need to bring in. You go on ahead.'

Then it dawned on me as the lift door closed, sending him on a solo journey: he was the same black man I had caught looking in the back of the van. Perhaps he had spotted the contents and was waiting an opportunity to get the bags? What if his gang was here, waiting? I watched as the lift button lit up, stopping at floor six. As Pat entered the corridor I told him to wait, keep an eye on the bags, something wasn't right.

'Where're you going? What's wrong?'

But I was gone, running up the stairs like a madman, taking the stairs two at a time, the adrenaline giving me "super powers". I was going to find out, once and for all, who this bastard was, what he was up to.

What if he has a gun? A knife? The voice of common sense asked as I reached the sixth floor, panting like a dog. But I didn't want to hear that, just get him, grab him by the throat and give a good tight squeeze. He'd soon tell me all that I wanted to know.

But he wasn't there. The floor's area was deserted. Just the sound of my breathing remained untouched.

'Bastard,' I said, loud enough for him to hear. I knew he was there, somewhere, and it wasn't my imagination or nerves, as Pat implied after we entered the apartment, bolting it shut.

'It could simply be stress,' he reasoned. 'Probably the janitor. Something innocent. That's usually how it is.'

But my gut told me he was wrong. I told Pat he would receive at least ten per cent of whatever amount was final. Before he could protest at not wanting a penny, I said, 'Think of what you could do for the homeless with that.'

And suddenly his mind began to calculate. 'They'll be safe here. I've something more permanent in mind, but this will do for now,' Pat assured me as we dropped a couple of US Army duffle bags on the bare floor, making a dead-thud sound.

'We need a money-counter,' I said, after we'd brought all the suitcases into the room. 'I still haven't a clue how much there is.'

I doubted if he believed me.

'I'll have one, probably by tomorrow, Tuesday at the latest,' he said.

We left the apartment, agreeing to meet in the morning, knowing the laborious task of counting piles of money lay ahead. I wasn't looking forward to it at all and wondered how long it would take to count it, get it out of my sight. The smell was making me physically sick, making my head swim.

From the safety of a café door, New York City detective, Garry Beekman, watched as we stepped out into the sunshine.

'They're leaving,' he whispered to his commander via a small mouthpiece.

No sooner had we left the apartment than ten FBI agents – part of the 100-strong team sent to capture us – alighted on the building, while others followed us home. They worked like ants, the remaining Feds, placing surveillance cameras in and around the tenth floor common area. In the "EXIT" sign, directly facing the apartment, they placed a "pin-head" camera, smack in the middle of the "X". Within minutes they had locked-in to their command centre at One Police Plaza, and were quickly given the go ahead for *Candid Camera* to proceed.

'Perfect,' came the static reply. 'Just perfect.'

35

Caught by the Balls. Again

August 1993

"Whatever befalls you was prepared for you beforehand from eternity . . ."
MARCUS AURELIUS

"Our offer now stands at $750,000 for information."
BRINK'S INC.

The money-counter made the soft hum of an insect's wings. So soft, yet I thought it could still be heard above the skull-penetrating sound of New York traffic, screaming from outside the windows. Pat said he couldn't hear the hum, and I put it down to my own paranoia as I watched dollar bills blur at the speed of light, consumed by the greedy mouth of the counter.

Later on, one person would agree with what I had just said. She was a female FBI agent and she was right outside the apartment door, her ear glued to it, giving the thumbs-up to the "X" in the "EXIT" sign, an enormous grin on her face that said, "We've got them". We continued on, blabbering away, while Keyhole Kate strained her neck, grinning.

213

'We have a bit of a problem,' said Pat, as we stopped for a well-earned cup of tea. 'That Englishman, Ronnie, has been about my place. He wanted to know if I had seen you lately and if I knew where you were now living.'

My face remained expressionless but my stomach knotted. I knew it was only a matter of time before he came sniffing. 'What did you say?'

'Told him the truth. That I hadn't seen you.' He smiled. 'It's never a sin to tell a lie to an Englishman. But I am worried. That sneaky grin of his implied that he knows something.' Although Pat tolerated Ronnie, he neither liked nor trusted him. Ronnie's Irish blood meant nothing to Pat, and he often referred to him, abjectly, as the Englishman.

The whirling whisper of the counting machine continued unabated, highlighting the silence. Pat wanted to ask where Ronnie fitted in, but for the moment he allowed the silence to torture me. Finally, I said, 'He's trying to get rich on another man's balls – forgive the expression, Pat – but he's a coward, a dog returning to its own vomit to see what it can find.' I was shaking with anger.

'I never did trust him, you know,' replied Pat, wrapping an elastic band around a brick of $100 bills. 'Never trust an Englishman. Trust the Devil first.' Pat sipped his tea while I wondered.

Then Keyhole-Fucking-Kate almost came crashing through the door as she slipped against it, just a little bit too eager.

I spilt the tea. 'What the hell was that?' I said, almost in a whisper, as I walked to the door, dreading that it might be Ronnie, believing he had followed Pat. Worse: the black man with a gang, all waiting to charge in. I peeped through the spy-hole before pulling the door. Nothing. The crashing sound of someone throwing crap down the garbage disposal echoed up from the basement, making me laugh a nervous sound.

'What was it?' asked Pat, edging on his chair.

'Garbage.'

I closed the door, bolting it, keeping monsters out, while Keyhole Kate – two stairs away on the landing – released the air from her lungs, making a sorry face at the "X". *Shit! The boss would have something to say about this.*

'What should we do about Ronnie?' asked Pat, returning to the subject I had hoped to avoid.

'Nothing for now. He can't do any damage at the minute.'

Still, I thought, sitting back on the chair, when all had been said and done, Ronnie had been good to me, and despite being a pain in the arse, he had treated me more than fair in the casino. If only he had seen it through to the end, he'd be laughing now, the Ragged-Trousered Philanthropist, handing out money to the poor. I was grinning now, thinking of him squeezing his face against the restaurant window, laughing as we rushed for the door; grabbing boxes full of rotten bananas, thinking he had it made; stealing a brand new van as a bewildered Pakistani chased after him down Tenth Avenue. Far too many memories.

I knew there was only one alternative to stop him sniffing any further, and to stop the tiny pang of guilt I felt: Money. He'd get a cut, even though he didn't deserve it. 'I'm goin' to have to give him somethin', Pat. It's the only way. Otherwise we'll never get rid of him. Gather one of those bags and stick a few stacks in it'

'You can't be serious? He'll think he's got you running scared. Better that he thinks you've left the country, because no matter how much you give him, he'll want more.'

'No, he doesn't think like that. I know him that way.' Or so I thought.

'But you thought you knew him well enough at the start, but look how he turned out. I'd advise against it. He's only bluffing.'

I was already packing the money. It was done. No point in counting it. It made little difference to the piles in front of us.

'An awful lot of money . . .' said Pat, resigned.

$100,000 is a lot of money, now, not then. I was simply glad to see it go. The smell of it was getting worse, as were my headaches caused by the talc-like stench from rotting paper.

'Okay,' said Pat, resigned to the inevitable. 'I'll see that he gets it.'

'Soon,' I advised. 'He'll be over the moon with that. Get him out of the picture.'

We'd left the apartment to the plants and piles of money and made our way down, taking the elevator, but as we descended, a coterie of Feds ascended, taking the steps two at a time. They had at last, it transpired, been granted a "sneak and peek" search warrant from a federal judge and in the few minutes that it had taken me to get to my truck, open the door and turn the ignition key, the agents were inserting their master key in the door of the apartment, video recorders in hand, ready to film the mess we had left behind: suitcases and duffle bags resting on the floor, their contents spilling out like paper vomit; the money counter sitting grinning at them; scraps of paper with the so-far money calculated.

We hadn't even bothered to close the living room window with the fire escape neatly attached outside, begging for someone to come in. That would have been funny, said one agent to the other as he checked his list of serial numbers against some of the piles stacked naked on the bed. They all held their breath, waiting, as one of their comrades slowly checked the numbers on his note pad against the numbers on the money. If they didn't match, the feds were in trouble and they knew it. From the piles of money they searched out the $100 bills, hoping to find some of the $200,000 worth of marked bills.

Each agent in the room froze as the black man spoke, barely a whisper, '*Series 1990; Mint: Richmond, Virginia; serialized E07510010A to E07510061A. Gentlemen, there is a God.*' His grin dominated his entire face. '*We have a match.*'

They slapped each other on the back, grinning like Halloween lanterns. This meant big promotions. Yes, sir! Fucking *big*! The black man eased them all out, nice and quiet, not wanting to disturb the sleeping money. In a couple of weeks, hopefully, it would be time to close down shop, make the arrests, alert the media, go home and have a nice hot bath. Eight weeks he had been dressed like a homeless man and he was beginning to smell like one. He would appreciate a good long soak. After that, well, he would want to have a word with me . . .

36

Arrest and Diesel Therapy

12 November 1993

"Federal agents have suddenly netted a veritable Sean O'Casey farce of circumstance and suspects. Bags of money scattered in a dim tenement apartment; Millar, an Irish revolutionary hiding out in America as a comic book dealer in Queens, New York; O'Connor, an Irish American cop and 'Father Pat', a classically ascetic Irish priest."

FRANCIS X CLINES, columnist for the *New York Times*

It was Friday, two weeks later. Everything was going well. Pat had just returned with me from the "leafy suburbs" of Westchester County, where I planned to buy a $300,000 home. He told the estate agent not to worry about the money as the Church was funding the payments. We both thought that funny.

Of course we wouldn't have found it so funny had we known that every spoken word had been recorded by the four FBI agents sitting only a couple of feet away, eating lunch, at the next table. One of them, a staunch Catholic, boiled with anger at the remark.

After dropping Pat at his home, I entered the main post office in Jackson Heights, a fist full of money-orders in my pocket.

219

"Loose change", comprising of $30,000, rested in the inside of my coat. It was the down payment for a Fredrick Remington statue that I had my eyes on.

The sky overhead was threatening, giving this Friday afternoon a nasty Monday flavour. As I walked towards my truck, I failed to notice how unusually taciturn the normally boisterous streets had become. Usually, the Chinese merchants would be screaming their heads off at potential customers, telling them not to miss this once-in-a-lifetime deal, holding up decapitated chickens and tiny pigs still wet with blood. Tiny drops of rain began to fall, making me quicken my pace.

No sooner had I reached for my keys than I went flying, hard, against the truck. It felt like being hit by a rhino and the first thought it my head was that I was being mugged. My arms were shoved as far up my back as possible without them being broken, all the while voices screamed, 'Where's your fuckin' gun!'

I was dazed, and for a moment I thought I was dead as I floated somewhere out to sea.

'Sam? *Sam?* Can you hear me? Do you have a gun?'

Why, yes. Of course I do. It's in the back of the truck along with the machine guns and flame-thrower. 'No,' I managed to say as they handcuffed my wrists *and* thumbs before lifting me up and bundling me into the back of a car, one of six that had cordoned off the top and bottom of the street, preventing movement.

'You know who we are?' inquired the same voice, this time much calmer.

The rain came in force, banging against the car, making it sound like hollow tin. It made me think of the dole, Sundays in Belfast, the RUC, and Celtic beaten by Rangers. A million other horrors that only rain can conjure up.

The repetitive voice went on and on: DO DO DO YOU YOU YOU KNOW KNOW KNOW WHO WHO WHO WE WE WE ARE ARE ARE . . . ?

The normal 45-to-60 minute drive into Manhattan took less than twenty minutes, as the convoy of cars, their sirens blaring, sliced through the buttery traffic like a hot knife. At One Police Plaza, my hand and thumb-cuffs were removed as the bad cop good cop was insultingly brought into play.

'We're givin' ya the chance to get down first, Sam, because ya've gotta wife 'n' kids,' said the beefy Fed, attired in a college blazer, shirt and tie.

At that very moment, when he was so concerned about my family, his associates were smashing in the door of our home with a battering-ram, pointing their guns at the head of my nine-year-old daughter, screaming at her, 'Where is all your father's money! If you don't tell us we will take you away and you will never see your mother or father again!'

"Getting down first" is an American euphemism for informing on ones associates. The FBI has a 90 per cent success rate of convictions, mainly due to people turning informer against each other. It can all be summed up in the words of a spokesperson at the US Treasury Law Enforcement Academy explaining to new recruits: *"Gentlemen, in this business, you're only as good as your rats."*

'Don't be a fall-guy for the rest of 'em,' advised Good Cop. 'We've already got Maloney, O'Connor and McCormack. They'll spill their guts out if you refuse our one-time offer.' He got up from the chair and opened the door. 'Listen.'

From next door, I could hear Pat talking away, like a parrot. It sounded all dark and whispery. But he wasn't trying to "get down first". Far from it. He was simply maintaining his innocence and stating a fact that he had never heard of this man O'Connor or Simmy Mullar, as a Bostonian-twanged FBI man had pronounced my name.

What was really baffling was the McCormack. Who the hell was he?

'Maloney's begging us to let him get down first, but you're married – just like me – and I don't want to see you go to the penitentiary for the rest of your life. Understand? Do you?'

He was so concerned about my welfare, it was almost touching. *The RUC would have a field day with these guys*, I thought, as Bad Cop entered the room. If I wasn't careful, he might force me to listen to Country and Western or blow smoke into my eyes, something really terrible.

While the Feds were telling me that Pat was spilling out his guts, and vice versa, in Rochester, they were telling Tom he was *"on a sinking ship. Your two friends down in New York have said you were the mastermind"*.

'Listen, you dumb mick,' said Bad Cop, an inch from my face. 'Where you're goin' to be spendin' the rest of your life is in the arms of a big fuckin' nigger, fuckin' you in the ass, night and day – and three times between meals, and he'll make you floss with his dick. Do you understand *that*?'

I remembered that line from a movie, but couldn't quite remember which one. I wondered if Bad Cop would tell me if I asked. All the Feds seemed to have Irish sounding names, with large "O's" stage-coached between them.

The "interrogation" went on for about an hour at the end of which Bad Cop and Good Cop left, mystified at not having their "offer" jumped at by either Pat or myself or the mysterious McCormack. As a last resort, one of the Feds showed me a note they had taken from Pat, throwing it down on the table, contemptuously.

'Is that what a priest carries with him, in his pocket? You should be ashamed of him, not protecting him.'

I glanced at the note, but quickly erased it from my thoughts. I would talk to Pat, later, about it. Right now I wasn't playing their game. The mirror in front of me, I presumed, was two-way and that a handful of Feds stood behind it, analysing my expression.

I remained alone for about fifteen minutes, when in walked the black man who had shadowed me for so long, munching a Hero sandwich in his hand. He didn't speak for some time, simply contented to munch, licking his lips with delight – at the sandwich or capture, was hard to tell. He studied me for a minute, oblivious of the mayonnaise falling on his shirt.

'My name is Louis Stith, Special Agent and leading investigator for the Federal Bureau of Investigation.' He waited for my reaction. When none was forthcoming, he continued. 'Between you and me, off the record, when did you start to suspect I was following you?' His voice was very low as he continued the self-conversation. 'I think I screwed up at the elevator, that day. Remember? You refused to get in with me? Was that it? Did you suspect I was FBI?' He smiled.

The only thing I wanted to tell him was how the other feds referred to him as "that boy". That, plus he had some lettuce trapped in his teeth. I stared at the two-way mirror, checking my own teeth.

'You know you will not survive our prison system, don't you? It's not like those pussy British prisons that you came from, everyone answerable to some Human Rights group.'

I wondered what brochure he had found *that* one in, but quickly realised he was simply goading me for an answer – any answer – to break the silence, to prove that all his years of training, his law degree, his belief in himself, could bring home the bacon. I hated to disappoint him, but he wasn't frying tonight . . . or any night.

For the next twenty or 30 minutes I had to endure his soliloquy until, resigned, he got up, shaking his head, mumbling, 'You're a mystery. I'll see you in court.'

What really was a mystery, I realised shortly afterwards, was what had happened to the $30,000 that had occupied my pocket for such a short period? It was a mystery never to be solved, at least not by me.

Shortly after our "discussion", I was removed from One Police Plaza to the court. In the elevator, Pat was placed beside me. We didn't speak. The elevator stopped at another floor and a young man stepped in. Just like Pat and myself, he also was handcuffed. I presumed he was simply another prisoner about to be charged in the court, same as us, and was shocked when he sat beside us at the table. Was he an undercover Fed, still trying their luck to obtain some information? I slowly eased away from him as if he were a leper.

I was even more shocked when the young man, whom I had never before seen, was charged along with us. I glanced at Pat with a what-the-fuck's-going-on look on my face but he simply ignored me, correctly so, under the circumstances. A few minutes later and the mystery was cleared up, if only a little bit.

The young man's name was Charlie McCormack, a schoolteacher. He was the owner of the apartment, not Pat. He had been out of the country, visiting family and had asked Pat to keep an eye on the place for him. Fuck! I almost pissed myself laughing at the irony of that. *Sure I'll keep a good eye on it for you, and you don't mind, do you, if I leave a few million scattered about while you're gone?*

Shortly after the hearing, Pat was granted bail. Charlie had the charges withdrawn after Pat admitted that Charlie knew nothing about the money. As for myself, I was quickly introduced to what is fearfully known amongst American Federal prisoners as "diesel therapy".

Diesel therapy is the name given to the mental and physical torture of prisoners whom the government is desperate to break in the hope of securing a confession or obtaining some vital information that can be used in court at a later stage. This punitive travail consists of moving the prisoner from prison to prison – as much as three times a day – disorientating and isolating him in the process, breaking down his resistance.

I'd been taken down this road before . . .

I was shackled, hands and feet, with only a jump suit to help stave off the elements of winter. After a seven hour "journey" in the back of a converted pick-up truck, ball-freezing, I would arrive at a prison, usually at about 2.00 or 3.00 in the morning, gratefully receiving a bed pack, just wanting to sleep. No sooner would I have my bed made when a guard would shout for me to get dressed, I was being moved again. This time I'd be hoisted aboard a bus that had been stripped of all its "comforts", legs chained to the floor along with fifteen to twenty prisoners, and told in no uncertain terms by the shotgun-hugging guard what would happen if even the *word* escape entered our tiny brains.

The bus drove us all the way back to Manhattan, past all the hookers on Tenth Avenue who waved and shouted at the zombies inside. Zombies. That's what we had all been relegated to, a scene from *One Flew Over The Cuckoo's Nest*. The diet of spam sandwiches and watered milk, twice a day, didn't help. I didn't care. All I wanted was sleep. But the lights from the tiny spotlights above our heads, combined with the canned C and W music blaring, made sleeping impossible. I promised myself to never again listen to Jim Reeves.

When we reached the prison, the bed-pack was once again handed to me. I went through the routine, making the bed, picturing what it might be like to be between the sheets, waking up in my house, realising that this had all been some sort of terrible nightmare.

But enough of that! It was time, once again, shouted the guard, for my scenic trip to Upstate New York and to wonder at the beauty of snow-capped mountains and shivering trees naked of leaves. And when the two armed guards stopped at *McDonald's* for Big Macs, hot fries and coffee, leaving me shivering in the back of the pick-up without shoes or socks, I thought I had earned, at least, a Happy Meal for my endurance.

I watched as they came back, squeezing their massive bulks into the seats, checking that I was still there. I could hear them turn on the heat full blast, knowing the glass panel prevented me from benefiting from it.

'How do you like your coffee, Sam?' said the smallest giant, a smirk on his face.

I wanted to give him a smart answer, but my teeth refused to stop chattering.

'Here. You're gonna have to drink cuffed and in motion. Understand? If it burns your balls off, you can't sue us, or *McDonald's*. Understand?'

They were both laughing now, unwrapping the fiendish spam sandwich and watered milk. My stomach was turning at the thought of one more pink and white.

'Here.' He opened the glass panel, and even though the heat

blasted in I couldn't feel a thing; not even the hot, beautiful coffee that burnt my greedy lips or the salty taste of fries in my mouth could be tasted. They left the panel open for the remainder of the journey, thawing me out as night trucks skimmed past us, their headlights colouring us.

I was all roasty-toasty now, as eye-lids became heavier and heavier. Fatigue slowly seeped through me while the two guards talked in a whisper, as if not wanting to disturb me. We could easily have been three buddies venturing out on a hunting trip, except for the fact that they had already captured their quarry.

Tiny spikes of insomnia interrupted my flow of sleep, but these were mercifully few. These were the bad days of diesel therapy, a testing time of things to come. I slept, if that's what it could be called, for the first time in over three weeks with the taste of salt and coffee in my mouth.

37

A Lawyer. A very expensive one

January 1994

"Now I lay me down to sleep . . ."
ANONYMOUS

The diesel therapy continued, unabated, for three more months until my lawyer, Anthony F Leonardo, finally was able to put a stop to it, getting a court order to have me housed in the Monroe County Prison, affectionately known as the House of Pain, where I stayed for the next two years awaiting trial. The billboard as I entered Rochester said *welcome and we hope you enjoy your stay*. This time *she* winked at *me: Thought ya'd be back . . .*

Tony was a high profile lawyer who loved the burn from publicity and dressed impeccably for it. An imposing a 6 foot 4 and more than 200 pounds, he looked every bit the part of the Hollywood lawyer. His father, Anthony F Leonardo Sr, had been a police detective with a reputation for being street savvy and tough as they came, a legend in the police force with the nickname "Captain Fearless". From 1985-6, Tony had won five straight homicide acquittals and in 1991 he had been asked to represent John Gotti, the reputed Mafia boss. In addition David Bowie asked Tony to represent him when accused of possessing marijuana, the charges eventually dropped.

'How long am I looking at?' was the first question I put to him, knowing it was probably 30 to 40 years, to which he quickly and tersely answered, 'Don't ever ask that again. We're beating this. That's all you need to keep in your head. Now tell me about this priest . . .'

He sat there as I relayed all I knew about Pat, explaining all the work he had done for the poor, and how he had nothing to do with the robbery.

'Bullshit. Did you put a gun to his head?'

'No. Of course not. But –'

'What was he doing with almost 200 grand hidden in his bedroom?'

This was the first I had heard about the money in Pat's bedroom, and it showed.

'I gave it to him . . . to pay someone off.'

'Then why was your face shocked when I asked you that?'

Because Pat had told me he had given the money to Ronnie. But that was only $100,000. Where did the rest come from?

'That's none of your business.'

Tony eased himself from the chair and stood over me. 'Look, let me make this as clear as possible. Everything to do with this case *is* my business, my reputation, and your freedom. Now I don't know how they do things in Ireland, but over here you play by my rules. I've destroyed the Feds so many times in court they hate my guts. They've even tried to set me up, but that's another story. If you want me to represent you, then you better think long and hard, because once I take a case, it becomes personal. I want to beat these people almost as much as you. Now, I know you're tired after all that travelling, so I'm going to let you sleep on it for a while. I'll see you on Tuesday.'

He put out his hand and I shook it, not knowing if I really wanted him, after all. Before he left, his nostrils took in the smell of "dinner".

'Meatloaf.' He made a face. 'Only in here could they make it smell like shit.'

I slept that night, for the first time in almost three months, undisturbed for sixteen hours, free from the monster of diesel therapy. It was the greatest sleep of my life.

38

Hey! What the hell are you doing with all those bags?

Spring-Summer 1994

"Always suspect everybody."
DICKENS, *The Old Curiosity Shop*

As the weeks turned to months, Tony began to accumulate small amounts of the prosecution's discovery – evidence – against me. Each visit was like waiting for an executioner as he explained that the prosecution had all these pieces of an enormous jigsaw puzzle sitting in their office, slowly being shaped to what fitted where. They needed that picture to show the jury. The clearer the picture, the easier the chances of securing a conviction.

'There are a few other, tiny, but not unimportant bits of the puzzle sitting in their lap,' he stated, sitting down at the table, placing his briefcase on top. 'They've traced your job in Park Avenue as a doorman. They know that you were absent on the night of the robbery.' Before I could open my mouth, he delivered a knockout punch. 'They've got tire marks from the van that was used on the night of the robbery. Just like fingerprints.'

'Fuck . . .' was all I managed to say.

'And, they claim, to have the tires.'

He watched my reaction as my mind flashed back to a *McDonald's* and grinning cops not believing their luck. My stomach felt heavy. I had known all along it was hopeless. Tony had simply confirmed it.

I started hating his visits. He was worse than the Angel of Death. 'Do you ever bring good news to your clients?' I asked.

'Analysis revealed that there were similar characteristics between the recovered tires and the photographs taken of tire marks at Drink's. Similar, but not identical. That's a very big plus for us.' He smiled. 'I haven't even begun to fight back yet, and those cock-suckers know it. They're frightened of me – and for good reason. Right now, at this very minute, they're sitting over in their warm office wondering if all these pieces will fit nice and snugly for them. Their jobs are on the line: their careers. They see this case as a ladder to further themselves, maybe in politics, perhaps with some big Wall-Street firm. Between you and me, Sam, I'm going to do my best to ensure that their dreams never materialize.'

He then started to explain how much effort the Feds had put into the case. 'Officially, 40 FBI agents were on the case, watching all of you at all times totalling 20,000 man hours. Another 60 were brought in intermittently when needed. The FBI has more than 100 alleged "witnesses", some from as far away as California and Florida. This isn't counting the dozens of FBI and New York detectives.'

Why was he filling me with this death-row talk? Was he secretly a sadist, laughing at the look of defeat on my face?

'I know,' he continued, as if reading my mind, 'that this may all seem overwhelming, disconcerting to you, but you must believe me when I say we have a chance of beating this. Initially, there was a lot of infighting between the New York Feds and the Upstate ones. Everyone wanted the glory of the case because of the high publicity surrounding it. An FBI agent has already admitted this to me.' He smiled, a Christopher-Lee-type smile. 'Would you believe the Feds from New York called the Feds up here "rednecks and hillbillies" when the decision was made to allow them to take the case? I can assure you that *that* didn't go down too well.'

He knew, by reputation, the prosecuting attorneys, Christopher Buscaglia and Christopher Taffe. 'They are both hardworking and meticulous to detail, but they are under a lot of pressure from their boss, Patrick NeMoyer, US attorney for the Western District of New York, to come up with a conviction. A lot is at stake here. Not just your freedom, but also the reputation of the FBI – especially the local ones. If they fail, then the Big City Feds will have been vindicated.

He brought some other pieces of news with him. 'The Feds have rearrested the teacher, McCormack. These pricks know the poor guy is totally innocent, but they want to ironclad their conspiracy theory for the jury. The more charged, the better it looks for them. But it all so tells us that they are not 100 per cent confident. This can help us in the long run. I mean, I feel for the poor guy, but it shows how desperate they have become with all the pressure mounting.'

Charlie's fingerprint had allegedly been found on a piece of cardboard. The simple reason being he lived in the apartment and his fingerprints would have been everywhere, including an old piece of cardboard that we had taken from beneath the sink to do some scribbling on. The Feds, of course, knew this. Knew, in all probability, that Charlie was totally innocent. That was something their conscience could overlook if it meant convictions for the rest of us.

'I thought we were the ones under pressure?'

He ignored this snide remark. 'One of the witnesses for the Feds, Louis Niger, apparently jumped to his death, last night, in very suspicious circumstances. He was the barman who called the ambulance for O'Connor the night he was abducted, and helped him to a barstool after a stiff shot of *Southern Comfort*.'

'Will it help or hinder us?' I asked callously, not worrying for a minute about the unfortunate man.

'Time will tell the answer,' replied Tony, slightly less callous. 'Now, if all the prosecution's witnesses were to follow the same path . . .' He grinned, and once again Christopher Lee came to mind. 'O'Connor invoked the Fifth Amendment when placed in front of the Federal Grand Jury. He declined a polygraph test, also. Anyway, in a few minutes you'll be taking a walk with me over to the Kenneth B Keating Building. That's where the trial will be held. I want you to study the video tapes the Feds have of you and your buddy Maloney.'

'Video tapes?'

'Oh. I thought I'd told you about them. They've hundreds of hours of tape allegedly of you and Maloney leaving and entering the apartment.'

I must have turned white, because he laughed and said, 'Don't worry. It doesn't prove too much against you. But I'm sure Maloney will have some explaining to do . . .'

Over at the courthouse, I sat down in a tiny room while Tony rolled out a massive TV complete with VCR.

'Sorry, Sam. No popcorn, I'm afraid,' he said, laughing. He was laughing just a wee bit *too* much for me at that particular moment in time. It seemed very peculiar.

The screen came to life and there I was, my Belfast dander, walking in and out of the apartment, not a fucking care in the world. I felt myself go red. Sweat was trickling down my back. What a dick, not even knowing they had been watching me. I wanted Tony to turn it off.

'Wait. It only gets better,' he assured me, grinning.

Turn the TV off and *that* fucking *grin*, also, please.

Now it was Pat's turn, walking up to the apartment door, disappearing inside. Suddenly, Tony fast-forwarded one of the tapes. 'Watch this.'

The tape was dated four days later after we first entered the apartment. Pat could be seen coming into the corridor, looking about. I thought nothing of it until the two black men appeared beside him, carrying empty bags under their arms.

'What the fuck is goin' on?' I said out loud, baffled by the presence of the two men. I hadn't known Pat had told anyone about the apartment. What was he playing at?

Tony froze the picture and flicked on the light. 'I take it they weren't part of the plan?' he asked. 'Do you recognize any of them?'

'No,' I said, livid.

'Okay. Let's get it over with,' he replied, turning the lights back off.

It was the same day on the tape, about an hour later. I could see the door open and Pat's head popping out slowly. Then came his two friends, carrying bags – full-to-the-brim bags. *Like a nice hot cup o' tea.*

'I don't fuckin' believe this!' I wanted to put my foot through the screen.

'The scene repeats itself, Sam, over the next two days of taping. In and out with empty bags, leaving with full ones. Would you like to see them?'

I sat in silence for a few moments, then said, 'No . . . I've seen enough . . .'

As Tony cleared away the TV, he explained that this would all be shown at the trial, for the benefit of the jury. 'Make the Feds look professional. Show people where all their tax money goes. The jury will be watching your reaction, so it's imperative that you remain calm, expressionless.'

It really didn't matter any more. I didn't care. It was bad enough that Pat hadn't given Ronnie the money, now he had this to explain.

'We have to be careful how we handle this guy,' advised Tony, reading my thoughts. 'We don't want to alienate him at this crucial moment, lest he does something. His hairs were all over the place as were his fingerprints. The ink used to write down the money totals was quickly traced to pens he kept in the church. An

Empire Safe located in his bedroom contained thousands of dollars. The list is endless.'

It was all becoming clear now. For months Pat had kept writing to me, asking – *telling* – me to drop Tony as my lawyer. He didn't trust him, he said. He had heard a few things about him. If I dropped him, Pat would get me another lawyer, one who would work hard to get us all free. Not like this "shyster" who was only after fame and money.

I had almost believed him.

He had even asked that we petition the court for a change of venue, to be moved back to New York City where we had been arrested. He claimed his health was suffering from having to make the eight-hour journey up to Rochester each time he had to appear in court. But more importantly, a trial down in liberal New York would grant us a far better chance of beating the whole thing than that redneck cop-town of Rochester.

God! I had almost succumbed! A few weeks ago I had contemplated dropping Tony just to please Pat, hoping to keep us united for the trial. It wasn't that he didn't trust Tony; he simply feared him. He knew, by now, that Tony would leave no stone unturned to get me off. He must have known, also, how angry I would have been at seeing the tapes.

'Look on the bright side, Sam,' said Tony as I prepared to return to the jail. 'You're only on the video twice, and with nothing in your hands. Maloney is the one who will have to explain to the jury what was in all those stuffed bags. My guess is he won't take the stand for fear of incriminating himself. Want to bet?'

'I would, except you and the Feds have taken every dollar I have.'

He laughed. I almost cried.

'Confidence. Have confidence. Oh, did I tell you that some guy from Buffalo is suing *Brink's*? He claims he squealed on O'Connor but never received a cent from the reward money. What a scumbag! If there's one thing I hate, it's rats – the human kind. I suppose I'm a bit like Indiana Jones.' He smiled, and I waited for him to produce a whip. 'Anyway, remember the key word: Confidence,' he said, waving goodbye.

Confidence? Why was I not filled with any, I wondered as I was escorted back to my cell by a cop/guard who kept reminding me I had the best lawyer in Upstate New York, and that I should be grateful he was willing to take me as a client. How did this cop/guard know that Tony was the best lawyer in upstate New York? Simple: he had been one of Tony's clients, also.

'Some niggers claimed me and six other cops in town violated their civil rights by slappin' them about a bit. Can ya fuckin' believe these people? Aim a shotgun at your face and *we're* the violators?'

I remained silent for a while. I was having a rough enough time without getting the cops in the jail to make it any harder by expressing any liberal views of disgust.

'So you beat the rap?' I asked eventually, trying to keep out of my cell for as long as possible. It was like stealing time from the Feds.

He grinned. 'We all beat the rap *and* the niggers. You'll do well by Tony. He's the fuckin' best lawyer in the world.'

The subsequent weeks and months following the TV screening saw a dent in the "united front" we had initially established. Pat and I barely spoke a word to each other. I began to receive hate-mail from some of his supporters, accusing me of "duping" him into the mess he was now in. Nonsense, of course, but he did little to dispel such notions. It suited him perfectly, the gullible martyr. It was beginning to gall me. I had done my best to give him a plausible excuse for getting involved, giving my gambling history to his lawyers in the hope it might secure his release, despite the fact that Tony went ballistic on hearing what I was doing.

But once Pat started to claim he knew nothing about where the money came from or, as some of his starry-eyed supporters claimed, that perhaps the money was "going to Ireland" and that he had been duped, then it was time for me to defend myself. If they thought he had being duped, then why did he go with me to purchase a $300,000 house? He claimed the money found in his bedroom – almost $200,000 – came from illegal aliens! Surveillance notes had recorded Pat giving out money like Santa. $3000 here, $5000 there, $8000 to Jason, a young man he had adopted. He also attempted to deposit $21,000 in cash at a bank in Florida but thought better of it when told by the bank official that he would have to fill in a Currency Transaction Report; other names popped up at an alarming rate, all given large amounts of money.

One of the many letters I received was from a nun who declared that "You will be going to Hell very soon, unless you repent your terrible sin against Father Pat". I wrote back that I had already been there and it wasn't such a bad place after all, *thank you very much*.

It was all becoming clear why he had wanted me to drop Tony for a lawyer of his preference. But it was all too late. The chickens were coming home.

'Have you heard of William Sherman?' asked Tony as we sorted through tiny mountains of legal papers in a tiny office in the county jail.

'The name sounds familiar. Didn't he win the –'

'He's a famous writer who won the Pulitzer, along with a load of other awards. Anyway, he has asked me to allow you to collaborate on an article for *Esquire* magazine. He says it will be sympathetic to you, put a "human face" on you for his readers. What do you think?'

'I kind of like the face I already have. But I don't know about doin' interviews. Isn't there always the possibility of saying the wrong thing?'

'You've echoed my thoughts exactly,' said Tony. But I thought I detected a slight disappointment in his voice. Did he see his smiling face on the cover? 'It *would* be a blunder. That's why I've recommended to the priest's attorney that his client refuse, say nothing that may jeopardize everyone. Why are you grinning?'

'You don't know Pat. He'll love all this, all the publicity. There's not a hope of him sayin' no.' And perhaps Tony didn't want either of Pat's lawyers on the cover either!

'Well, I think you're wrong. I've convinced his lawyer of the folly of it. I was pretty adamant about it. I doubt if it will go ahead.'

The article, two months later, was titled "Blood Money" and almost every page carried a picture of a grinning Pat.

'I can't fucking believe this guy!' shouted Tony, throwing the magazine on the table. 'He's trying to get us all hanged. The Feds love this sort of shit. What a fucking asshole! Can no one speak to this guy? Ask him to shut his mouth?'

No, not Pat. He loved it; even if it damaged our case he would still continue talking to reporters. And the Feds loved it. Sooner or later he would say something incriminating.

'We'll weather this one, Sam. I'll personally go down to New York and speak to Maloney.'

Tony needn't have bothered. There was more to come. Pat was now on the TV, giving interviews to all the well-known celebrity chat-show hosts, radio stations and newspapers. There was no stopping him now, I thought, as I watched him carry a child in his arms, for the cameras. He could have been a senator running for office, a fire-fighter saving a child from a burning building. Even the *Late Night Show* wanted him. And when I phoned him on one rare occasion, asking him to tone it all down, he simply told me not to worry, Hollywood would pay for everything.

I put it all down to a nervous breakdown, the strain, and the pressure.

Tony was less diplomatic. 'He's full of shit. He thinks the more people hear him, the more they'll believe him. Our only concern is what twelve people think . . . not David-fucking-Letterman.'

It was then that Tony hit me with a devastating piece of bad news.

'The Feds have arrested Bernie.'

He spoke so softly I could barely hear what he had just said. 'What did you say?'

'Look, there's no easy way to say this. The Feds ordered Bernie to appear at the grand jury this morning to give evidence against you, to give an account of anything she allegedly knew about the robbery. She refused to testify, citing the spousal-testimonial privilege which excuses spouses from offering adverse testimony against their partners.'

Bernadette's first marriage had lasted only months and had been annulled by the Catholic Church after a long battle from us. She had been my common-law wife of ten years as we were still having problems in the North over divorce procedures.

'What the fuck happened? Why has she been arrested?' I was frantic, despite trying to remain calm.

'New York does not recognise common-law marriages, but exceptions are made for those that began elsewhere, in a place where common-law unions are legally recognised. Judge Larimer said after researching the law, he did not believe such relationships are recognised in the North of Ireland.'

'That fuckin' cunt! What the fuck would he know about the North!'

'He told Bernie he didn't relish this proceeding. But he must hold her in contempt if she still refused to testify. She refused and was led away.'

'No. I can't allow this. We've three kids. What will happen to them? No way will I go along with this.'

'You can't allow the Feds to get to you,' said Tony, trying to instil something into my misery. 'This is how they work. You're stronger than they are. Now they think they can get to you through Bernie. They know she knows nothing, just like McCormack. But they're desperate, Sam. Believe me, you don't know *how* desperate.'

At that moment, I was rock bottom. Tony knew in my state of mind I was no longer thinking rationally. He didn't want to leave the room.

'Listen. Bernie has an excellent lawyer, Robert Napier. He's a fighter, just like me. Neither of us will sleep until we overturn this. You have my word on that. But I need your word that you will stay strong. Deal?'

I muttered an agreement that he could live with. Lucky for him I had yet to see a copy of the evening's newspaper with Bernie on the front page, handcuffed, being led away by federal agents: 'Under no circumstances will Bernadette agree to answer questions about Sam. They are in all ways, spiritually and emotionally, married people. She will not violate that relationship in any way,' said Robert Napier sombrely, to the awaiting reporters. 'A jail-house wedding ceremony appears to be the best option for her early release.'

It made little difference that Tony repeated to me each day: 'We think we have something . . . this could work. I told you this guy was good . . .' I knew he was simply stalling me, trying to keep me focused. 'I've got to tell you this, and it's no bullshit. But the Feds have a grudging respect for you, they're hitting you with every single thing they can and you're still standing. I've talked to a few of them and they are totally baffled by your action. They know if you'd been an American, you'd have collapsed a long time ago.'

'Is that suppose to be a compliment?'

'In a backhanded way, yes.'

'Well, the next time you're talkin' to your great buddies over at the Feds, tell them I said to stick their compliments up their hole. Okay?'

He left before I could deteriorate any further. His remedy was having the opposite of the effect desired.

Eventually, one month later, after obtaining proof of our relationship in Ireland by way of a divorce decree it was presented to the court and studied by Judge Larimer. Bernie's lawyer asked the judge to vacate the contempt order so that she could apply for a marriage licence at Rochester City Hall.

'Four kids and ten years together speaks for itself in my mind,' argued Napier, studying the judge's expressionless face.

'This puts me in a Cupid-like position,' said Larimer, studying the documents. 'But I approve it, and I wish the couple happiness on their wedding day.'

'Didn't I tell you he was a fair judge?' claimed Tony, later that day, all smiles.

I said nothing, just savoured the moment. A great weight had been lifted.

'A fair judge,' reiterated Tony, not knowing, at that moment in time, that soon he and the judge would be at each other's throats and making all the headlines.

39

Our Strategy

October 1994

"The investigation has run to over $1,000,000 so far
– and that's not counting the trial."
DEAN ANDERSON, spokesman for the FBI

Before the trial began, a process of jury selection was implemented.

'Are you kidding me? *We* get to select the jury?' I asked Tony, as we all sat in a tiny strategy room, over in the Kenneth B Keating Building, mapping out the best strategy to beat the charges.

'More or less. The prosecution gets to pick some, we get some. They get a couple of chances to bar the ones whom they believe to be biased in our favour, and vice versa. It's all very democratic. Not like back where you come from.'

We all sat in the room with our lawyers, fiddling with notepads. Pat had *both* his lawyers, Charlie had his, as did Tom. Tony began his ideal profile of potential jurors. He believed the personalities, beliefs and opinions of potential jurors could be crucial at the end of the day. 'No blacks on the jury,' argued Tony. 'They're out to prove they're tough on crime because they're frightened of being stereotyped as criminals themselves. I'd put twelve blacks on the jury if I thought they'd be sympathetic, but I can tell you now, they'd be a disaster.'

The other lawyers wrote something down, neither agreeing nor disagreeing. Everything would be ironed out, later. Someone suggested that this being a cop town, perhaps getting relatives of law-enforcement people on the jury might be a plus for Tom. There was laughter at this.

'No,' advised Tony. 'They'd be like the blacks, out to prove that not all cops, and I'm not implying anything by this, Tom, are corrupt.'

Tom just smiled his Gary Cooper smile.

'Also,' continued Tony, 'I recommend that we try and get all females on the jury. We have four good-looking guys here and no all-female jury will convict.'

More laughter.

'That's not going to happen. The Feds would see right through that. In addition, there is no proof that it will work, Tony. I personally don't subscribe to the jury profile theory. The whole case could explode in our faces,' said an unconvinced lawyer, staring at Tony over half-moon glasses. 'Besides, women can be more prosecutorial than men. Picking all women . . . and I doubt if we can do it, might just backfire on us. It's a big risk that could turn everything into an unmitigated disaster.'

Tony laughed. 'Are you kidding? You're telling me, put twelve women in a room, for maybe two months and they're still friends? By the end of this trial they'll be killing each other. The least we can expect is a hung jury.'

'Or hung clients.' Tiny laughter.

'It can't work. The Feds will not allow it to happen,' stated Felix, Tom's lawyer.

'It's up to us to *make* it happen,' replied Tony, calmly. 'And I'm going to give it my best shot. What about the rest of you?'

'I think our biggest problem is Buscaglia. There's nothing flashy about him but he keeps coming at you like a glacier,' said Felix.

John Speranza, Charlie's attorney, summed his own feelings up. 'The conspiracy statute gives considerable leeway to prosecutors in linking defendants in a conspiracy. It takes into account the whales and the minnows. The net is a fine net, and it's very broad.'

The debate went on for two more hours, each lawyer voicing his concern, each trying to map out a strategy beneficial to all, yet keeping their client's acquittal at the top of the list. It would be a thin tightrope to be walked and I doubted very much if any person in that room believed we would all stick to the selected path. We could only wait and see when jury selection began in earnest.

I wanted to talk to Tom, apologise for the mess I had placed him in, but Tony advised against it. 'The less you communicate with other defendants, the better it'll be in the long run. O'Connor's a big boy. He'll understand . . .'

40

Jury Selection

2 October 1994

*"The court is obliged to submit the case fairly, but let the jury
do the deciding."*

CHEKHOV

Each potential juror was brought in individually and asked to sit
in front of us while our lawyers fired questioned at him or her.
Most looked nervous to me, dreading the "interrogation", but
Tony told me not to be fooled by appearances. 'Oh, they want to
be on this trial. Make no mistake about that. This is probably the
most exciting thing to happen to them in all their life, something
to tell their grandchildren.'

The first hopeful walked in, spoke his name, sat down. He was
covered in gold, from head to toe. Tony quickly ran a line
through his name on the list. 'Maybe *he* was the one who robbed
the *Brink's!*' whispered Tony, trying not laugh.

Another was a toolmaker. He was quickly disposed of for fear
of knowing too much about the *Brink's* security.

247

One had a sheriff for a cousin. Everyone quickly shook their heads.

Get him out of here!

Another potential had a father who had worked for *Brink's* and had been a "model employee".

Goodbye.

The prosecution asked a female if, as a Catholic she could convict a priest if she thought he was guilty. She looked at Pat for a few moments, studying his face. Pat stared straight at her gaze, his back stiff, fingers slowly rubbing his "worry beads".

'Yes. I could. If he were guilty . . .'

Pat sagged and his lawyers moved quickly to have the woman's name removed.

'Don't be too hasty,' whispered Tony to the other lawyer. 'I think she could be fair. Something tells me the evidence would have to be overwhelming for her to convict. We may not have much of a choice as the list gets smaller. Think about it.'

After a few minutes of consultation between themselves and Pat, they decided to allow her to stay on the list.

One woman on, eleven to go . . .

Another male potential juror sat there without a blush telling us he hadn't heard about the *Brink's* case. 'Can you believe this guy?' whispered Tony as he quickly scribbled Mister Never Heard from the list. 'I know some of them are desperate to get on the jury for their 60 seconds of fame, but you'd think they'd come up with something original.'

Another woman, immaculately dressed, sat down on the seat that Never Heard's arse had just warmed. Her expression gave little away, and the routine questions directed at her were answered thoughtfully, yet almost indifferently. She would be next on the list. I had no doubt about that. Then came the shocker. 'You have a nephew in the police force. Is that true?' asked Felix.

There was complete silence. The woman's face wasn't moving.

'Is that true?' asked Felix, once again. He balanced a pencil between two fingers and a tiny smile appeared on his face.

'Yes. That's true,' replied the woman, breaking the silence.

'And your husband? He's a retired police officer?'

'Yes.' There was a hint of pride in her voice at this.

'In all honesty, you would not look too kindly on policemen who allegedly broke the law. Would you?'

She didn't miss a beat. 'No, sir. I wouldn't,' came the honest reply.

'Thank you for your candour, Madam. Your honour, I move to have her name removed from the list.' The prosecution tried to retain the woman, for obvious reasons, but to no avail. The judge ruled in Felix's favour.

The day progressed slowly; a name dropped here, one added there. The novelty was wearing off and everyone – judge included – was getting a bad dose of itchy arse, wiggling in his or her seat, trying to stay focused.

'How much longer?' I asked Tony.

'As long as it takes to get what *we* want. All week, if necessary. Any problems, seeing as how we are doing it for you?' Christopher Lee was back with an acerbic tongue.

'No. Of course not. I appreciate it.'

Eventually, all the men were out. I couldn't – nor anyone else – believe the prosecution team were letting us get away with it. Maybe they had the same plan, believing women would be more sympathetic to them. Whatever the reason, when the twelve women were finally selected the newspapers gave it their undivided attention making the Feds feel foolish.

They had walked into the trap set by Tony and the other lawyers. Trying to regain some lost ground, the prosecutors quickly asked the judge to review the choices the lawyers made in selecting an all-female jury in that men had been discriminated against. After a closed-door session, Judge Larimer said he had extensively reviewed the choices and found no basis for the feds concern. The all-female jury would be sworn in the next day and the trial, after almost two years, would commence.

A last meeting with Tony prior to the trial brought me some news. 'Ten is the max you can get. But you will more than likely be given about eight years, *if* you are found guilty. Now this is the last time we discuss this. I'm going in there to win – so are you. I don't want to hear any more about doing time. Agreed?'

Eight years? I doubted if he was telling the truth. I could handle eight years, but I knew it must be in the region of 60. I tried not to think about dying in an American prison, but I had to be realistic. I put my smiling mask back on and shook his hand. 'I appreciate all that you've done, Tony, irrespective of what happens.'

'Get a good night's sleep. I want you to be looking your best for tomorrow.'

He smiled, and I wondered what was behind it. Did he know, deep down, what I was truly heading for? Soon it would be all over.

41

The Trial Begins

11 October 1994

"If it takes 100 witnesses to prove your case, you don't have one."

LAWRENCE ANDOLINA, New York Lawyer,
commenting on the trial

The courthouse was packed. There wasn't a seat to be had. The Press was allocated a certain number and our families and friends tried to squeeze into a few more. The remainder went to that breed of morbid people who have nothing in their life except the expectation of someone else's demise – the perverse high brought about by the fallen. The same type of "citizens" you would have found during the French Revolution, sitting with their knitting needles at the guillotine.

FBI agents were trouped in, conveyor belt mode, non-stop, by the prosecution. They were impeccably dressed and strolled down the centre of the room with the confidence of actors receiving an Oscar. Each read carefully from notebooks that had logged our movements over a ten-month period.

I tried to keep my thoughts elsewhere knowing what the

inevitable held. I wasn't going to sit there in self-mutilation, humiliated by all the mistakes I had made. Instead, I had gone fishing in the Waterworks in Belfast. I think my father was there, eating a big, thick strawberry-jam sandwich, giving me the thumbs-up. "Chin up, son. Don't let them get you down." I returned the thumbs-up, smiling –

Tony was nudging me. 'You've got to pay attention,' he hissed. 'And stop sitting there with that silly grin on your face. The jury might think you're not taking this seriously – or laughing at them.'

'Sorry,' I mumbled. 'Where are we at?'

'They're testifying about McCormack. About the sheet with all those amounts of money on it, allegedly in his hand writing.'

The "sheet" contained figures from an essay Charlie had written years previously in Fairfield University, for an accountancy class. In a strange twist of fate, the figures he had written all those years ago were almost identical to the amount of money taken from *Brink's*. This was enough to have him arrested by the feds on a conspiracy charge. It didn't help that the essay was titled *"For the Love of Money"* and jokingly signed, *"Jesus Christ Millionaire"*.

Of all the people at the table, Charlie was the only one I really felt sorry for. He didn't know what was happening to him. Every now and then his parents would stare over at Pat, ice in their eyes. Who could blame them? Not me. They probably felt the same way towards me. I would, if it were my son.

'I would like to call special agent . . .' The prosecution had an embarrassment of riches with the federal witnesses. Not only were they FBI, these were the elite "special" agents: the *unfuckingtouchables*. They knew what they were up against and sent only the best to capture us. The jury was becoming hypnotized each time the word "special" was mentioned. *Special* agent this, *special* agent that. You could see some of the women blush each time a "special" agent glanced in their direction. Suddenly, the prosecution wasn't looking so daft after all. They could beat us at our own game with new, "special" rules being brought in by the bucket load.

It was then, just as the tide was turning in the prosecution's favour, that Tony decided to burst *all* our bubbles. 'Special Agent Stith, you claim in your testimony that my client refused to enter the elevator after you were so kind to open the door for him. Is that true?'

'Yes, sir.'

The questioning of Stith lasted for about 40 minutes. Just as he was about to leave the stand Tony asked, '*All* agents of the FBI are titled "special", regardless of rank or experience. Is that true?'

Stith frowned at the question, but nodded.

'Is that a yes or a no, *special* Agent Stith?'

'Yes.'

'Thank you. No further questions for this witness . . . for now.'

As the days turned to weeks, speculation began to mount on which, if any, defendant would take the stand. Tom was already committed to testifying in his defence, as was Charlie. Only Pat and myself remained undecided, neither one of us allowing the other to peep over the fence to see if we had any aces up our sleeve.

'It never looks good if you refuse to take the stand,' said one of the lawyers during a well-deserved lull in the proceedings. 'Don't pay no heed to what you see on *Matlock*, that you're presumed innocent until proven guilty. A lot of bull. Each one of those twelve people is thinking the same: If he's truly innocent, why the hell isn't he up here telling us his side of the story? And you've got to admit, they do have a point.' He smiled, just as the trial recommenced and Danny Calemine, a New York City detective took the stand and testified to having seen Pat and myself come from a bar, drunk, staggering up the street!

I couldn't restrain myself. 'That's a lie,' I said to Tony, a bit too loud. Everyone knew Pat never touched a drop of alcohol, let alone be seen staggering in the street, drunk. He had probably never been to a bar in his entire life, and certainly not with me.

'Just let me do the questioning,' whispered Tony. 'Another outburst like that and they'll have you removed.'

'But the bastard's lying through his teeth. He's making it all up. You can't let him get away with this.'

Tony initially began his questioning of Calemine routinely enough, asking the usual mundane and predictable, nothing dramatic. How many years had he served in the force? Any medals for bravery? Was he having problems with his eyesight? And was he certain about having seen Pat and myself doing an Irish jig, drunk as two skunks on a Saturday night?

It was about this moment when the judge intervened by pointing his finger at Tony, saying, 'You know better . . . you're testifying.'

'Don't point your finger at me!' exploded Tony, spinning on one heel, glaring as he walked towards the judge.

Mouths dropped open. No one said a word. Everyone in the court – lawyers, prosecution, jury and public – looked on in amazement.

'You're a better lawyer than that,' said the judge, red spreading on his face.

'Judge, I would think you would be a better judge than to interrupt me. I'm going to protect my client's rights,' responded Tony.

'You'll be held in contempt of court for being flagrantly abusive to this court. We will take a short recess,' said the judge, obviously shaken, scowling from the bench. 'Mister Leonardo? I want to see you in my chamber.'

'Get a cell next to you ready for me,' whispered Tony. 'I might be over there tonight.'

Tony was already in trouble from a previous case for accepting $75,000 from a client without advising him to seek independent legal advice on the transaction. 'No court or jury should have to endure such rude, disrespectful conduct which infects the integrity of the entire judicial process,' said Larimer to Tony in the chamber. 'When I admonished you . . . you exploded and engaged in a lengthy tirade against the court. You violated the state Code of Professional Responsibility and federal rules. The reason I do not hold you in contempt immediately is the possibility of your client not getting a fair trial. But your conduct was so unprofessional and offensive that some action will be taken at a later stage.'

Tony smiled, as he emerged from the "meeting", relieved, but still defiant. He would now have to wait for the reply from the Appellate Division to find out if he would be suspended from practising law, or worse, disbarment.

'You've got to calm down, Tony,' I advised as he sat beside me. 'I don't want to be losing you at this late stage of the game.'

'Don't worry.'

'Still think he's a fair judge?' I asked, smiling, packing up to go back to the jailhouse.

'Hell, yes. He's just doing his job. I wouldn't have it any other way.'

The next day's proceedings began with Tom's lawyer questioning a representative from *Brink's Inc.*, getting him to admit that between $40,000,000 and $50,000,000 was sometimes kept in the Rochester depository on a Wednesday and that if it was an inside job – as the prosecution charged – wouldn't it be more sensible to raid the place on *that* particular night instead of the one in question?

Of course I knew the answer to that better than the representative. I had known about the vast amounts of money held on a Wednesday, but what would I have done with it? We could barely take the almost eight. How on earth could we have managed 40 – 50? Opting for the more "conservative" Tuesday was the only realistic option available to us.

The questioning of witnesses continued relentlessly throughout the day. The judge, at the end of his patience by the constant repetitive evidence demanded the prosecution speed up the process by eliminating all witnesses, with the exception of those with vital evidence. 'Enough is enough if we are to conclude this trial sometime this year.'

'Yes, your honour,' mumbled the prosecution, sheepishly, quickly leaving the room to inform the small army of agents, to their dismay, they might not all get to testify.

The next day, shortly before noon, mixed news came for Pat's attorneys. George Thompson, a private investigator for Pat's team informed them that he had been able to track down two people in New York who had worked at the casino, but that the INS had threatened one of them by checking if his Green Card was in order. He quickly disappeared from the scene. As for the other one, he would be willing to testify about the gambling provided he received word from me via Tony that it would not harm my defence.

Tony was adamant. 'No. We can't allow this guy to testify. The jury will see it as a pattern. I'm trying to make you out as this poor guy whose only sin was to believe the American dream and in walks this guy saying you were running illegal casinos in New York. Think about it, Sam. Maloney's team has to get him out of this mess, but not at your expense.'

But I was just as adamant. Despite his underhanded way and doing nothing to discourage the innuendoes, I still wanted to see Pat get out of this. 'Who is the witness?' I asked, curious.

'Patrick Farrelly.'

The prosecutors were taken totally by surprise. Typically, both sides share documents before a witness testifies. This gives either side the chance to do their homework for the cross-examination, and to prepare any relevant question for the witness. This time it did not happen, and the prosecution let their frustration be known.

'Your honour, we have had no notes of this witness given to us.'

Over the objections from the prosecutors and outside the

presence of the jury, Pat's lawyers asked the judge to allow them to present evidence about my work in the casinos. 'We believe our client thought any money that might have originated from Mister Millar may have come from the casino, your honour.'

'Your honour, lawyers for the defendants can not present evidence about one defendant's action to try to establish another defendant's state of mind. It's nonsense,' replied Buscaglia.

Larimer nodded, as if in agreement, but said, 'The court has to be very cautious about letting him put in his defence. I'll allow the witness.'

When Patrick took the stand, it was obvious he was anything but comfortable. He took a long drink of water and waited for Pat's attorney to commence questioning.

'What is your occupation, Mister Farrelly?'

'I'm a reporter for the *Village Voice.*'

'Have you had any other jobs involving journalism?'

'I was the editor of an Irish newspaper in New York.'

'Do you recognize any of the men sitting at that table, Mister Farrelly?'

Patrick looked at me, and then quickly glanced away before nodding.

'I'm sorry, Mister Farrelly, but you can't nod. A simple yes or no will do.'

'Yes. Mister Millar.'

'And where do you know Mister Millar from?'

'I was a journalist covering a story about illegal gambling casinos in the Irish community in New York. I managed to get a job in one of the casinos by way of a friend. I hoped my experience of working there would add authenticity to my article.'

'Could you please tell the court what role Mister Millar had in the running of this casino?'

Patrick looked at my impassive face before answering. 'He held the highest responsibility.'

'And what was that responsibility, Mister Farrelly?'

'He was the box manager.'

'The box manager? Could you explain to the court exactly what that means?'

'He was the one with sole access to all the money that was dropped into the boxes. He was the only one with the key to open the boxes.'

'How much money would be in these boxes at any given time?'

'Thousands of dollars.'

'What did Mister Millar do with all this money?'

'Normally he would count it along with the owner. Afterwards, it would be transferred out of the building by him to prevent the police from confiscating it in raids.'

'Did you personally see Mister Millar count the money.'

'Yes, on numerous occasions. Sometimes he'd send for a *Coke* or coffee. I worked as a barman in the casino and brought it to him quite a few times. He was always there with the owner. If the casino was having a tough night – losing a lot of money – he was the one to see. Didn't make any difference. It could be noon or 3.00 in the morning. He was the one that was sent to bring or take money. No one else.'

'That wasn't the total disaster I thought it might turn into,' said Tony as we prepared to leave the courtroom.

'Could've been worse,' I agreed, standing up.

'We're not going anywhere just yet. Clauss and Feldman are going to put a motion to the court.

'What kind of motion?'

'To have all the charges dropped.'

I laughed. I thought he was joking. 'You're not serious, of course.'

'Just wait and see.'

It was almost 3.00 pm when William Clauss and Jonathan Feldman, Pat's lawyers, dropped the bombshell.

'Your honour. We move to have all the charges dropped against the defendants.'

The prosecution seemed bemused.

'Under what grounds?' asked the judge.

'There is no proof that money was moved in interstate commerce. The prosecution has not offered a shred of evidence to support this, your honour.'

'Mister Buscaglia?'

'Your, honour, I believe we have brought more than enough evidence into the court to support and justify the charges. It would seem, to me, that this motion would be a waste of the court's time. Why was it not brought at the initial stage of the trial instead of now? I would strongly question the motive behind this motion.'

Judge Larimer fingered through some paper, peering intently at the words, studying them. 'Well, it's a bit late in the day to make a ruling, gentleman. I'll take these documents home with me and hopefully I'll have an answer for you tomorrow.'

'This isn't goin' to work,' I said to Tony before being escorted down the stairs. 'So what's the point?'

'Wait and see,' replied Tony, smiling. 'You heard the judge. Hopefully, he'll have an answer in the morning. Hopefully, it'll be the one we want.'

That night, I tortured myself, hoping against hope that perhaps the judge would suffer a bout of madness, dropping the charges. It was almost farcical, the motion. But this was America, not the North of Ireland. Who the hell knows what could happen over here. You read about it in the newspapers all the time. Why couldn't it happen for us?

I'll not sleep tonight . . .

'Did you sleep last night?' asked a grinning Tony as we sat down at the table. The courtroom was full, mostly with media wondering what the judge would rule. The noise was intolerable. I was irritable through lack of sleep.

'Like a baby,' I replied.

As the judge entered, the noise died and everyone rose in a Mexican wave.

'I have looked carefully at the motion forwarded by the defence. After long hours and meticulous studying of the Constitution, I rule in favour of the defence. The prosecution *failed* to prove that defendants O'Connor, Millar or Maloney, possessed stolen money that moved in interstate commerce. Furthermore, prosecutors failed to prove that the defendants possessed stolen money in the Western District of New York. The money had been found in New York City, the Southern District. The right to be tried in the venue where a crime allegedly occurred is cited twice in the Constitution. Charges Two and Three are dismissed.'

The ruling was a disaster for the prosecution and it clearly showed on their faces. In the belief that it would be easier to secure a conviction upstate, the prosecution had cut its own throat by removing us from New York City, violating our rights in the process. Pat, Charlie and myself now faced the lone charge of conspiracy. Tom's charge of actually committing the robbery, remained.

I was thankful Pat had not succeeded in having the trial held in New York for his own convenience. Had he succeeded, not one charge would have been dropped. I couldn't help but rub it in a wee bit. 'I hope you're happy now that you didn't get your wish,' I said. 'Good job Tony knew better.' He could only look at me sheepishly, relieved a major hurdle had been cleared.

Back in my cell I hovered from the ground, reading the late edition of the Rochester *Democrat and Chronicle*:

"Prosecution's case fading in Brink's trial."

Earlier today, prosecutors took a major blow when possession charges against Millar and Maloney were dropped in U.S. District Court for lack of evidence.

By all accounts, The Brink's Inc depot robbery case was one federal prosecutors here wanted.

Armed with a mountain of evidence, they lined up more than 100 witnesses, several flown in from as far away as Florida and California, not to mention the dozens of New York City FBI agents and detectives brought here to testify.

But there was a tug-of-war between the New York feds and the local feds . . . everyone wanted the glory . . . the prospect for glory, however, appears to be fading."

But there was still life left in the prosecution. In his final summing up, the next day, Buscaglia began by urging the jury, 'Use the common sense that you have developed over your lifetime. Bring it into this courtroom.'

He seemed frail, as if the trial had taken its toll on him, as well. He occasionally stopped for a tiny sip of water, giving the impression of someone deep in thought. His career was probably on the line and he desperately needed this speech to sway any juror who might still harbour doubts as to guilt or innocence.

'Does your parish priest have suitcases full with money? Is this what your parish priest does? Is this man the pious priest we have been told about?' He glared at Pat. 'Does Mister Millar look like a poor immigrant whose only crime, according to his lawyer, was to seek the American Dream?' A cynical smile appeared on his face. 'And remember Mister McCormack's so-called spoof essay? Was it just a coincidence, the amount he claims he wrote in college just happens to be close to the amount stolen from the *Brink's*? Can you really believe he was just an innocent bystander? And what about O'Connor? He refused a polygraph.' He shook his head, and for a moment, I thought he would laugh out loud, like a madman barking at the moon. 'Can you buy his story that he had a paper bag placed over his head by the kidnappers who were kindly enough to drop him outside his favourite bar? Picture that, folks. A guy sitting in the front passenger seat with a bag over his head! Does that have a ring of truth to it? Use your common sense . . .'

With those final words, the prosecutors rested their case. Everyone's fate was now in the hands of the jury. All we could do was wait.

42

The Verdict

29 November 1994

"No praying, it spoils the business."
THOMAS OTWAY

The jury deliberated over the next three days, for a total of twenty hours, occasionally requesting some piece of evidence to be shown to them. We were, for the most part, relaxed. But sometimes the atmosphere became one of frayed nerves soothed by gallows humour. The look of anxiety on all our faces – the defendants, the prosecution, the FBI and lawyers – was equal, each for a different reasons.

Pat and myself were polite but wary of each other. A fat sandwich of silence sat between us for most of the deliberation. Each of us had cut just a little too deep with our knives to pretend.

Sometimes I lost myself going over the litany of mistakes I had made, marking the miscalculation and questioning my judgment of trust. It was impossible to fathom retrospectively, but at the time, necessity dictated, clouding my judgment.

Charlie lay sprawled out on the evidence table like a corpse waiting to be dissected, his hands behind his head, tilting it slightly. Occasionally, he would smile to himself, then frown as if just coming to terms with the nightmare thrust upon him by Pat and me. Pat massaged his worry beads, occasionally placing them in front of him on the table, only to scoop them back again to the safety of his hands. When our gazes met, they were those of strangers. Tom? Well, Tom just continued being Tom, nodding and smiling at anyone who glanced his way – including the FBI agents and prosecution. The smiles were not returned. His blasé, laidback style was infuriating them. A good kicking wouldn't go amiss, said the expressions on their faces.

Reporters entered the courtroom looking about, hoping for news. The prosecution and defence lawyers milled around each other, laughing softly, like old buddies reunited at some embarrassing wake of a person they had long forgotten.

On the third day, the announcement that the jury had reached a decision sent everyone back to their original seating positions. Gone were the smiles and jokes, replaced quickly by the cool professionals in suits and leather briefcases, their ties firmly knotted, just like our stomachs. We waited as the jury streamed in through the door, their expressionless faces impossible to read. Soon it would all be over. The classic denouement was at hand. All the tiny noises which had accumulated into an annoying hum, suddenly filtered out of the room, leaving a white sound of silence in all our ears.

'Do you have a verdict?'

'Yes. We do.'

'What is that verdict?'

I slowly stilled my breathing and felt my skin tighten with tension. I knew what was coming next, and like a freight train in the night, there was little I could do about it . . .

43

Thoughts from a Court – a Gathering

November 1994

"Justice is only as good as the case that can be made, and in the case of the Brink's trial that ended Monday, the case wasn't very good. No doubt prosecutors did their best with what they had, but it wasn't enough. It didn't provide the key convictions and it didn't provide the answers.

Important questions remain about the January 1993 robbery. Not least of them is the whereabouts of the money – at least the remaining $5 million. Then there are the mysterious gunmen who took $7.4million from the Brink's depot, along with Thomas P. O'Connor as hostage.

The FBI plans to continue pursuing answers in the Brink's case. That's reassuring. But unless there is new and substantially stronger evidence, the culprits, whoever they are, might just get away with this one."

Editorial from the DEMOCRAT AND CHRONICLE

"There are at least two gunmen still at large who robbed the Brink's depot in January 1993."

TIMES-UNION, FRONT PAGE, after the verdict.

"We felt bad about McCormack. He could have been out of there for Thanksgiving. But I have a question for Maloney: Do you think God dropped the money in to your suitcase?"

JUROR, after the verdict.

265

ON THE BRINKS

"We always liked him. He was a hardworking guy, straight and narrow."

DONALD BRUCE, squad commander of the Rochester Police Force, speaking about Tom.

"To me, the police officer who was taken as a hostage shouldn't even have gone to trial."

BERNICE COOK, owner of *$4.99 Cookery*

"I'm just really stressed out. It's been nine weeks, and I really don't want to talk about it right now. Maybe I'll want to talk about it another time."

JUROR, after the verdict

"I felt there was sufficient evidence to get this case before a jury. That's my duty."

CHRISTOPHER BUSCAGLIA, Federal prosecutor

"I wouldn't characterize it as anything going wrong. It's the nature of the system. It doesn't mean the prosecutors did a poor job."

PAUL MOSKAI, FBI spokesman

"When you take on the United States government, it's mind-boggling . . . to see the FBI just trooped in one after the other. It's always nice to beat the government. In this case, more than any other, it was a close call."

FELIX LAPINE, Tom's defence lawyer, after the verdict.

"Millar's gambling arrests – brought up by Maloney's lawyers – will be taken into account."

PROSECUTORS, speaking – ominously – after the trial.

44

Execution

23 February 1995

"No man can lose what he never had."

IZAAK WALTON

Judge Larimer waited until only the sound of his power settled in, taking control in the courtroom. I stood beside Tony as he and Buscaglia glanced over the papers in their hands. He had assured me that I would receive no more than five years, but I still doubted him.

'It is a fact that you, you know, you were up to your eye-balls in this case, and I have no doubt of that.' The judge stared at me for a second before continuing. 'The evidence here, in my view, was strong and certainly justified . . . Your attorney worked hard . . . This Court and the prosecutor worked hard to make sure this trial was done to proper procedure, in I suspect a trial that looked quite different to those "trials" you faced over in Northern Ireland.'

I couldn't argue with that.

267

'Therefore, it's the judgment of this court that you receive the maximum allowed under the law, 60 months . . .'

60 months. I was relieved. How easily it could have been 60 years. But, of course, it wasn't over yet. They still had two more years, before the statute of limitations ran out, to find another piece of the puzzle. Or another snitch willing to wear a wire.

I couldn't complain about the outcome. Pat received a few months less than the 60 but had threatened to go on hunger strike. I felt bad for him, but advised him it was senseless even talking that way. Fortunately, after cooling down and talking to his family, he decided against the notion. As for Charlie and Tom, both were found not guilty. Charlie went back to New York, hoping to return to teaching; Tom returned to work, though not at *Brink's*, it should be added.

Two more years. I had no other choice than to wait, hoping my luck would hold out.

Two more years . . .

Epilogue

"Millar's Crossing"

"You heard it here first. Sammy Millar, the stone-faced former IRA man whom the FBI believe was the mastermind in the 1992 Brink's robbery in upstate Rochester, New York, has been told he can return to his native Ireland, in spite of the fact that about $5 million of the $7.2 million is still missing."

Editorial in NEW YORK'S *IRISH ECHO*

"I, for one, know of no sweeter sight for a man's eyes than his own country . . ."

HOMER, *The Odyssey*

It was sixteen months after the verdict. I was still counting down the days, hoping the federal five-year limitation would run out. The FBI continued relentlessly and actively to pursue any leads. The robbery was still high on their priorities, though any new information had been scarce. Every now and again the prosecution would make a request through my lawyer, hoping I was still open to some sort of deal. Their offers were politely refused.

269

'Kill someone in this god-awful country, and it's forgotten about in weeks – if not days. But steal the "government's" money and they'll hunt you down until every drop of blood, sweat and tears is removed from your body.'

The jailhouse sage giving me such uplifting advice was a lawyer – at least he used to be one before he was caught laundering money for some shady people in New Jersey. His stomach was quite large from having sheltered so much good food and wine, thought it had to be said he was seeing very little of that here. He was now doing 50 years because he refused to "get down first". His former partner, apparently, had no such qualms. 'I pray to God each day that the cock-sucker gets cancer in the face. But first his wife and kids . . .' As one can imagine, he was bitter at having received such a harsh sentence for a white collar – no violence – crime. He was not the sort of person you wanted to have a conversation with if you were feeling down, as it always eventually turned to the subject of his ex-partner. 'That mother-fucker, telling me each day how we were going to beat this, provided we stayed united, all the time he's rattin' to the Feds. *The mother-fucker.*'

He spat something from his mouth, shaking his head like one of those little dogs at the back of a car, before continuing the "conversation" with me. 'I know what you're thinkin', Sam. This guy's a lawyer, he should have known better . . . and it's true. But we'd been friends for 30 years – can you imagine? 30 fuckin' years, and he sticks it to me. If his mother were alive, I'd pray to God to give her cancer, before his wife and kids . . .'

The only reason I was "listening" to him was the baseball game in progress between the prison inmates and "visitors" from another nearby prison. It had been a good game, both teams fairly even, and a few home runs had been hit across the electric fence. Each time a ball went sailing into the air, over the wire, pass the watchtowers and sending the Canadian geese squawking for their lives, a massive cheer would erupt as if the ball were one of us, escaping like angels in leather.

'Yes. You take those fuckin' cock-suckers' money and they

will hunt you down like a dog,' reiterated the lawyer, just in case I hadn't heard him the first ten times. 'You should have killed somebody, instead. I know I should've, starting with that cocksucker, then his wife and kids . . . maybe his mother . . .'

I needed to get away from Mister Depression as quickly – and diplomatically – as possible. No point in offending someone who might be able to help with some sticky part of the law at a future date. I was saved by my cellmate, a Derry man, who was waving frantically from the top of the hill.

'Got to go, Peter. Mickey wants me. I'll see ye later.'

'Don't worry. I'll hold your place, Sam. There's plenty of time left in the game.'

'That's great. See ye in a wee while,' I lied, racing up the hill.

'You've made legal history,' said Mickey, as I reached the top. 'You're on the front page of the *Irish News*.'

'Are you ballsing about?'

'Read for yourself. You're on the way home.'

He handed me the newspaper and I read it. Re-read it. Then studied it again, wanting to believe, but doubting every word the ink had formed:

"Exclusive:
US Jail Move Of Belfast Man
Marks Legal History

A Belfast man, Samuel Millar, is to be the first person transferred from an American prison to serve the rest of his time in a prison in the North . . ."

The story went on to give the facts behind the case, and how members of the SDLP – but principally Martin Morgan, the local councillor in my area of North Belfast – had worked behind the scenes to persuade the American Justice Department to give their assent for my transfer back to the North of Ireland:

". . . Mr Millar will be home by October."

And pigs will fly, I thought, handing the paper to Mickey. I didn't believe a word of it and wouldn't until I smelt the inside of an airplane somewhere over the Atlantic. Even though I knew that other people were working to try and secure my release – including Paul D McGuigan, a lawyer from Fife, Washington, who had been relentless in his "harassment" of the Justice Department, bombarding them with legal questions and papers on my behalf, never taking a penny for his services – all reasoning questioned the folly of it. I was staying here for the remainder of my time, and no amount of pressure would change that. I was simply torturing myself. I had to be realistic, and reality said I was odds-on for more charges. The hourglass was running out for the prosecution. They were in the sadistic habit of waiting to the very last hour of limitations running out, before hitting you with a new charge. Even if they had little or no proof, it would be worth it – from their point of view – to see you remanded for a few more years in some county jail, not forgetting a good diet of diesel therapy.

Two days later, I was summoned to the governor's office. I expected to see someone from the prosecutor's office, smiling, hitting me with the new charges. Instead, the phone was handed to me by an uncomfortable looking gentleman. Reluctantly, I took the phone while a mysterious woman's voice at the other end informed me that Bill Clinton was sending me home, irrespective of protestations from the FBI.

I knew it was an elaborate trick, hoping to break my mind, winding me up for a fall. 'Thank you,' I replied. 'And you have a nice day, also.' I placed the phone down gently on its cradle and walked calmly from the office, feeling acid burn my stomach. It would only be a matter of time before the diesel therapy began. Probably this week.

I shuddered at the thought, dreading what lay ahead, tasting the diesel in my throat, along with the spam sandwiches . . .

Later, that same week, a reporter from the *The Washington Post* asked for an interview. He was doing an article about an upcoming trial concerning an armoured car robbery, and would I be willing to give him an "insider's" view? The "simple" questions would range from the mundane: What makes a person want to rob such a place, knowing the risks? (Answer: *the money, stupid*), to the more sinister: How long did it take for you to load all the money into the van, on the night of the robbery?

The request, coming at such a late stage in the game coupled with the questions, only helped to arouse my concerns that the Feds were trying to set me up. I quickly declined the interview and waited for the diesel therapy to commence.

The next day's newspaper confirmed my suspicions:

"BRINK'S CASE REOPENED" claimed the headline.
"'*Nobody, obviously, thinks that it's totally solved,*' said Dale Anderson, supervisor of the FBI. '*We certainly would be interested in talking to anybody who would have information about it.*'"

Two days later, at about 4.00 in the morning, it happened.

'Pack up, Millar. You're being moved to MCC (Manhattan Correctional Centre). What fits in the bag goes; what doesn't, stays.'

The memories of the bad old days in Fed pick-up trucks came flooding back, laughing at me, singing, *We'll meet again, don't know where don't know when.* I could almost smell the fumes dancing in my nostrils, see the faces of Feds with their told-you-so grins, taste the dreaded spam sandwiches lounging in my throat waiting to throw-up.

Six hours later, I occupied a cell at the reception in MCC. Outside I could see the yellow cabs zipping in and out of the New York traffic and it broke my heart. It had been years since I last saw the Great City and all the memories – good and bad – were still there, like a painted shadow that had never fully dried. If I had been on the roof, I would have been able to see the street where we had the first casino operating 24/7; Queens was just across the East River, I would have been able to see my apartment, the store I once owned, a few neighbours . . .

'Are ye goin' to give us any trouble on the plane, Millar?' asked a voice from behind the closed door, breaking my daydream.

The voice was rough Ulster, mixed with mellowed distain. It was familiar, but I failed to put a face to it.

'You don't want to answer? Maybe ye want to stay here? Is that it?'

The door opened and I couldn't believe my eyes. Had the pope been standing there in the nude I wouldn't have been as shocked. Ape Face, accompanied by six American guards and three other screws from the Kesh. He had aged terribly – which lifted my spirits a bit – and the old nastiness was no longer as keen, as if, like all the rest of us, he had become a bit wiser with time. The white shirt of promotion probably helped.

'I've told these boys there'll be no trouble from ye. Behave yerself and ye'll be treated correctly,' he said, believing he was John Wayne.

'Not like on the Blanket, eh?' I answered, the cockiness returning.

Ape Face flushed, but bit his lip. 'We'll be back tomorrow morning to get ye. Try not to be goin' anywhere,' he laughed, but no one else did.

The Americans probably couldn't understand a word he said and proved it when they asked me later, 'Was that Gaelic, you guys were speaking?'

I couldn't sleep all night, pacing and pacing. My heart had stopped but not my stomach. I wondered if it was a trick or, perhaps, had the "diesel therapy" caused me to hallucinate? Had Ape Face really been there? Outside the cell, the night's noise hummed with traffic and people going to cafes and bars; the smell of coffee filtered to me and I swear I could taste it in my mouth. I thought I heard Bronx Tommy tellin' me, *Watch it kid, these cock-suckers will try anything.*

Then the darkness slowly melted revealing the most beautiful rising sun I had ever seen. It warmed my face, and my stomach remained calm for the first time in hours. Something told me everything was going to be just fine.

And what became of the rest?

PAT

In 1998, after spending 40 months in prison, he returned to live at the drop-in center for troubled teenagers and illegal immigrants in lower Manhattan.

He was still giving those interviews. He told the Rochester *Democrat and Chronicle*: "A movie producer approached me earlier this year and said my story would be bigger if I were convicted. I've shied away from two movie offers and two book offers."

I thought that funny, having never "shied" from publicity in his life, always having a penchant for it – just like the interviews before, during and after the trial. Even *The News of The World* granted him front-page headlines, claiming he was part of a new organization who had recently joined together to send millions of dollars to free Ireland, hoping to bring down the Good Friday Agreement.

CHARLIE

Charlie went back to try and pick up his life, *never* forgiving *Pat* for bringing him into this.

TOM

Tom went back to try and pick up his life, *never* forgiving *me* for bringing him into this.

"MARCO"

He was untouchable. Just like the rest of the loot.

The lawyer "friend" – the one whose house we had used to stash the proceeds that night of the robbery – had claimed all the money had been stolen, *all* $5,000,000 of it, by a cocaine-addicted friend who stumbled on it "accidentally".

After months of spending and snorting, the lawyer's friend eventually returned home, threatening to tell the Feds should any harm come to either him or his girlfriend, whom he indicated was the instigator of the whole mess. He also indicated that the lawyer had actually stolen most of the money, and used him as a scapegoat."

'Who's going to believe a coke-head over a lawyer,' he replied to questioning. 'I got about half a million – he got the rest . . .'

Over $4,000 000 in small, unmarked bills!

It was the "perfect" crime . . .

TONY

Three familiar figures sat in the Kenneth B Keating Building. Each was a seasoned veteran from numerous "battles" fought out within that imposing structure. The three men had once sat together as a legal team during the *Brink's* trial: Tony Leonardo, Jonathan Feldman and John Speranza. Now they sat as "enemies".

Tony's tan had shaded slightly and gone were the expensive suits. In their place he wore prison garb: an orange sweatshirt and blue pinstripe sweat-pants, ragged from excess wear. The handcuffs had been removed from his wrists, but telltale whelps still remained. He was now being charged with conspiracy to distribute cocaine and having a firearm, a life sentence if found guilty. Most of the "evidence" would be from an FBI informant who had worked for them for over two years. The informant had made almost 200 secret tape recordings for the Feds over those two years. 90 of them would be against Tony.

Tony's good friend, John Speranza – the same man who had worked so hard for Charlie – was now going to have to work doubly-hard to prevent Tony from spending the rest of his life in prison.

It wouldn't be easy. The man occupying the judge's chair was none other than Jonathan Feldman, Father Pat's attorney. Feldman, who had successfully motioned for most of the major charges to be dropped against Pat and myself, was no longer a lawyer but a US Magistrate Judge. Feldman nodded to both men, business-like yet friendly.

In the summer of 1999, Tony had opened an exclusive nightclub called Club Titanic, in Charlotte, at 4775 Lake Avenue. He, along with his partner, Anthony Vaccaro, had sunk $200,000 into renovating the 15,000-square-foot building. Vaccaro saw little of the new business. Within a year, the club closed. Shortly afterwards, Vaccaro was gunned down in an execution-style murder.

Despite a $1,500,000 offer for bail from Tony's family, Feldman opposed, believing the lawyer "too dangerous" for the public domain and that there was "clear, convincing and chilling" evidence that Tony was dangerous.

The headlines and smiles, down below in the US Marshall's room, said it all: *The Arrest Of Superman* and *A Stunning Reversal*. The Feds couldn't conceal their delight as they escorted Tony back to Monroe County Prison – the House of Pain. The smell of meatloaf filtered through the jail like raw sewage on a hot day. Tony had been right: only they could make it smell like shit.

Perhaps it was that smell, perhaps it was the thought of spending the rest of his life with people he preferred to defend rather than associate with, or, perhaps, the realization that the movies were just that – movies, and that prison has no happy ending. Whatever the reason, two days later, in exchange for a 12-year federal prison sentence, Tony pleaded guilty to the murder plot of his ex-partner and agreed to testify against his co-defendant, Albert M Ranieri.

He told the FBI that the plan was to have a hit man hide inside

Club Titanic and wait for Vaccaro, a business associate, to show up for work. Then Vaccaro would be killed. Tony admitted that he gave his co-accused, Ranieri, a key to the club and the security-alarm code to assist in the murder, which was not carried out that night. Vaccaro was killed six weeks later when seventeen shots were pumped into his car as he drove home. "We got to kill him", Tony is captured on undercover tape as saying before the killing of Anthony. Tony then asks the guy if he could kill, if asked. Ranieri answers that he would "pop the guy in a second' and would "cut off his fingers and eat them too if I had to".

Tony, the man who had hated rats more than Indiana Jones, had grown a tail.

RONNIE

It was hot, that August morning in 1995, as Ronnie drove up to a restaurant called Appleby's in a red Toyota Tercel. He had borrowed the car from a friend in New York and there was little fuel in the tank. He just about made it. As usual he was on a shoestring budget.

After about twenty minutes of standing conspicuously alone in the car park, nervously glancing at his watch, a black car, driven by a young man, pulled up alongside him and the window slowly opened. Sun reflected from the car's gleaming metal, stinging Ronnie's eyes, slightly. Less than a minute of conversation took place before Ronnie reached in through the window of the Toyota and removed the keys. A few seconds later he entered the passenger side of the black car and was driven out from the parking lot, heading north, evidently in the direction of Buffalo. His last known words were: "I'm meeting these guys in the morning. If anything happens to me, give my family a call. Tell them who it was. See you later, pal."

Some believed he had borrowed from "wise guys" and had not been able to cover the bill. The Feds, still smarting at their defeat, tried to pin his disappearance on Tom, which was strange considering, to my knowledge, neither had ever met.

The red Toyota, inexplicably, sat in the restaurant's parking lot for *two weeks* before someone decided it was time to call the cops. A tiny bird had made its nest beneath the car, feeding on insects attracted by the shade afforded them by the unmoving bulk.

"No damage. No suspects", stated the police report.

MYSELF

We drove in a convoy of FBI cars and vans at near-death speed, towards Kennedy Airport, sirens blazing. The usual 90-minute ride took less than 30, as the convoy sliced through the New York traffic. It was Hollywood and the FBI were flexing their muscles for the screws, loving every minute of it, as was Ape Face and the gang from the Kesh, who grinned like kids at a carnival.

The usual over-kill of the Feds quickly came to the fore. Snipers lined the roof of British Airways and cops on duty were told: "Watch yourselves. These guys are more dangerous than Arabs . . ."

As I sat in the plane waiting for take-off, the FBI and stewardess were still arguing with Ape Face that I should be handcuffed. To Ape Face's credit, he told them he was in charge and that no one would be getting shackled. The argument became more heated when the Feds insisted that they had jurisdiction because the plane still sat on American soil.

I let them argue and picked up a copy of *USA Today,* reading last night's report on the New York Nicks, when I stopped at a column just screaming to be read: *"Milton Diehl, one of three winners in the New York State $10 million lotto . . ."*

The name automatically registered in my head. A tiny footnote on the page explained that he was one of the guards who had been held at gunpoint by masked raiders in the *Brink's* robbery.

'What's the smile for?' asked Ape Face, sitting beside me, victorious in his argument with the Feds.

I didn't answer him, simply continued smiling, thinking how Milton Diehl, old Trigger Happy himself, must be feeling just about now, all that money sitting on his lap. The tiny headline summed it up: *"What goes around comes around."*

I loved it. It was simply beautiful; poetic justice. I had always loved irony and a good Greek tragedy, and I had to admit the Greeks would have had a hard time outdoing this one.

'Are ye gonna tell me what's the grin for?' persisted Ape Face.

But he no longer existed, just the beautiful sound of engines purring then roaring with frightening power.

Soon they would be taking me home . . .

Publisher's note

Sam Millar was released from Maghaberry Prison, Northern Ireland in November 1997.

He won the Brian Moore Short Story Award for his short story *Rain* in 1998.

His first novel, *Dark Souls* was published by Wynkin deWorde in April 2003.

Also from Wynkin de Worde

Sam Millar

DARK SOULS

ISBN: 0-9542607-6-7

www.deworde.com